Scheyville Speaks

Biography of a national park

by

Roger Donnelly

© Roger Donnelly 2021

Scheyville Speaks – Biography of a national park

All Rights Reserved

Copyright © 2021 Roger Donnelly

Reproduction in any manner, in whole or in part,
in English or any other language, or otherwise,
without the written permission of the copyright holder is prohibited

For information address roger21donnelly@yahoo.com.au

First Printing 2021

ISBN: 978-0-6468394-4-8

Published by The Mickie Dalton Foundation
NSW
Australia

Scheyville Speaks – Biography of a national park

Acknowledgements

Dedication

Preface

Foreword

A piece of dirt that would only support one bandicoot to the acre! 1

The Dharug, the Hawkesbury Commons and a man called Schey 16

From Pitt Town to Scheyville – agricultural training begins 23

Dreadnoughts 1909 to 1939 53

A training farm for Australian boys – Scheyville in the 1930s 81

White fingers and red berets 109

A memory meadow is foreshadowed 133

The role of the churches 177

Training officers for Vietnam 201

Vietnam and its aftermath 237

Four battles and a National Park emerges! 257

References 293

Appendix A: Scheyville Centre School reports 301

Appendix B: Giving the Migrants a Profile 313

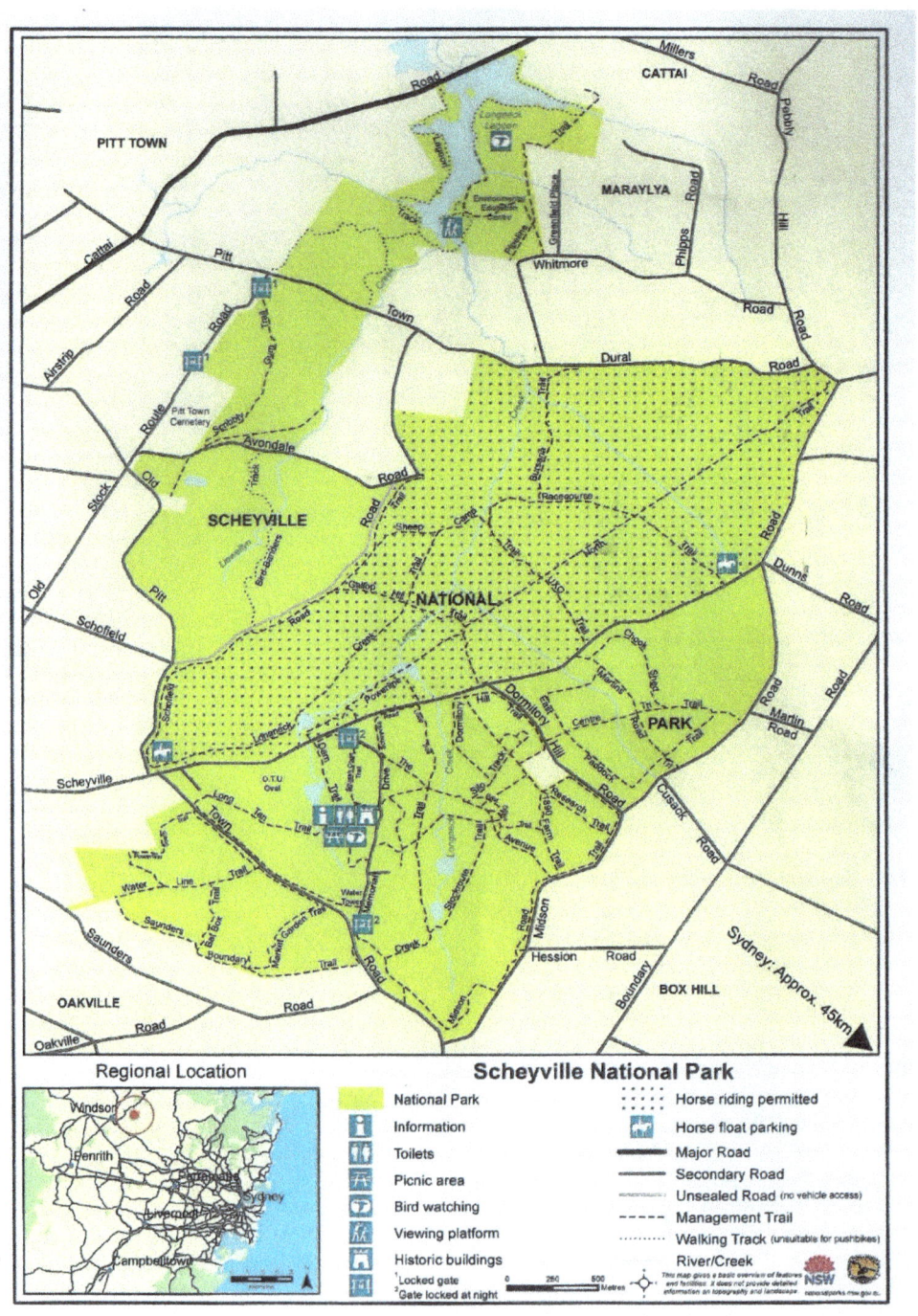

Permission to include the map received gratefully from Ms Mary Gaudry of the National Parks and Wildlife Service of NSW, 13 April, 2021

Acknowledgements

Firstly, the patience and guidance of my wife, Jill is appreciated and never taken for granted. Secondly, daughters Anita and Bianca for their encouragement, even if they felt the need to stir me for taking so long to complete the project. Thirdly, to Michael Davies, author and publisher 'extraordinaire' for volunteering to do the necessary steps to bring my words and photos to publication and printing standard.

The lesson has been learnt again that you are more publishable if my manuscript has had a very good edit and all sources traced so that copyright is not infringed, footnotes done correctly and a limit to paraphrasing of others. This wouldn't have happened if it wasn't for the tough but thorough work of Elizabeth Spiegel. To rest easy from a legal point of view, I was mentored once again by specialist defamation lawyer Geoff Gronow.

Members of The Officer Training Unit Scheyville Association and its National President and Committee have continued their support. Of note is Neil Leckie who corrected mistakes on the Vietnam chapters sourced photos and has always given constructive thoughts and suggestions along with his time. Laurie Muller for his encouragement, especially belief in my ability to write both an entertaining story for the general readers and to have written and researched at the PhD academic level. According to Laurie, few people can manage both.

Frank Miller, President of the O.T.U. Association for his support over the years.

Robyn Dodd, granddaughter of William Francis Schey, for once again loaning me photos and supplying additional stories and information on Mr Schey.

Former O.T.U. graduate and Vice Chancellor of the University of West Australia, Emeritus Professor Allan Robson for taking the time to read the manuscript and write an entertaining Foreword for the book.

Emeritus Professor Geoffrey Sherington of the University of Sydney for his friendship and encouragement over a period of ten years and his peer review of the Dreadnought chapters.

Emeritus Professor Grace Karskens of the University of NSW for reviewing the Introductory Chapter and the Early Hawkesbury Chapter.

Sebastian Condon of the Roman Catholic Vicar-General and Chancellors Office for reviewing the Church Chapter.

The staff of the Presbyterian Church Archives and the Ferguson Library Sydney for their introduction to Deaconess Betty Eady and help on Reverend Ayling.

Rose Good for her encouragement and generously giving of her time and supplying photos for the Migrant and Church chapters.

Elvie Suviste and members of the Estonian Society for contacting former refugees and smoothing the path to introductions with those who still needed to trust an unknown researcher.

Helen Ord, Administration Officer at Scheyville National Park for being an unending source of contacts and research help.

Jonathan Sanders, former Manager of Scheyville National Park who has always been a great source of information, and introductions to former Scheyville residents as well as showing initiative to hold a Centenary Celebration in May 2011.

Jo Robertson and Pauline Garland of St Marys Cathedral Sydney Archives Office for their help and interest in my research.

The many former residents of Scheyville from the different eras of its human occupation who have given freely of their time and stories.

Michelle Nicolls of the Hawkesbury Regional Library for her assistance on the history of the Hawkesbury District.

Mary Gaudry, Publications Manager at National Parks NSW for her ongoing interest in fostering the project and permission for use of National Parks Department material.

The Archivist at the former Hawkesbury Agricultural College for access to its records.

The staff at the Mitchell Library Sydney, NSW Records Office, National Library Canberra, the Australian War Memorial Canberra, the National Archives Offices in Canberra, Chester Hill and North Melbourne for their assistance and being accommodating for my visits.

Tim Overall for information on Colonel Overall, Commander of the First Australian Parachute Battalion and Richard McCooey, CEO of the Australian Parachute Association for permission to quote from the history of Skydiving and Parachuting in Australia.

To Grant Buggy, my workmates Stan Milosevic, Bis Mitra, Managers Karl Meadows and Colonel Michael Chapman and Master Gunner mates David (Reg) Grundell, and Dion Hawkett for their encouragement.

Every endeavour has been made to trace copyright. Being human, I am sure to have made some mistakes so I would be happy to hear from authors of my unacknowledged sources.

Dedication

This book is dedicated to my wonderful family; Jill, Bianca and Anita, and to the former residents of Scheyville who "didn't let the bastards get them down" and to those who saw to it that the site is preserved as a National Park.

May the present and future decision makers of NSW have the wisdom to preserve Scheyville National Park. Since white people arrived, the site started out as one of Governor Macquarie's Commons, and as a National Park that really is what it is again. Common Land to be enjoyed by all people and as a protected habitat for the many species of plants and animals that inhabit the place.

Preface

This is a site history that encompasses the story of Australia since British settlement. The main period covered by the story is from the depression of the 1890s through to the Scheyville site being declared a National Park in the 1990s. That was a happy ending after a number of battles were fought to save it from development. Subsequently it has been listed on the New South Wales Heritage Register. This is a better outcome than it being the site for Sydney's second international airport, a waste dump, a large prison or a new suburb of twenty thousand people. All of these uses were pushed by various groups and governments between the mid-1970s to 1996. Approximately one per cent of Australia's population can claim a direct link to Scheyville.

Other writers have recounted parts of Scheyville's story, each focussing on a particular era or group. My own book *The Scheyville Experience* (published by QUP 2001) is about the national service officers of the Vietnam War. This book brings it all together, adding much new material to the site's existing history. Scheyville has been involved in each phase of Australia's political and cultural evolution. The storyline of this work extends from 1890 to 2000. The site was the home of a socialist experiment in the 1890s and an agricultural training institution from the early 1900s to 1939. It was used for various military purposes during World War Two and became a home to a national servicemen's Officer Training Unit during the Vietnam War. At other times it was a migrant holding centre for refugees and European migrants. Although 'the State' has always been involved, this book focuses on the stories of the people who have lived at Scheyville.

Foreword

Roger Donnelly has written an excellent account of Scheyville, a place which has had many uses over the more than two hundred years of its recent history. As he says, the account is a biography of a place. His approach to this biography is very well articulated in the preface where he outlines a number of common themes which he brings together as he considers the changing uses of the site.

The site was frequented by the Dharug Aboriginal people who hunted in the woodlands and wetlands. In 1804 the site became the Pitt Town Common and in 1893 the Pitt Town Co-operative Labour Settlement was established on the site as an experiment in socialistic living for unemployed men to develop farming skills. In 1906 it became a place to introduce city boys to agriculture. The site was named Scheyville after Schey a former parliamentarian and Labour Commissioner in 1911.

The first Dreadnought boys arrived in 1911. In this scheme, boys from England were given a three-month period of farm training by a trust which had initially been established to fund a battleship. The scheme was suspended in 1915 and recommenced in 1921. During World War One the site was used for training women to go upon the land. The Dreadnought Scheme continued until 1939.

In 1939, Scheyville was used as a training ground for Searchlight Batteries and then as a site to train paratroopers. After the Second World War Scheyville became a Migrant Holding Centre until 1964. In 1965 Scheyville became the home of the Officer Training Unit established to train National Service officers. The last class at the unit was in 1973.

In 1977, the site was leased to the Hawkesbury Agricultural College with the lease ending in 1983. Since that time a number of uses have been proposed for the site; a second airport for Sydney, a waste dump, a maximum security prison and a residential estate. All of these suggestions were fiercely resisted by the local community and the site is now a National Park.

This chronology is presented here to illustrate the many uses of the site. For each of these uses, Roger Donnelly examines many aspects of the use, and with painstaking research and interviews he presents a fascinating and insightful account of each period. He places the uses in the social, political and economic climate of the time.

I read the account with great interest. I was a resident of Scheyville for six months in 1970 while training to be an officer at the Officer Training Unit but I had no idea of the history of the site. I was mainly concerned with surviving. I was a very poor soldier who hated camping, who was hopeless at drill and who has never fired a rifle before or after Scheyville. Every morning I waited at breakfast for the names to be read out for those cadets to report to the Commandant prior to them leaving Scheyville. When the list got beyond "R" I felt always a great deal of relief. I had survived another day. In the end I won the Commandant's Prize for the cadet most determined to graduate so you can make your own conclusions. I can say that my class (1/70) was collectively the most able group that I experienced in my career. I also have used many things I learnt at Scheyville in my career. Imagine the reaction of many academics when I told them this as Vice-Chancellor.

I also greatly enjoyed the book because I am an agricultural scientist having completed a B.Agric.Sci. at the University of Melbourne and a PhD in Perth. The accounts of the agricultural uses of the site are very insightful and reflect many issues that are relevant to the agricultural history of Australia.

I thoroughly recommend this book. It is a very scholarly account of the history of an important site. The book is very easy to read being very well written. Roger Donnelly is to be commended for this very valuable history.

Alan Robson, AO CitWA

Emeritus Professor

The University of Western Australia.

Scheyville Speaks

A piece of dirt that would only support one bandicoot to the acre!

If history were taught in the form of stories it would never be forgotten.

Rudyard Kipling

Imagine being able to explore the history of a piece of land in a number of different contexts. Firstly, you are writing a biography of the site. A kaleidoscope of different people having different experiences, but all those different people had those different experiences at different times in the history of this site. Each person who lived on this piece of land had their life transformed in some manner. It was an intense transformation. Each group of people sacrificed something to go there, or were required to sacrifice something whilst there. Attending activities on this site also involved the person in some form of initiation. The multitude of uses this site has had over the past one hundred and fifty years have all involved people being involved in some form of training.

No matter which group an individual belonged to, there has been a feeling of belonging to the place for many of them. Each group has had reunions and individuals have made casual visits on a casual basis. Yet, each group saw only a small slice of the site's history. As Anna Woods stated in her pamphlet, the Scheyville site is a *Field of Memories*,[1] this is especially true for the European migrants who came after World War Two and the young British boys who came as Dreadnought Boys to learn farming skills.

This book 'puts all the pieces of the cake back together'. It chronicles the changing uses of the Scheyville over the past one hundred and fifty years. Each change reflects the political decisions and social forces that have transformed and shaped Australia. These decisions mirror the evolution of Australia's cultural and

---

[1] Williams, Anna, and Picket, Charles, *Fields of Memories*, Migration Heritage Centre, Powerhouse Museum NSW, 2006

social heritage. The site has acted as an incubator of these ideas and decisions. Those decisions have dictated the uses of the site. Both the NSW and Australian Federal Governments have projected their expansionist hopes for development and desire to tame both people and the land, onto this site. The Roman Catholic and Presbyterian Churches have also intervened and influenced the lives of the people who resided at Scheyville.

Scheyville is approximately fifty kilometres north-west of the Sydney CBD, and about five kilometres from the historic town of Windsor and some ten kilometres from the RAAF Richmond air base.

In the 1800s the site was common land, and in the 1890s was used for a socialist share farming experiment. This government-backed venture failed, and in the first decade of the twentieth century young city boys were sent there for farming training.

From 1910 to the outbreak of World War Two, boys brought to Australia under the auspices of the Dreadnought Scheme were given their initial farm labouring skills.

During World War Two the Commonwealth Government took control of the site and used it for training artillery personnel in a number of Search Light Batteries. Following World War Two, the Commonwealth kept control of the site and used it as a migrant holding centre from 1949 to 1964.

During the course of Australia's involvement in the Vietnam War, Scheyville functioned as an Officer Training Unit. Twenty-year-old conscripts graduated as Second Lieutenants in a matter of twenty-two weeks.

Following the Vietnam War, the institution then known as Hawkesbury Agricultural College used the site for some lectures and as overflow accommodation. When the Agricultural College became a campus of the University of Western Sydney and no longer had any need for Scheyville, the site fell into disrepair. Much debate ensued with a number of proposals considered, some of which were vehemently pursued, such as the four thousand home real estate development. The land was also considered as site for a prison by the New

South Wales government and by the Commonwealth as forming part of a proposal for a second major Sydney airport to relieve pressure on the Botany Bay site.

As a biography, this book explores and weaves together the social history of the various groups that have inhabited the site, delving into the roots of the place. A memorable cast of characters has graced this parcel of land. All the players of the past one hundred and fifty years have been of British or European origin. It is almost as if the land gives 'white fellas' a sense of place. Just as Martin Welch wrote in *Biography of a Place: Passages Through a Central Oregon Meadow*, this book has 'a storyline that flows across overlapping circles of connection among people and place'.[2] You will witness the evolution of a changing cultural heritage in Australia. The tale of this large 'meadow' called Scheyville is tracked from the 1800s to the present day. The 'meadow' has become a National Park.

This history of the Scheyville site and its various historical layers is a study of the site over time and provides a lens onto the periods studied. Due to the site not being as significant as others in Australia to our Indigenous people, there is only a small piece on Aboriginal history.

Colonial-era primary sources, newspapers, official government records, Australian Army records, and various publications are drawn upon. The oral history testimony of post–World War Two migrants and Officer Cadets is accessed.

State control of Scheyville has always existed and now the state is concerned with Heritage Management of the site. Government policy regarding immigration, national service, Labour Policy and heritage and the environment have shaped its existence.

Concepts applicable to the Scheyville site include its place as a place of agricultural education, as an institution for boys, as a co-operative settlement, as a defence training site, and a reflection of the changing face of Australia's immigration policies and practices. This is mirrored in the white, Anglo-Saxon,

---

[2] Welch, Martin. *Biography of a Place: Passages Through a Central Oregon Meadow*. Deschutes County Historical Society, 2006.

mainly Protestant make-up of the Dreadnought Boys who came between 1910 and 1940, and the Roman Catholic majority of the migrants who arrived post–World War Two.

The activities carried on at the site were also of an 'initiation' type; whether that be an introduction to Australia as a migrant, or a recruit into the Army. Training was certainly a common theme of site use.

Mantras adopted by people who have passed through Scheyville make it out to be 'a place where men are made' and to survive you must adopt the attitude of 'don't let the bastards get you down'.[3] This mindset applied to whatever institution was functioning at the time whether that be a military unit or a farm training scheme.

The influence of the Church appears through the book. The role and experience of women at the site is also discussed. Scheyville is best read as an historical palimpsest. This is a good way to 'unpack the story of a site'.

It can be interesting to reflect on what sort of Australia we might have had if the various activities had not been carried on at Scheyville. What if the fifteen-year-old young British boys had not been seduced in the early 1900s by the sales spiel to come to Australia to start a new life as trainee farm hands in the first part of the twentieth century? What if the refugees and other post–World War Two migrants hadn't left war ravaged Europe to help populate Australia and fuel an economic recovery? Many of them had the opportunity to emigrate to Canada or the United States. What if none of those conscripted into the Australian Army during the Vietnam War had decided to have a go at officer training? (It was about the only thing they could volunteer for!).

A short answer is that the nation would be poorer. The experiences of these people mean that the history of the piece of land known as Scheyville can be explored in a number of different contexts.

---

[3] Donnelly, Roger. *The Scheyville Experience. The Officer Training Unit Scheyville 1965-1973*. University of Queensland Press, 2001. 'don't let the bastards get you down' quoted to and by all graduates of the O.T.U.

Scheyville Speaks

The idea for this book germinated over a decade ago after writing the book, *The Scheyville Experience*.[4] That book explored the experience of some three thousand men who had been conscripted to serve Australia when the nation was engaged in the Vietnam War. The site is listed on the NSW Heritage Register. Its role in Australia is shaped by the people who called Scheyville home for anything from a week to many years. In this book I explore and weave together the social history of the various groups that have inhabited the site, delving into the 'roots of the place'. A memorable cast of characters has graced this parcel of land. Those players include former Deputy Prime Minister, Tim Fischer, former Victorian Premier, Jeff Kennett, Victoria Cross recipient Keith Payne, modern-day adventurer Lang Kidby, and former Qantas pilot, Brian McCarthy. McCarthy incurred the wrath of former Prime Minister Bob Hawke when he was head of the Federation of Airlines Pilots during a bitter national dispute in 1989.

Further, the final use of this site as a National Park reflects the accumulation of layering of memory, meaning, history, political decisions and heritage built up over the nineteenth and particularly the twentieth century.

It is now a National Park because its historical significance dictated it had to be considered as such by the then Carr Government of New South Wales in the late 1990s when it was implementing its campaign of environmental awareness and protection.

This book demonstrates the impact of political decisions, social forces and a changing attitude towards cultural heritage on and through the site. The research explores a number of concepts such as co-operative settlement in Australia, institutions for boys, agricultural training, military training, the 'populate or perish' mentality that pervaded Australian economic and immigration policy after World War Two, and the 'greening' of the Australian mind.

Australia's indigenous people speak of their tribal lands as giving them a feeling of belonging – a sense of place. The majority of people who have inhabited this site during the past two hundred years may have only experienced the site on

---

[4] Ibid.

an itinerant basis, but somehow, the Scheyville Experience as I call it, instilled a sense of belonging.

It explores how different people have connected to the site. On this site a kaleidoscope of different people having different experiences performing vastly different activities for a multitude of uses has occurred. A picture of the twentieth century as a century of memorialisation in Australia emerges. Shortly after the white invasion the site was known as Nelson Common. The site has become a 'Memory Common'. However, there is no common memory between the people who went there.

A more profound appreciation of our political, social and cultural history is gained by comparing and contrasting the Leongatha Labour Colony in Victoria to the Pitt Town Co-operative Settlement (Scheyville). Dissecting the evidence of the parliamentary inquiries in each colony on their respective labour camps adds to the understanding of how communism and socialism played out in Australia's late nineteenth century.

At least 250,000 Australians can claim a link to Scheyville.[5] That represents approximately one per cent of the population. Add that to the fact that it is an area of some nine hundred hectares within fifty kilometres of the Sydney CBD and has been able to escape the urban sprawl, makes it unique. Each group who has inhabited the site attaches a different meaning to the site and has a different meaning of the national identity. Each group is bound together by different cultures and by the culture of their generation. When they visit the site, the remaining built environment and surrounding vegetation enable them to readily re-connect with the site.

In her book, *The Rocks – Life in Early Sydney*,[6] Grace Karskens wondered 'What were these people like? What kinds of lives had they been able to make

---

[5] Donnelly, Roger, email to Jonathan Sanders Manager Scheyville National Park May 2011 "At least 250,000 Australians can claim a link to Scheyville". The method of calculating this figure is in the email.
[6] Karskens, Grace. *The Rocks: life in early Sydney* Melbourne University Press, Carlton, Vic, 1997

here? What individuals, families, communities existed here?'[7] and went on to explore an urban world of the nineteenth century. Like her, I realised I had only glimpsed part of Scheyville's history. Professor Geoffrey Sherington of Sydney University focused on the experience of the Dreadnoughts, and Anna Williams carried out oral history interviews with some former migrants. That work is celebrated in a booklet titled *Fields of Memories*. There is such a wealth of information about Scheyville that settling on the content of the book seemed harder than finding evidence to support the interesting stories of any facet of the site's history.

Whereas Karskens 'telescoped' her work from a complete history down to covering the early colonial period to about 1830,[8] I wanted to cover each period to illustrate the layering of the history. This shows how the site has been involved in each phase of Australia's political and social evolution. It was used as a common and is now a site that reflects a contemporary society that values National Parks and shows regard for the environment.

I have consulted with and had discussions with the various Associations that have been closely connected to the site, and whose members have been residents of, or directly affected by the activities at the place. These include the Dreadnought Association, CRADLE (Concerned Residents Against Development of Longneck and Environs), the New South Wales National Parks (now the Department of Environment and Sustainability), and the Officer Training Unit Association.

In my early research I came across articles and documents relating to prior uses of the site, and found that the term, 'a place where men are made' was used when the Dreadnought Trust had trained young men at the site between 1911 and 1939. This term was also used when Army Officer Cadets were trained there between 1965 and 1973. One activity was agricultural in nature, the other military, yet common threads were emerging. The site was intriguing with remnants of

---

[7] Ibid., p5.
[8] Karskens, op.cit.p. xiii

various phases of occupation remaining. Silos, sheep dips, the original road, the remains of the draught horse stable left from the Dreadnought phase, the flagpole of a school that existed more than 100 years ago, the parade ground, the SAAR huts that had been used as dining rooms and as a gymnasium during both the Officer Training Unit phase (1965–73) and to feed the post–World War Two migrants (1949–64).

One of my aims was to describe and contribute to an understanding of the shifts in use which brought Scheyville to the way it was in 2011 (Scheyville's centenary year). It seems appropriate to consider the site in relation to the evolving character of the region and connect those uses to the character of Australia's political and cultural history. There was a change in the religious affinity of people who have occupied the site. The Dreadnought Boys were predominantly members of the Church of England, (ninety per cent), whereas the majority of migrants who occupied the site between 1949 and 1964 were Roman Catholic. Most of the Estonian and Latvian refugees who arrived in the site's early days as a migrant camp were Lutheran, but those of Polish, Dutch, Italian and Hungarian descent who came in the following ten to twelve years were mainly Roman Catholic. A reliable approximation is that seventy-five per cent were Catholic.

Hence the connection with Grace Karskens' work. She had been invited to do archaeological work at the Rocks and 'turned on the need for an overall history of the place'. Some of the same questions intrigued me about Scheyville as they did Karskens: Where did it begin, how old is its name? How did it get its name? How has the environment altered? Were the residents just victims of circumstance?[9] I believe it is not always necessary to dwell on the negatives and hardships in understanding the complete story. Just as Karsken's subjects emerge as human beings with hopes, aspirations, loves and loyalty and disagreements, the Scheyville residents over the various eras reveal small things that give an insight to their cultural affinities. Just as the convicts came here with nothing, the post–World War Two migrants came with nothing more than a suitcase, and very little

---

[9] Karskens, op. cit., p 5.

else. The site has a gendered history: while it was used for training women in horticulture during World War One, when men were trained in farming pursuits the work was heavier and involved animals. Again, the gender lines were drawn after World War Two when the women stayed at the camp minding the children and doing embroidery and other crafts, whereas the men were sent to 'build the nation', working on projects such as the Snowy Mountains Scheme and Warragamba Dam. They were only allowed home at weekends. The building of the Warragamba Dam also alleviated the flood threat in the Windsor Richmond area which affected the Scheyville site. Until the dam was completed, Scheyville was always cut off from the townships by floodwaters. Here, we have links between gender roles, the geography of the place and infrastructure needs of the local region.

A variety of approaches, research tools and techniques to collect evidence were used because the aims of each chapter have lent themselves to different approaches.

I 'walked the land' early in my research. The Scheyville National Park manager, Jonathan Sanders, took me on a guided tour of the 850-hectare site, pointing out remnants of earlier occupations such as the silos, the remains of the original school flagpole, the remains of the stables, sheep dips, water storage and where roads and a bridge had existed. Aerial photographs and maps were also used to get a sense of the layout of the site as used by different groups.

Judy White's book, *Tocal, The Changing Moods of a Rural Estate*,[10] provided an entry point to looking at a site that has had multiple uses. The title of that book says a lot that is similar to the thrust of what this book sets out to accomplish.

Just as Tocal is a 5000-acre estate on the Paterson River near Maitland New South Wales; Scheyville is a 2150-acre site near Windsor and close to the Hawkesbury River.

---

[10] White, Judy, *Tocal, the changing moods of a rural estate,* The Seven Press, Scone, 1986.

Tocal traces the agricultural history of the nineteenth century in the Hunter Valley, the achievements of an early explorer, the site's time as a cattle and thoroughbred horse stud and the establishment of the C.B. Alexander Agricultural College. The personalities of the people who inhabited the landscape are also captured to help us understand the changing influences in agricultural, rural and social history of the Lower Hunter Valley of New South Wales.

Just as Tocal might be a site with a number of layers, Scheyville is a site that has a multi-layered history influenced by, and dictated to by national events, political decisions and personalities from a multitude of nations. Both this book and *Tocal* are 'biographies of the land, and the achievements and failures of the residents. The arrivals and departures have in many cases been dictated by the land and climate'.[11] Yet the land is patient in the background as this history takes place and the patterns of life unfold. The aims, ideals, habits of life and aspirations of those who have passed through Scheyville in the last 150 years are interconnected, yet so different. As Miss Marguerita Curtis of Tocal said, 'It's like living in a Story Book when you add it all up.'[12] Having been a resident at Scheyville is a bit like having lived in Australia's National Story Book. The natural grasslands and remnants of the forested parts of the site may still be there but the land use has altered from agricultural training to military training to migrant accommodation to military uses to becoming a National Park.

Similarities exist in as much as the colonial Governors of early white settlement had input to the development of the areas.[13] For example, direct descendants of Assistant-Surveyor Henry Dangar of New South Wales contributed to the Dreadnought Trust that helped some 7500 boys train as farm labourers at Scheyville.

James Webber, one of the early owners of Tocal, 'considered that Australia had a flourishing community that could benefit the mother country in many ways.'

---

[11] Ibid.
[12] Ibid.
[13] White, op. cit. p 24

As well as providing fine wool 'he saw New South Wales as a means of outlet for the surplus population of England'.[14] This sentiment and similar such as 'the populate or perish' cry of Australia's post–World War Two government has been echoed a number of times since. Scheyville was involved in the ramifications of policies that gave force to such sentiments, with boys being brought out to train as farm labourers between 1911 and 1939. Other common elements to the Tocal and Scheyville stories are the involvement of the Presbyterian Church and involvement in agricultural training. Tocal became the C.B. Alexander Presbyterian Agricultural College from 1965 to 1969 and the Principal of Hawkesbury Agricultural College assisted the first Board of Control of the Pitt Town Co-operative Settlement in the 1890s, while in the 1970s the College used the Scheyville site as overflow accommodation and for some training. Religious affairs were administered at the Pitt Town Co-operative Settlement by Mr Ayling, the Presbyterian Minister from Ebenezer Church, Pitt Town in the 1890s. From 1952 to 1962, Deaconess Betty Eady helped the migrants at Scheyville and was a live-in resident of the site.

This book explains how newcomers to Australian society have altered and contributed to the cultural, political and social development of the nation. An interplay of religious, social and political forces through government, philanthropic and not-for-profit organisations has been at work. The book is also about how the concept of 'the place of Scheyville' has manifested itself in people's lives and the political ramifications have left an historical legacy. It is also a story of how the landscape has been utilised for many purposes, how that landscape has adapted and how those from foreign shores who have resided there have adapted to our Australian landscape.

New South Wales was only one of a number of large areas undergoing transformation by European settlers; the study of its development is a contribution to the larger theme of nineteenth century colonisation which takes in, as well as the rest of Australia and New Zealand, the two American continents and parts of

---

[14] White, op. cit. p 31

Africa. Not all newcomers to Australia whose initial place of residence was Scheyville found advantage or fulfilment, not immediately, but a majority have adapted to their adopted, once alien environment.

There have been harsh years, such as the 1890s and the 1930s, in which the optimism of previous decades was destroyed. The evolution of suitable uses for the site has been determined not only by the manner of initial settlement – which was affected by the climate and soil, but also by later land legislation which has been the subject of a struggle by vested interests at different times. This outcome ended many decades of struggle, particularly the years from 1973 until it was proclaimed a National Park in 1996, perhaps realising the egalitarian ideals of some reformers.

Jeans states that New South Wales built its railway system with a view to cornering all the trade of its border regions for Sydney, and that the colony used tariffs more sparingly and preferred the Imperial Government's inclination toward free trade compared to the protectionist policies of Victoria towards its manufacturing and rural industries.[15] Yet, this free-trade government also supported the experiment in the 1890s of the socialist co-operative settlement–style share farming for the unemployed. When the co-operative settlement failed, the New South Wales government didn't hesitate to hold a parliamentary inquiry into its demise. It then used the site as a Casual Labour Farm for destitute men until the Dreadnought Trust began using it for training young British boys. The Commonwealth Government took control of the site in World War Two, using it for military training during the war, as a migrant camp from 1949 to 1964 and once again for military use to train conscripts for the Vietnam War. The history of this plot of land shows that the different and varied uses that it has been put to, are as a result of political decisions by both successive state and Commonwealth governments. Thus, its history is entwined with an emerging political history and the changing cultural face of Australia.

---

[15] Jeans, D.N, *An Historical Geography of NSW to 1901,* Reed Education, Sydney, 1972.

McCalman states that, 'the essence of human memory is that it is selective and, like written history, the basis of that selectivity is value-laden; hence the sins are of omission rather than commission'.[16] Scheyville is a memory ground for a number of diverse groups.

Laurajane Smith's concept of the 'authorized heritage discourse' (from *Uses of Heritage*) and who owns it[17] applies to my participatory observations at the Scheyville Centenary. One group; the former soldiers, 'hogged' the official commemoration functions on the day, although they were numerically insignificant compared to the former migrants. This group has stamped its claim to the ground for commemorative purposes by ensuring an obelisk with a number of plaques has been erected at Scheyville, whereas specific memorials have not been erected by, or for other significant groups of former inhabitants.

Rodney Harrison also explores the aspect of heritage that relates to the idea that 'things tend to be classified as heritage only in the light of some risk of losing them.'[18] 'Places become more saturated with meaning when they are threatened' and the clichéd 'you don't know what you have until it's gone – or almost gone' apply to Scheyville.[19]

When Scheyville fell into disrepair from 1973 onwards, it was almost lost to at least four major bids for redevelopment as a prison, as a waste dump, as an airport and as a town of 20,000 people. The potential for loss of both built and natural heritage was huge. The battle to protect the area involved many groups.

This book demonstrates that Scheyville has intrinsic value and that different people have attributed value to it.

---

[16] McCalman, Janet, *Struggletown –Public and Private Life in Richmond 1900–1965*. Hyland House Publishing South Melbourne 1998. p 184.
[17] Smith, Laurajane, *Uses of Heritage*, Routledge, 2006
[18] Harrison, Rodney, *Understanding the Politics of Heritage*. Manchester University Press, 2009. It also explores the aspect of heritage that relates to the idea that 'things tend to be classified as heritage only in the light of losing them'.
[19] Harrington, Jane Therese. *Being here: heritage Belonging and Placemaking. A Study of Community and Identity Formation at Avebury (England) Magnetic Island (Australia) and Ayutthaya (Thailand)*. Thesis submitted 2004. James Cook University. P316.

In explaining how, where and when different groups connect with their past at Scheyville I have increased what Harrison terms 'a form of cultural capital'.[20]

Scheyville is a site where 'a sense of historical continuity exists' (Pierre Nora). It is also a site where 'there are as many memories as there are groups, that memory is by nature multiple and yet specific; collective, plural, and yet individual.'[21] Scheyville is a site of memory in the three senses of the word quoted by Nora: material, symbolic and functional.

Stuart Hall claims 'a shared national identity thus depends on the cultural meanings which bind each member individually into the larger national story'.[22] There is a community shared by all who went to Scheyville: they all call themselves Scheyvillians. It was a place of initiation into the Army, or into the Australian way of life. Each group may consist of people from different cultures, but each is bound together by the culture of their own generation, their shared ideals, ideas, experiences and memories.

In Hall's words, they are helping 'the nation slowly construct for itself a sort of collective social memory'. This storytelling of random incidents and contingent turning points of their lives, such as going to Scheyville, mean they are selectively binding their chosen high points and memorable achievements into an unfolding national story.

This book provides evidence that the site's present status as a National Park should not be challenged or changed. Serious consideration should be given to listing this site on the National Heritage Register. The pressures that were recognised in the various Sydney Metropolitan Growth and Development strategies drafted since 1980 will not diminish. However, the reasons that surfaced

---

[20] Ibid.
[21] Nora, Pierre, '*Between Memory and History: Les Lieux de Mémoire, Representations*, Spring, 1989, No. 26, 7–24
[22] Hall, Stuart, 'Un-settling 'the heritage', re-imaging the post nation. Whose heritage?' *Third Text*, 13.49, pp 3-13, 1999. Stuart Hall claims 'a shared national identity thus depends on the cultural meanings which bind each member individually into the larger national story'.

in the debates during the 1980s and early 1990s as to why Scheyville should not be developed are still relevant.

The following chapters talk about the changing uses of the site, and provide a lens to examine the evolution of Australia's heritage. One per cent of the population has a direct link to the site. To know there is such a layering of individual and collective memories of the people who have lived part of their lives there makes the Scheyville site significant in terms of the effects of political decisions, an environmental awakening and cultural capital.

The majority of people who went there 'volunteered' for the experience. They all had to overcome fear of the unknown, but not all have regrets. Perhaps the saying: 'Fear is temporary. Regret is permanent' applies to those who have had a Scheyville Experience.

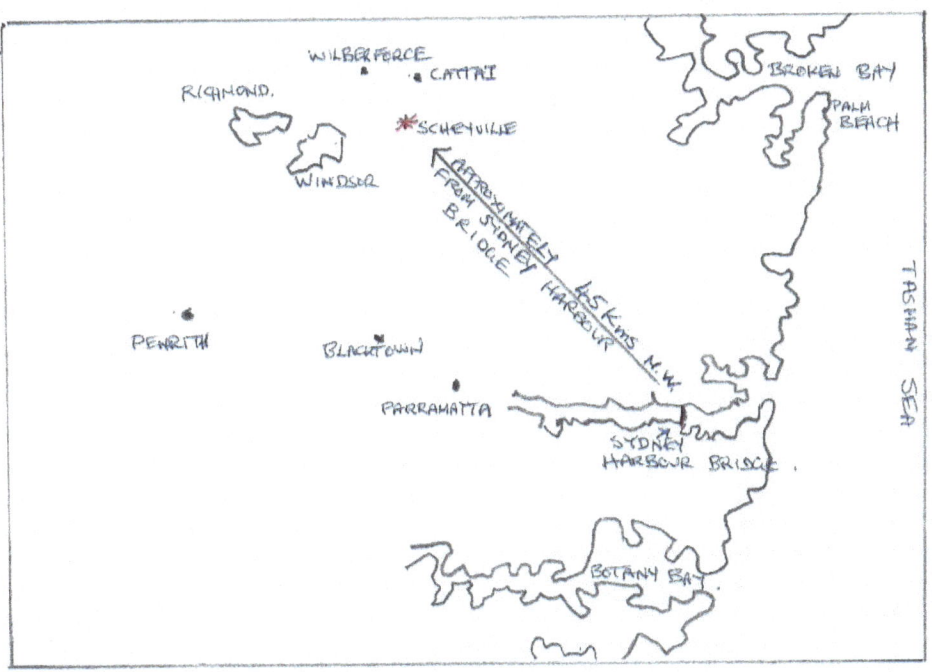

Hand-drawn map of Scheyville

The Dharug, the Hawkesbury Commons and a man called Schey

The stories in this book and the physical area that has been used since white occupation relate to meadows that contain remnants of Cumberland Plain Grey Box or Ironbark woodland. In the north-west corner of Scheyville National Park is Longneck Lagoon. This area contains endangered and vulnerable species of vegetation and wetlands.

Evidence indicates that the Dharug Aboriginal people frequented this area because fish, tortoises, birds and eggs would have been available to them. It is believed a substantial, mobile Indigenous population inhabited the area. They would have hunted in the surrounding woodlands. The Park Conservation Plan notes that the long history of European occupation and use of the area has heavily disturbed some areas and 'is likely to have destroyed many Aboriginal sites. An archaeological survey recorded 16 sites with most of these concentrated on the margins of Longneck Lagoon and along Longneck and Llewellyn Creeks'. These days the area is located in the area of the Deerubbin Aboriginal Land Council. 'On-going liaison is maintained with the Deerubbin Local Aboriginal Land Council in regard to management of Aboriginal sites in the Park'.[1]

Kohen writes that 'the Aboriginal occupiers [of the Cattai Region] combined their use of the area with seasonal migration to other areas such as the upper Blue Mountains in the summer months'.[2] Different articles on life before European settlement places the existence of Aboriginals in the area for anywhere between 13,000 and 30,000 years.

Kohen notes that there were probably 5000 to 8000 Aboriginal people in the Sydney region before 1788. Of these, about 2000 were probably Dharug, with about 1000 living between Parramatta and the Blue Mountains. They lived in bands of about fifty people each and hunted over their own territory. Kohen's research

---

[1] *Scheyville National Park Conservation Management Plan,* Department of Environment and Climate Change, 2009.
[2] Kohen. J. as quoted in Appendix 1 of Proudfoot, Helen. *The Hawkesbury - A Thematic History.* Hawkesbury City Council. 1987.

indicates 'there may have been 100 inland Dharug alive by the 1850s, which appears to tally with what appear to be numbers of non-Christians in the 1856 Census'.

A rarely recognised fact is that the Surveyor-General, Mitchell, generally employed Aboriginal names for newly mapped natural features. He argued that a map became more useful when the settler could fix his position by asking local Aborigines their name for a feature and checking it against the map. Other explorers used the names of public figures, perhaps likely patrons, with Oxley, for example, distributing the names of British officials about the Liverpool Plains. This policy, reported by Jeans, is the probable reason that New South Wales has more placenames today with an Aboriginal meaning![3]

Research from a few decades ago suggested that disease and fighting after the arrival of white man had unfortunately decimated the Indigenous people of the area. However, current research by Grace Karskens confirms that 'they continued to live in the area over the 19th and 20th centuries and used the commons in particular to camp on. Thousands of Dharug as well as other Aboriginal people live in the region today, including the people I am working with.'[4]

Pitt Town Common

Research by Helen Proudfoot informs us that:

> The land grants which opened up the fertile alluvial lands of the Hawkesbury Valley in 1794 were largely initiated in Pitt Town. These are the earliest grants in the colony outside Sydney and Parramatta area and the allotments at Pitt Town Bottoms are the oldest farms in Australia still under cultivation.
>
> At Pitt Town the vital farming connection between the floodplain where the best crops grew and the adjacent upland where cattle, sheep, goats and horses could graze above flood level was reinforced by the creation

---

[3] Jeans, D.N. *An Historical Geography of NSW to 1901*. Reed Education, 1972. p 36.
[4] Karskens, Grace. Email to Roger Donnelly 4 January 2021.

of Nelson Common by Governor King in 1804. By demarcating common grazing land to the east of what is now Old Stock Route Road, King defined and delimited the settlement along Wilberforce, York and Canning Reaches. Governor Bligh established a model farm on the land sloping down to York Reach, a highly significant act of practical assistance to the standards and techniques of the ex-convict settlers around. This model farm was the earliest of its sort in the colony, it was created by a controversial Governor who had a special affinity with the Hawkesbury.[5]

When Governor Macquarie created service towns, securely above flood level, Pitt Town was one of the five sites chosen. The creation of the new town in 1810–11, then re-sited in 1815, regularised the symbiosis between lowland and upland, which farmers had already been developing. The insertion of a small urban service centre immediately above the floodplain with a street which is still entirely apparent 190 years after 1815 consolidated the community along the reaches. An important element of this consolidation was the tying of the town allotments to floodplain farms. Despite a degree of subdivision and realignment, the earliest farms are still legible as the street system of the Macquarie town.

"The area also reflects the later growth of citrus and stone-fruit orchards on the upland, which for much of the twentieth century provided an alternative cash-crop after wheat had been wiped out by disease in the 1860s.

Such indications of the intensely rural character of the Macquarie towns are now rare elsewhere".

As settlement expanded, three main clusters of farming districts developed, centred around Sydney, Parramatta and the Hawkesbury.

Pitt Town Common lies east of the village of Pitt Town and stretches between Arndell's Cattai grant and the Hawkesbury Road to Windsor. It grew from

---

[5] Australian Heritage Database at www.environment.gov.au/egi-bin/ahdb. Pitt Town District Cultural Precinct, Pitt Town Rd, Pitt Town, NSW. Hard copy obtained 15 August 2008.

5650 acres (2620 hectares) to 8950 acres (3580 hectares) by 1835. The quality of the land was described by Surveyor Felton Marhew as 'middling forest land' to the south, 'undulating land' across the centre of the common, with 'high rocky ridges to the north and swampy near Cattai Creek'. The elevated land would have been doubly useful in time of flood.[6]

Helen Proudfoot notes:

> In the 1846 Parish map, the names of John Larkin Scarvill, William Johnson and Joseph Smith are written across the common and probably refer to the 'three persons resident in the district' who acted as holders of the lease on behalf of the settlers. The legal situation remained similar in the following decades. By 1894, small 'Homestead Selections' of between forty and 65 acres had been parcelled out in both the northern and southern parts of the Common, with some even smaller blocks of about ten acres [four hectares].[7]

Macquarie's towns

Although the Pitt Town area was some of the most productive arable land in the colony, it suffered from the frequent loss of crops to floods in the early years following its establishment.

On tours of the district in December 1810 and January 1811, Governor Macquarie selected and marked out the flood-free sites of Windsor, Richmond, Castlereagh, Wilberforce and Pitt Town. He located these on high ground against flood dangers, and four of the five sites he selected were approachable along the river by substantial vessels.

The necessity of siting the town above the 16-metre level regarded as the minimum height to ensure safety from future floods meant that Pitt Town had originally been positioned on high land too far from the river farms to be of use in

---

[6] Proudfoot, Helen. The Hawkesbury Commons 1804-1987 *Heritage Australia,* Summer 1987, p 24.
[7] Ibid.

sheltering the settlers in flood time. Originally laid out on either side of today's Old Stock Route, much of the town was in what is now Scheyville National Park. It had to be re-sited because the lowland settlers refused to move into it because of its distance from their lowland farms. As a result, Macquarie re-sited it in 1815, lower down the ridgeline and closer to the lowland farms. Little detail of the original town remains in the historical record and no physical remains constitute any archaeological evidence of its existence. Because of the topography of the new 1815 site, Macquarie was unable to plan the new Pitt Town in the rectangular grid form of his other towns and its triangulated grid follows the narrow line of the ridge. Macquarie could only mark out a single long road which led from and effectively bisected his planned town into two roughly triangular portions, allowing just nine street blocks, before the allotments slid into flood-prone lands on three sides. It also incorporated an existing burial ground, and has an unusual triangular public 'square' reserved for open space. The original plan for the re-siting of Pitt Town still exists, signed by Macquarie himself.[8]

Bruce Baskerville informs us that Pitt Town Common income was mainly derived from various fees for loads of wheel-wrights' stuff, slabs, shingles, palings, rails, posts, firewood licences and stone, as well as rents of various paddocks on the common.[9]

The Park Conservation Plan tells us that the quarrying of building stone was apparently being carried out on a commercial scale by the mid-nineteenth century.[10] St James Anglican Church in Pitt Town was built of this stone in 1857, and later Victorian stone homes in Pitt Town such as Bona Vista, built in 1889, are said to be made of blocks quarried on the common.

---

[8] Barkley, Jan, Nichols, Michelle & Hawkesbury (N.S.W.) Council. *Hawkesbury 1794-1994: the first two hundred years of the second colonisation.* Windsor, N.S.W: Hawkesbury City Council, 1994.
[9] Baskerville, Bruce. The Hawkesbury Commons, *HistoryMatrix*. https://historymatrix.wordpress.com/2013/07/15/the-hawkesbury-commons/ 2006.
[10] *Scheyville National Park Conservation Management Plan,* Department of Environment and Climate Change, 2009.

Another result of the drought of the early 1890s was the 1893 establishment of the Pitt Town Village Settlement on the Nelson Common which was intended to help agricultural labourers and their families.

William Francis Schey, 1857–1913

It would be remiss if a history such as this was written without some information on the individual after which it is named.

The name 'Scheyville' was given to the area in recognition of the work of New South Wales MP William Schey, who was instrumental in the development of State-sponsored welfare for the unemployed and disadvantaged. He had been interested in the area since the inception of the co-operative settlement. Schey actively promoted the settlement, visited the area several times, and presented the views and complaints of the settlers to Parliament.

In 1911 whilst serving as the Director of Labour, NSW he authored a book titled The Government Agricultural Training Farm, at Scheyville, near Pitt Town, New South Wales. The Descriptive Account, as he calls it, includes a list of rules the boys have to abide by, accounts information as at 30 June 1911, an application form to attend the Farm, a Bill of Fare for the students and much other information. It is quite a marketing tool.

Schey was born in London and attended the City of London Middle Class School. Having a yearning for the sea life he served an apprenticeship in the White Star Line. At nineteen he qualified as a second mate. Ill health caused him to leave the merchant navy and for a short time he took a billet as schoolmaster at the naval training school at Kohi-Marra, near Auckland, New Zealand.

It was the end of 1876 that he settled in Sydney. He worked as a chainman under the Harbours and River Department helping lay out the retaining wall round the Sydney Botanical Gardens. He then worked for the railway service for approximately six years. An addendum of good character certificate granted him by the railways commissioner, Mr Goodchap, upon leaving the Parramatta Goods Shed states, "I desire to add to this certificate that during the period of Mr Schey's service in the Railway Department of New South Wales, it became evident that he possessed abilities fitting him for a higher position than the one he held, and had he elected to remain in the service, I should have taken an early opportunity of promoting him."

Schey first entered Parliament in 1887 as the member for Redfern. Many resolutions he put before the Parliament called attention to the woes and wants of the unemployed, and he constantly urged the passing of State Pensions for Aged and Infirm Persons.

Most of his time in Parliament he was a Protectionist. In 1894 he won the Darlington seat for Labor, held the seat as a Protectionist the next year and was defeated as an Independent in 1898.

In 1901 he was appointed Chairman of a Royal Commission on Labor matters and became State Director of Labour in 1905 when the State Labor Bureau was created.

Outside of politics his main interest was Freemasonry. He was a past Master of Lodge United Service, and a member of Mark Master Lodge.[11]

---

[11] Dodds, Robyn. (Schey's grand-daughter) notes and an article in The Patriot Newsletter July 20, 1898 supplied to Roger Donnelly.
Consultation was also made of :Audley, R. M. 'Schey, William Francis (1857–1913)', *Australian Dictionary of Biography*, National Centre of Biography, Australian National University, http://adb.anu.edu.au/biography/schey-william-francis-8356/; paraphrased from Donnelly, Roger. *The Scheyville Experience*. UQP. 2001. pp 199-200.

From Pitt Town to Scheyville – agricultural training begins
Responses to the 1890s Depression

The New South Wales colonial government announced in the Government Gazette on 13 June 1893 that part of the Pitt Town Common would become the Pitt Town Co-operative Labour Settlement. This area once formed part of the former Nelson Common.

Pitt Town was one of three co-operative settlements established in the 1890s. The other settlements were at Wilberforce and Bega. A form of socialism played out in late nineteenth century Australia.

The State expected certain outcomes for the unemployed, by establishing the three settlements. Pitt Town was the largest, most controversial of these, and was referred to as an 'experiment' in socialistic living. The unemployed and their families also had expectations.

Reverend Benjamin Backhouse was influential in the colony. He explained to the 1896 Pitt Town inquiry that 'in 1892 a committee was formed with a view to obtain from the Government such assistance and concessions from the Government in the way of land as would enable a number of people to be put on Village Settlements in the country. Just at this juncture, the Reverend Tucker from Melbourne came to Sydney and illustrated what they were doing in Victoria. This gave impetus to the movement, and the committee of which Backhouse was a member organised a large meeting in the Town Hall on 22 May 1893. There were eighty influential men on the platform and about 5,000 people in the body of the hall. At that meeting a village committee was appointed, principally to induce the government to frame an Act and get it passed by Parliament.'[1] Dr Roseby drafted, and the committee eventually published this model for the Labour Settlements Act. The Pitt Town Settlement was officially inaugurated on 23 September 1893.[2]

---

[1] Progress Report from the Select Committee on Pitt Town Settlement. Legislative Assembly NSW. 1896. Minutes of Evidence. p 22.
[2] State Records of NSW Archives Investigator Details on Agency 2395. Government Labour Camp, Pitt Town. start date: 13 July 1893; end date 17 June 1896.

A testing time

By the early 1890s, two thirds of New South Wales' population lived in urban centres. The gold rushes of the 1850s ignited an economic boom which lasted a few decades.

The Argus newspaper editorial of 26 January 1888 wording was, "Australia confronts the world today with a record of 100 years, with a marvellous past, a prosperous present and a future of boundless possibilities." Eighteen months later trouble arrived in the form of a maritime strike over the right to unionism. This was followed by a bitter shearers strike in Queensland in early 1891. Later that year the first of the local banks failed. The banking situation worsened during 1892 and the lowest point came in 1893.

1893 saw the establishment of the socialist farming experiment at Pitt Town (Scheyville) there was no welfare system as we know it and unemployment levels exceeded 25 per cent. The onset of drought and low primary produce prices exacerbated the situation. Prosperity would not return until the turn of the century. The conditions of this decade fostered a rise in national sentiment, socialism, and formation of the Labor Party.

The Man from Snowy River and Other Verses by Banjo Paterson was published as was Henry Lawson's While the Billy Boils. Art schools flourished and many impressive buildings such as The Queen Victoria Building and the Sydney Hospital were built. On the sporting front the Sheffield Shield cricket competition began in 1892.

Brian Dickey informs us, in his history of social welfare in Australia:

> In the critical years of economic and political evil of the 1890s, the problem of unemployment received mixed and intermittent attention alongside efforts to support destitute families, children and aged people. The depths of the depression around Australia throughout the 1890s saw the question handled firstly through relief payments to destitute families, secondly through the creation of government funded publicly sustained employment bureaus, and thirdly by the provision of strictly limited

opportunities for relief. When the better conditions returned the issue tried in government was one of getting development under way again. In New South Wales, the Labour Bureau became a permanent feature of the administration under various guises. It eventually became located in the Department of Labour whose principal charter was to police the Factories and Shops Act of 1896.[3]

The State makes a move

It is necessary to understand the seriousness of the unemployment situation that led to the decision to establish the Pitt Town Co-operative Settlement.

A Government Labour Bureau was established on 18 February 1892. This Bureau opened at the Post Office stables for two months and was then granted use of the Exhibition Building from April to 29 September. Between 500 and 700 slept here nightly in the winter months, blankets being supplied by the Government. Bathing, cleaning etc. was carried out by a committee of the unemployed, under the direction of the Superintendent. Many of this large crowd were described as "habitual loafers – and some worse – who would not work, and to whom compulsory bathing and cleanliness was a terror".

On 2 October 1892 the Bureau moved to premises at the rear of No 2 Police Station, at the junction of George and Pitt Streets. In that first six months, the cost of rations was £2324; the average number of families getting relief was 220, and the average number of rations weekly was 520.

When the Bureau opened there were thousands of unemployed in and around Sydney appealing to the Government for employment, holding public meetings, and canvassing the general public for aid to assist them to live, and at times the situation was desperate and indeed dangerous.

---

[3] Dickey, Brian. *No charity there: a short history of social welfare in Australia.* Allen & Unwin Sydney 1987

During the first six months of the Bureau's operation 13,447 were registered for work and 5,867 sent to work. In an effort to find out the probable number of unemployed, in August 1892 old registration tickets were called in and re-registration took place. The total sent to work for the year February 1892 to February 1893 was 8,154. Tradespeople of all kinds as well as station and farm hands were sent to all parts of the colony. It was reported that '206 married families' permanently settled in the country. A large number of boys averaging twelve to sixteen years of age were also sent to farmers with the consent of their parents.[4]

The objects of the Pitt Town settlement

The committee of twenty-eight had five ministers of religion as members. The main, but not exclusive object of the scheme was: 'to provide the means of living for the present large numbers of persons out of employment, by settling them in a Village or industrial Settlement, on suitable blocks of land, under the direction and management of a Board of Control, appointed by the Government, consisting of no more than sixteen, nor less than eight persons, of whom one fourth may be females.'[5]

The Board would be granted leases by the Government for any term not exceeding twenty-eight years. The Act made no provision for purchase, the tenure being exclusively leasehold. No rent would be payable for the first four years, but at the expiration of that time, as well as a rent charge, the Government advance would also become repayable, at the rate of eight per cent per annum.

Other features of this fully co-operative or communal scheme included the provision that so many hours per week must be done by each enrolled settler for

---

[4] Legislative Assembly of NSW. 1892-1893. Government Labour Bureau (First Annual Report) pp 957-958 of NSW Parliament Records.
[5] Parliament of NSW. Act No. 34 of 1893. An Act to establish and regulate Labour Settlements on Crown Lands 1893. Section 2 to Section 7.

the settlement itself. Any aggregated profits were only divisible after all persons in each settlement had received a fair allowance for maintenance.

The settlement was to be largely dominated by the idea of equality. As near an approach to this was to be arrived at as possible.

Settlers were to do forty-eight hours work a week for the benefit of the settlement. Beyond these hours fixed by regulation, a member's time would be his own. A settler might have a home of his own.

Attitudes to women

A clue to the role of women in the 1890s is given in the book on Reverend Ayling. His great nephew, Robert Ayling gives some thought to the role of Ayling's wife. He writes: 'It is noteworthy that there are few references in the public records to the part played in John Ayling's professional life by his wife. It is known she was hired as Assistant Female Teacher in partnership with him by the Presbyterian School Board and that she visited the village Labour Camps with him in Pitt Town. Apart from a few private letters these are the only known references to her public role. Perhaps, this lack of record is reflective of the male-oriented times, reinforced by the fact that she bore nine children and raised seven, much of the time in difficult financial circumstances. In the absence of modern conveniences, she was undoubtedly busy enough.'[6]

Officialdom had certain attitudes enshrined in it. For instance, when speaking to Electoral Act Amendments in the Legislative Assembly on 16 May 1894, Mr Barton, later Prime Minister, said that 'the principal qualification for electors in the act - the real qualification - is manhood with residence'.[7]

In June 1894, a visitor from Tasmania accompanied the Reverend J. Kinghorn to the village settlement on one of his usual weekly visits. After praising the male superintendent on the progress of the material improvements, visually

---

[6] Ayling, Robert I. *Rev. John Ayling Australian pioneer: the life of Rev. John Ayling clergyman, educator, beekeeper, 1825-1897* Robert I. Ayling Marco Island, Florida 1999. p 198.

[7] New South Wales *Parliamentary Debates*. Legislative Assembly, 16 May 1894.

accessible, he took the liberty of making suggestions to the board of management through the paper that 'one of the first things the writer noticed was the groups of healthy-looking women talking together without apparently the opportunity of occupying their time in any useful work.' He asked 'is it not possible to find work for so much idle female labour? The primitive nature of their homes prevents their spending much time on the domestic affairs, and I have no doubt the majority of the women would be delighted to have suitable work. Now it has occurred to me that the board of management might profitably send them wool for knitting into socks &c. If the Board have not funds for this purpose, private benevolence might very well step in and supply the want.'

Not content with implying that the women of the settlement were lazy, the article further states: 'another thing also occurred to me. Is not the system of each little household doing its own cooking a great waste of good food? Would it not be better to have one kitchen, with a large oven and a large boiler, where good soup could be made and joints baked, and the settler could have a good dinner at much less cost than at present? The kitchen could be run by five or six women, taking it in turns; it would give them a good knowledge of cooking, and utilise their time profitably.' This writer also expressed the opinion that the assistance of a local committee would be of assistance to the Sydney Board.[8]

The above gives an insight into the tone of letter that was published at the time, attitudes towards women, the fact that the success or otherwise of the settlement was being judged in the press, and pushing a case for the settlers that they wanted some input to their own affairs. Articles in the press of the time indicate that there were a lot of visitors to the site, both official and unofficial, observing progress. The idea of a communal cooking facility was used at Scheyville when it housed post–World War Two European immigrants between 1949 and 1964. The article does give a clue to the women at the settlement at least looking healthy.

---

[8] 'The Village Settlements.' *Windsor and Richmond Gazette* (NSW: 1888–1961) 9 June 1894: 10.

This was a time of greater inequality between class and gender than now exists. A time of rapid social change. A time for radical groups.[9]

What if we were to hold a dialogue between our past and present, as Scates suggests?

Some high-profile members of contemporary society are at the forefront of pushing for more women on the boards of Australian companies and government organisations.

These people have a case. However, The New South Wales Parliamentary Inquiry into the failure of the Pitt Town Co-operative Settlement, 1896, informs us that Reverend Roseby insisted that the rules of the Board of Control included a provision that up to twenty-five per cent of the members of the Board of Management could be female. The maximum number that could be on the Board was sixteen. To explore the reasons why no women ever nominated is not possible in this work, and no one from the 1890s is alive to interview, but the provision was there. Thus, there were some far-sighted males in the 1890s!

Daily life and schooling

In August 1893, all members of the settlement's Board of Control made a formal application for the establishment of a public school. A hand-written letter by John Roseby on the letterhead of the New South Wales Local Option League, Temperance Hall, Sydney was intended to help push for the establishment of the school. The President of the League was Reverend Bertie Joyce. More than half of the League Vice-Presidents, central committee members and representatives were ministers of religion. The remainder of the officials were Members of Parliament. The estimated school population was 130 pupils from a settlement child population of some 250.

---

[9] Scates, Bruce. *A New Australia. Citizenship, Radicalism and the First Republic.* Cambridge University Press. 1997. And Scates, Bruce. Mobilising Manhood: Gender and the Great Strike in Australia and New Zealand. *Gender and History*, Vol 9 No 2 August 1997, pp285-309.

On 20 October 1893, when completing a compulsory assessment sheet for the Department of Public Instruction, he wrote that 'the settlers are poor, but appear to have a very keen interest in their future', and that 'the prospects of the Settlement are encouraging', and he 'saw no good reason why a Public School should not be established at once'. In his Summary Report on Application, however, in December 1893, he was advocating that the 'interests of education would be well met by the erection of a cheap wooden building'. Cheap was the operative word as some 'facts and circumstances have come under my personal observation. I do not consider the Settlement has a very bright future before it and it would be unwise to erect a more expensive structure. ... The children are practically beyond the means of education and a community among themselves.'

On 4 April 1894, the school opened on a two-acre reserve within the settlement with a male principal, male assistant, one male pupil teacher and one female pupil teacher. The building specifications called for the 'best Colonial hardwood, seventy feet long and twenty feet wide with brick chimneys and fireplaces'. School teacher Bennett and his Assistant, Clements, applied for special consideration for a form of travelling allowance, as there was no accommodation on the settlement for them, and they incurred a cost of 'a minimum of fifteen shillings to keep a horse and travel from Windsor. The local Inspector of Schools, C.J. Pitt, supported the teachers in their application, but was ambivalent about the prospects of the Settlement.'[10]

The Windsor and Richmond Gazette reported that the settlement at Pitt Town Common was the site of a picnic on 22 June 1894 for 250 children of the school. The picnic marked the start of the two-week winter break which the children began after an unsuccessful assault on the mountains of food supplied by the ladies of the district.[11]

---

[10] The Settlement School and Pitt Town School. NSW Records Office Item 5/17356.2 Pitt Town Co-operative Settlement.)
[11] 'Picnic at Pitt Town Settlement.' *Windsor and Richmond Gazette (NSW: 1888–1961)* 30 June 1894: 6.

Although they may have been poor, the settlers knew how to enjoy themselves. Inspector Pitt was suspicious of the settlers intended behaviour; when the Board of Control wrote on their behalf to use the school building as a reading room, he replied to Reverend Roseby, 'the settlers have already urged on the Contractors to hand over the keys to them, so that they could hold their dance parties there. ... Once they got permission to use the school premises they would be used for every conceivable meeting and fad, and in my opinion, its condition each morning would never be fit for teachers and children. ... The settlers have a commodious marquee at their doors which they have used as a Reading or Meeting Room, and if that doesn't suit them it would be easy for them to erect a wooden hall for themselves.'[12]

Special permission was granted for the use of the school for a lecture on cropping operations by the Principal of the Hawkesbury Agricultural College. Inspector Pitt also approved that students be admitted free to the school, and that copy books be provided free. He considered it the Board of Control's duty to provide drawing books and other requisites.

A picture emerges of involvement of the Church, the State, a fair but firm schools Inspector, and poor people who deserved special consideration in certain contexts, but parents who couldn't be trusted to leave a school property in a fit, usable state if allowed to use the premises after hours.

When the Pitt Town Public School file was examined it was found that schooling was conducted in the area at least from 1875. For example:

'The Council of Education had agreed to the amalgamation of the Church of England School at Pitt Town with the Grono Park Public School in November 1875. New stone buildings had been erected by January 1879 and the school population was 105 pupils. A teacher's residence of four rooms and kitchen (if required) of bricks were provided.' (The Settlement school was wooden and no teacher accommodation provided.) The Local Board solicited 'the honor of the

---

[12] The Settlement School and Pitt Town School. NSW Records Office Item 5/17356.2 Pitt Town Co-operative Settlement.

attendance' at the school opening of the Secretary of Public Instruction and offered 'a conveyance to meet him at Mulgrave Station'. By 1881 an evening Public School had been established. By 1883 the school 'now ranks as a school of the Fifth Class' and a Sewing Mistress was to be appointed. The examiners report on the teacher showed that he had 'attainments in Alternative Subjects' such as geometry and algebra as well as the 'Ordinary Subjects' such as reading, writing, arithmetic and grammar.

In 1891, friends of the Pitt Town School contributed four pounds five shillings 'in connection with Arbor Day'. Not everybody though, was better off at the Pitt Town School. Written history records the beginning of the bad times as 1893, but labourer John Saraje was begging for cancellation of his debt for his children's Public School instruction in 1889. 'I am at work now, but that is nearly finished, and don't know of any other work to be obtained.' John had eleven children, 'one married, but I have to support all the others' he wrote. The Under-Secretary of the Department of Public Instruction also exempted a Mr Sullivan from arrears of fees in September 1889. In 1893 Mrs Smallwood, who 'is very old and nearly blind' had a report submitted on her arrears of school fees. The recommendation was 'to wait for a time and she would pay when her corn comes in'.[13]

Letters to the Department of Public Instruction in February 1889 concerning two orphaned boys at Pitt Town (Sydney and George Watt) indicate a special case was to be mounted if you cared for orphaned children and wanted exemption from school fees, whereas those children deemed as 'State Relief Children' were exempted from paying fees.

In 1893–94 the Inspector of Schools recommended the Settlement School children be exempted from fees! There was a means test for exemption from public education fees back in the 1890s. It appears you received more consideration if you had nothing!

---

[13] NSW State Records. Item 5/17356.2 and 5/17536.1 Bundle A. Pitt Town 1876-1934.

It wasn't just school fees that people were hounded for: a Government Gazette of 11 May 1894 announced that action would be taken to declare forfeited any conditional purchase (of land) on which instalments were in arrears on 31 May.[14] People who could not meet their arrears would forfeit their land, lose any money already paid and lose any improvements they had made. The Minister claimed that a large number of people wouldn't pay until the money was squeezed out of them. That year, an extension of time had already been given for 1,671 conditional purchases held by over 800 people. Although it may have been true that some wouldn't pay at all if the law wasn't administered, times were clearly still tough for those who had some means of buying land, let alone those who were so needy enough to be sent to Pitt Town.

The media

The settlement was on trial in the media from the outset. The 1896 Parliamentary Inquiry merely legitimised its closure. The locals, who had been in the district for a couple of generations by the 1890s, also had expectations. Overall, they were against the sort of people who were sent to Pitt Town. They and the activities at the settlement were viewed as an economic threat to the freeholders. They viewed the loss of part of their common for grazing as a legitimate cause for antagonism towards the newcomers who were thrust upon the area.

The Daily Telegraph, although it described the failure of the settlement as a 'fiasco', attempted to take a balanced view. It recognised there were 'real workers' at Pitt Town. It also had kind words for the Board, saying, 'The resignation of the Board of Control was in the peculiar circumstances they found themselves in, clearly inevitable'. It believed 'the public, on whose behalf they undertook the work, should give them credit for having done their best according to their light, and under circumstances exceptionally trying, to bring the experiment to a successful issue.' The Domain and Statue orators, who pushed for the adoption of their 'socialistic brotherhood' were to blame. 'Theoretically, co-operation in

---

[14] 'Overdue Payments on Conditional Purchases.' *New South Wales Government Gazette (Sydney, NSW: 1832–1900)* 11 May 1894: 3094.

farming is as practicable as co-operation in the factory or the store … but when the principle, as applied in the latter enterprises, is looked into … each co-operator is paid … according to the amount of his shares and purchases … the co-operators get in the proportions they give … [whereas] at Pitt Town … the co-operator who did little or no work demanded an equal share of the results with his fellows who did the most and best work.'[15]

The Sydney Morning Herald, a week earlier showed more sympathy with the Minister for Lands, who 'finds himself confronted by something like a dilemma.' He had received a favourable report on the character of some South Coast land for the continuance of the experiment but was being reminded of 'his duty to see that the public estate is administered in the public interest.' The paper claims that the Minister 'is also anxious to do whatever he can, that would tend without placing a burden upon the State to solve the difficulty of the unemployed.' He also can see that throwing open the reserved land, 'it would at once be taken up by people in the district who are accustomed to farming, and would work it to advantage without assistance from the State. … He has realised, he says, that he cannot do both these things.' If the unemployed were looked after, it would be 'an injustice to the hundreds of struggling settlers who, with perhaps but little more means at command than the means possessed by the Government protégés on labour settlements, had taken up land on their own account, and, fighting against all adverse influences, had managed to support themselves.' This article came but a month after another article – pushing the case of the 'bona-fide' settlers.[16]

Another article, (3 January 1895) in the Windsor and Richmond Gazette presented a special case for the freehold settlers. It conceded that those who accepted the responsibilities of office on the Board of Control did so with the good intention to assist 'their fellow colonists who were at the time in dire distress'. However, it took aim at the Reverend Thomas Roseby, a member of the Board of

---

[15] 'The Village Settlement Fiasco.' *The Daily Telegraph (Sydney, NSW: 1883–1930)* 22 February 1895: 4.
[16] 'The Sydney Morning Herald.' *The Sydney Morning Herald (NSW: 1842–1954)* 16 February 1895: 8.

Control. It referred to lectures he gave in April 1894 on the topic of Village Settlement in New Zealand. He had received a letter from the New Zealand Minister for Lands, explaining the reasons why their Village Homestead Special Settlement system was working satisfactorily and had been in operation for six years. New Zealand's experience proved that that you needed (1) the right locality to form a settlement, that is to say near a centre of population, or in a district where work can be found in the neighbourhood, (2) the right class of land, and (3) the right class of people. Prior to the settlement, a large number of very old residents of Windsor gained a fair living by wood-cutting and carting. They now found it hard to compete with the village settlers who had the unusual advantage of being provided by the government – out of taxpayers' money – with machinery, tools, food, clothing and a place to live, rent free. Further, clause 35 of the Board's Regulations stated that the board shall accept work on such terms as might compete on the basis of a lower wage with workmen outside the settlement. The article paints the older residents as the 'bona-fide settlers'.[17]

The Windsor and Richmond Gazette claimed on 13 June 1896 that 'from the time of its establishment right up to the last the Gazette has supported the settlement scheme, and despite the cavilling of captious critics, has held that under proper management and wise administration, coupled with a desire of the settlers themselves to work harmoniously together, it could have been brought to a successful issue.'[18]

Not all newspapers supported the settlement. The media were as scathing of the experiment as the individual opponents.

---

[17] 'The Pitt Town Village Settlement. By a twain of Erstwhile Settlers.' *The Windsor Australian*. 3 January 1895.
[18] 'Pitt Town Settlement.' *Windsor and Richmond Gazette (NSW: 1888–1961)* 13 June 1896: 7.

Pitt Town gets modelled on Leongatha

In the report on the Casual Labour Farm of the Labour Commissioners of New South Wales 31 August 1901, to the New South Wales Parliament, it was reported that:

> Under the Public Instruction Department an attempt was made to model the Settlement on similar lines to those in Victoria, notably, the one at Leongatha. A Manager was appointed, and the work of clearing, fencing and ploughing the land, and repairing certain of the huts was entered upon. This control lasted from 17 June 1896, to 30th June 1900.[19]

After the Parliamentary Report of 1896, Pitt Town was modelled on the Leongatha Labour Colony, Victoria, which functioned from 1893 to 1919. A Colonel Goldstein was the honorary Superintendent of Leongatha from 1894 to 1904, and his attitude towards the unemployed shows similarities to that of Schey. Aid wasn't to be given indiscriminately, but a system of relief for the destitute was needed. In the 1891 Annual Report of the Charity Organisation Society of Victoria, Goldstein stressed:

> … that the disproportionately large floating body of beggars and vagrants in these colonies is due partly to the rapid growth of the Colony, but chiefly to the unhappy practice in Europe of shipping family failures to Australia in the foolish belief that a changed sky would induce changed hearts ... The difficulties of the unemployed problem have been caused quite as much as by the presence of this latter body as by the existence of any extended area of labour disturbance.[20]

Some researchers, such as Metcalf and Forster, have pushed the case that, 'In Australia there is considerable historical evidence of governmental pressure

---

[19] NSW Parliamentary Papers. Government Labour Bureau Reports: for the year ended 30 June 1898 p5 in papers for second session 1898 Vol 3 p 837and for the period ended 31 August 1901. pp 12-15 in Parliamentary papers 1901 Vol 6 pp 380-383.
[20] Charity Organisation Society of Victoria. Annual Report 1891.

toward communal living ... official support and direct financial subsidisation of communes in Australia in the 1890s was partially undertaken because nervous colonial governments saw this as a way to get disgruntled radicals out of the cities – where they could make revolution – and onto the land, albeit as communards, where they were safely out of the way. Some of these nineteenth century communal groups, such as the Leongatha Labour Colony in Victoria, resembled concentration camps more than happy communes.'[21]

Hence the importance of comparing the two settlements and how they operated, using comments from the respective inquiries. The Select Committee Inquiring into the Leongatha Labour Colony in 1900 and the Minutes of Evidence of the 1896 proceedings of the Report from the Select Committee Inquiring into the Abandonment of the Pitt Town Settlement reveal that both the Victorian and New South Wales Governments had a similar objective of helping the unemployed but approached the problem and executed solutions differently.

Positives of Pitt Town

Extracts from the Committee of Inquiry into the failure of the Pitt Town Settlement 1896.

Not all the comments at the inquiry were negative. Reverend Backhouse claimed:

> ... under ordinary circumstances, the position of these settlers would be a drain on public charity while the present Depression continues. We cannot see men, women, or children starve. And how much better it is for us to help people help themselves than to feed them on the bread of idleness. It was seen as a great help if the Settlement was near some established centre of population to enable settlers to get work outside.[22]

---

[21] Forster, P.M. and Metcalf, W.J. 'Communal Groups: Social Laboratories or places of exile?' *Communal Societies Journal,* Vol. 20, 2000, pp. 1-11.
[22] Progress report from the Select Committee on Pitt Town Settlement. Legislative Assembly NSW. 1896. Minutes of Evidence. p 22.

Reverend Thomas Roseby also addressed the inquiry and made a statement:

> It wasn't a failure. There were elements of success in it. In the first place there were one hundred families, and they had not been idle. It turned out that the land was only suitable for orchard purposes. It was originally a common, and the timber left on it by the residents around who used it as a common was only good for firewood, the best having been cleared away before; and the distance from Sydney, the low rates ruling, and the railway charges made firewood getting unremunerative. The land was really only suitable as orchard land, where it was unreasonable to expect any return under five or seven years.
>
> The hundred families lived a wholesome country life, their children were educated, there was no drinking or gambling allowed, and there were few complaints of idleness. There were no social scandals, and a policeman visited the settlement only two or three times in the course of two years.
>
> The scheme did not fail due to any inherent weakness of socialism, for it was not really a socialistic experiment. Some members of the Board did not have the least sympathy with socialism but stood by the scheme as being an experiment in co-operation. There was an element of co-operation but the scheme was rather that of a mild despotism than of socialism. The Board had absolute control. Secondly, the failure of the scheme was not due to internal dissensions. Some disaffection did exist, but it arose from attempts to get behind the back of the Board by writing to the Minister. Third, the real causes of the settlements failure were: 'An experiment carried out with men on the lowest social grade, with no means and no social coherence, could only be expected to succeed under

especially favourable circumstances – namely, good land, Governmental, and public sympathy, and steady and adequate help.[23]

The land was declared to be orchard land, wholly unsuitable for agriculture, and the government never believed in the thing, and never treated it as if they hoped or expected it to succeed.

Roseby also spoke highly of the trust and probity of Superintendent Waite, and his ability to manage large bodies of men. He defended members of the Board, especially Backhouse, for making frequent visits to the settlement.

Roseby also explained, like Backhouse, that the land had been a common, and that the early settlers had much better timber to send to market and to build with, and would have been able to get the best of the land that was available, to be able to rely on activities such as dairying.

The capital mistake of selecting unsuitable land was not the act of the Board of Control, but the Minister only, and this action was guided by 'expert' advice.

He spoke of the other two Superintendents, Vaughan Jenkins and Mr Tressider, as having knowledge of agriculture, 'but in other respects there is no doubt that their management of the Settlement was anything but a success.'

It was intimated by the investigating Committee that the Department of Industry had proposed to transform the settlement into a Casual Labour Farm.

The inquiry also discussed the idea that the first Board of Control had recommended to the Minister that the number of men on the settlement should be reduced to somewhere about twenty-five families and they would have been able to make a living.

The Board had, according to Roseby, resigned because the Government had done an illegal act, that is, they had disenrolled settlers who had done no wrong.

The reasons for failure in New South Wales included:

---

[23] Progress report from the Select Committee on Pitt Town Settlement. Legislative Assembly NSW. 1896. Minutes of Evidence. p 22.

- The original Board of Control was composed of civil servants who had no sympathy with the co-operative concept. The second was also composed of civil servants and the third composed of farmers and civil servants.

- The farmers were locals who were opposed to the common being taken away from them. One of those farmers became the Chairman of the Wilberforce Settlement Board of Control. That Chairman had stopped the rations of some of the best men at Pitt Town.

- The press was used to eulogise the Wilberforce Settlement and condemn Pitt Town. (according to the first witness at the inquiry, James Watson)

- No alternative sites were considered by the Minister. The Pitt Town site had been recommended to the then Minister for Lands, Mr Copeland, by Principal Thompson of the Hawkesbury Agricultural College.

- The site was a bad site. (witnesses William Musto, Harry Packwood and Watson)

- The site needed irrigating.

- The Board of Control did not pay the settlers, it only provided rations. (Musto and Packwood)

One witness, Harry Packwood, didn't see anything wrong with the principle of co-operation but didn't think that co-operation could work with a large body of men. 'A certain class of men wanted to domineer over the others. About twenty per cent of the men were drones. One of the great faults was favouritism. A little officialism crept in. There should have been one man at the head who could command respect.' Packwood also claimed there were too many managers.

Reinforcing this view was William Stanley who stated that 'the management was unfortunate in that it was frequently changed. The constant changing of Superintendents was an unfortunate necessity. There were three boards of control and four superintendents over a three-year period.'

The attitude of the Superintendents also played a part. William McGuire advised that 'Jenkins, the first Superintendent, was a drunkard. The appointment of Mr Waite led to dissatisfaction amongst eighty per cent of settlers and Tressider knew his work but was affected by drink.'

The Casual Labour Farm

The establishment of the Casual Labour Farm on the property of the former Government Labour Camp at the settlement was proclaimed on 17 June 1896. The purpose of the farm was to provide temporary accommodation and employment for men who were unemployed and homeless. Residents received meals and were paid according to the hours of labour.

Mr A. Hutchison was appointed manager. The property was fenced, premises were erected for the accommodation of workers and the land was prepared for cultivation of fruit and vegetables.

Men seeking assignment to the farm were selected by the Government Labour Bureau and were required to abide by the conditions and regulations. The first men arrived in January 1898; by 30 June of that year the population was twenty-six. During the period there were changes of personnel due to residents obtaining permanent employment. In addition to cultivation, tree felling was carried out. There were plans to increase the population to sixty and to develop the farm into a training school for agricultural workers.

After two years the operations manager reported a maximum of thirty men in residence. The men stayed for a maximum of three months and were required to be away for two months before re-entry to the farm. The weekly wage was three shillings and three pence after deducting the value of food. Twenty acres of land was cleared and the wood was sold. The farm had diversified to pig raising. The manager reported in relation to the effect of work on the men: 'Men come here run down in body, and sometimes almost naked; many of them are very helpless. I can, however, say with confidence, all leave here improved in every way; good men often leave reluctantly.'

The Labour Commissioners of New South Wales took responsibility for the farm in September 1900. They reported that of the 2,140 acres only 160 were cultivated. The twenty-acre orchard was neglected. The soil was poor and therefore the crops and stock were of poor quality. The farm was irrigated by five dams which were inadequate.

The whole of the living accommodation was insanitary and of the rudest description. The immediate response of the Commissioners was to maintain the farm until it could be sold and another site be purchased for the purpose. Following investigation, however, it was determined there was no Crown land suitable for the purpose within a similar distance from Sydney. The Commissioners therefore began working the farm. In its first year under the Commissioners, greater efficiency was reported, the number of men in residence doubled and the living accommodation was improved.

During 1900 to 1901 the Principal of the Hawkesbury Agricultural College inspected the farm, preparing a comprehensive report. It was recommended that the pig raising be further developed and diversification into dairying, poultry farming and bee keeping be attempted.

In the immediately following years under the Labour Commissioners and the State Labour Bureau of New South Wales, productivity and efficiency increased and the number of men sent to work on the farm grew; fifty-four men were in residence as at 30 June, 1906.

Conditions appear to have improved by 1906. The State Labour Bureau Report for the year ended 30 June 1906, refers to the Casual Labour Farm, Pitt Town as 'this shelter farm' and notes that '182 (men) were admitted as ordinary residents, and that 54 were in residence on 3oth June. In addition, 195 "special" men (or casuals) were admitted during the year in connection with the food relief work.' Although not all casuals completed their two weeks term at Pitt Town, 'Among the ordinary residents, reluctance to leave was very noticeable, and practically one-half of those who took shelter stayed on the establishment for three months and over.' The notes to the General Statement (Profit and Loss Account) state that 'taking into account increases in stock and permanent improvements, this establishment paid the whole of its working expenses, and gave a surplus of 365 pounds, or a balance of one pound for each and every day right throughout the year.' From their earnings men had been able to purchase 361 pounds of tobacco smoking pipes, in addition to clothing items.[24]

A separate paragraph headed 'Attentive and Sympathetic Administration' proudly reported that the Director and Assistant Director had taken much trouble to bestow personal and sympathetic attention on every person who had a complaint or wished to make a suggestion. They had 'from time to time, patiently listened to and reasoned with many who really did not merit the time or attention bestowed upon them.' If a complainant was referred to 'this office, he may be assured of sympathy, full information, and such assistance as circumstances may require and permit.'

Loafers were not tolerated, however. Another initiative of the year ended June 1906 was the Unemployed Labour Bill. Although the Bureau's work 'can be and is done under Executive Authority, the new Act, modelled on the lines of the Unemployed Workmen's Act of Great Britain,' would 'for the first time in this State, thoroughly systematize all matters relating to the unemployed, will provide necessary treatment for undesirables – not at present possible except in gaol – and give the local authorities in all municipal districts an interest in, and a responsibility for the unemployed of their particular district.' It provided for 'the amelioration of distress caused by unemployment, the detection and deterrence of the loafer.'

It did, however, transfer the responsibility from the state government to municipal councils.

By 1907 the dairy herd numbered 171, a silo with a capacity of 150 tonnes of ensilage had been constructed and the dairy was capable of handling a hundred cows and contained a separator, concussion churn and butter worker. The milk was used by the residents, but some of the butter was sold. There were ninety-one pigs

---

[24] NSW State Records Authority. Agency Nos: 2419- Labour Commissioners of NSW,2407Casual Labour Far, Pitt Town (1896-1910/Government Training Farm, Pitt Town (1910-1911) 2438- State Labour Bureau of NSW (1905-1912),2395- Government Labour Camp, Pitt Town, 2448- Training Farm for City Lads (1905-1910)/Government Agricultural Training Farm, Scheyville (1913-1940). Annual reports of these organisations and administrative notes and files.

at the end of June 1907 and sties and other piggery equipment had been built. There were seventy-six sheep which produced income from wool and skin sales.

A sawmill had been constructed with two saw benches for milling firewood and sawing timber. Millet was also grown and sold. All of the horse-drawn vehicles and most of the parts were made on the farm as was some of the equipment for fruit and vegetable cultivation. The residential quarters were much improved with the addition of a recreation room and a library.

By 1908 dairying had become the major industry of the farm with butter and milk being sold commercially. Millet production had increased to the extent that a plant for the manufacture of brooms was acquired. By 1910, the farm was known as the Government Training Farm, Pitt Town.

A training farm for city lads

By 1906 it had been recognised that not only was there difficulty in obtaining farm and station labour, but that no effort to turn the surplus workers of the metropolis into rural workers was likely to meet with success. The men, it was claimed 'were unadaptable, and too often had neither desire nor incentive to learn.' That year saw the introduction of farm training for city boys.[25]

The idea of giving city boys some knowledge of farm work was actively taken up with Dr Arthur MLA by the Immigration League of Australia. The Hawkesbury Agricultural College wasn't interested in the idea, however, a scheme was 'propounded by Mr Schey, accepted by the [Immigration] League and approved by the Government. If boys were not daunted by four weeks at the Labour Depot Randwick, (from where they could go home each night), they could proceed to Pitt Town where they could stay for up to two months. A special dormitory was built for them, to keep them apart from the men, and a special foreman looked after them to initiate them into the mysteries of digging, hoeing, milking, churning, ploughing, sowing and feeding pigs, calves and poultry. It was expected there would be no trouble in placing them on farms in the country on advantageous

---

[25] 'Farm Training for City Lads.' *Singleton Argus (NSW: 1880–1954)* 26 March 1910: 1.

terms. It was reported that 'so far as the experiment has gone, it has been with the entire satisfaction to all parties interested'.

By June 1907 the Immigration League of Australia commenced a program of training young men from the city in elementary farm work. The boys spent one month attending the Labour Depot at Randwick daily for initial instruction followed by a supervised program of two months at the Casual Labour Farm where they gained practical experience in farming, dairying, piggery and poultry work.

By June 1907 approximately ninety young men had passed through the farm training program with most of them obtaining employment immediately or soon after finishing their training. Only seven had proved unsatisfactory. The following year the boys' program was so successful that the demand for those completing the course outstripped supply.

In 1911 the farm ceased to be a Casual Labour Farm and was entirely taken over by a program of training young men from the city for farm work. The Dreadnought Scheme started at this time.

Reverend Ayling – a spiritual leader and community activist

The Church has always had an involvement in Pitt Town or Scheyville.

The Presbyterian Church at Ebenezer (Pitt Town) is the oldest church in Australia still functioning. The work of Reverend John Ayling, together with his wife was important to the Labour Settlement, providing Pitt Town with its main religious influence throughout the 1890s. He had been inducted into the charge of the Presbyterian Churches at Pitt Town and Portland Head on the Hawkesbury River on 22 July 1885.

A book celebrating the minister's life helps give a localised viewpoint of life at the site. Visiting religious leaders such as Reverend Charles Strong from Melbourne were instrumental in creating interest in co-operative settlement ideas, both in Victoria and New South Wales. Religious leaders such as Reverend Roseby were on the Board of Control of the settlement, and involved in the schemes for the unemployed. There was a nexus between involvement of the State and the Church.

Ayling's biographer wrote that in 1893 Ayling had said that 'it is not a progressive place, but the village settlements of Pitt Town and Wilberforce may, it is hoped, be the means of infusing fresh life. ... He frequently preaches three times, taking two Sabbath schools, and travels a good deal over 20 miles on the Sabbath day.'[26] His was described as a 'Practical Ministry'.[27]

Ayling was acutely aware of the social problems of the day, as reported in the Gazette newspaper:

> On Monday evening John Ayling addressed the monthly Band of Hope meeting. He suggested that seeing the immense sum annually spent in strong drink, the misery and crime caused thereby; the consequent inevitable taxation for police, pauperism, lunacy, etc. would it not be an excellent plan for politicians of all shades to lay aside their difficulties, and unite in a grand crusade against the deadly curse of society everywhere, subduing that monster. The prosperity of the country would almost certainly endue, whether protection or free trade prevailed.[28]

Ayling commented on the lack of spirituality in the Windsor area as a whole. Yet, he also commented when an event 'proved that the heart of the Pitt Town public is good to the core when a really deserving case is brought beneath their notice'. Such an event was the concert held in the schoolroom on 20 November 1891, in aid of Mrs Stockings and family. The Sackville Minstrel Troupe had appeared with other performers to raise funds to assist the widow and orphans of the late Joseph Stockings.[29]

Reverend Ayling was also active in attempting to engender some community spirit. For example:

---

[26] Ayling, Robert L. *Rev. John Ayling Australian Pioneer. The Life of Rev. John Ayling Clergyman, Educator, beekeeper 1825-1897.* Florida. USA. 1999. P132.
[27] Ibid.
[28] Ayling, *The Gazette* 29 November 1888.
[29] 'Concert at Pitt-Town.' *Windsor and Richmond Gazette (NSW: 1888–1961)* 28 November 1891: 5.

A public meeting was held in the Church of England schoolroom 'for the purpose of discussing a scheme with the object of constructing a railway from the Hawkesbury through Pitt Town to connect with the Richmond line.' Ayling proposed the building of that rail line. Referring to the different views at the meeting, he noted: 'They wanted to see their scheme adopted. Things were in a state of stagnation in Pitt Town, and principally because they were broken up into a lot of petty cliques. They would have to agree and unite. There had been no progress in Pitt Town during the seven years he had been a resident there; he wanted to see it go ahead, and this without depreciating Windsor or Sackville Reach in any way.'

He also established a Mutual Improvement Society in Pitt Town. Ayling chaired the meeting and it was reported that 'With a strong working committee we are looking forward to making it a perfect success, and ere long to raise the once-designated "Sleepy Hollow" to a pleasant little township. The roads have been put in good order, … Our butter factory is in full swing, though there is still room for many improvements.'[30]

Ayling attended the inauguration of the Pitt Town Village Settlement along with a large party including Mr Copeland, the Minister for Lands, the Board of Controllers and local personalities.[31]

The Board took the opportunity of the Minister's presence to hold a ballot for 100 residential lots to much cheering by the settlers. John Ayling was asked to speak at the end of the meeting which he did in some unrecorded words.

In a separate item, the Gazette noted: 'On Saturday last, the day set apart for the drawing of lots for residential areas at the Pitt Town Common Settlement, there were on the ground 82 married men with their families, 13 single men, 119 boys, 109 girls, 20 infants (who are treated by the Committee as a distinct sex) and three dependent adults, making a total of 433 souls.'[32]

---

[30] 'Pitt Town.' *Windsor and Richmond Gazette (NSW: 1888–1961)* 22 April 1893: 10.
[31] 'The Village Settlements.' *Windsor and Richmond Gazette (NSW: 1888–1961)* 30 September 1893: 5.
[32] 'Notes.' *Windsor and Richmond Gazette (NSW: 1888–1961)* 30 September 1893

The Gazette of 27 January 1894 reported that

> 'Rev. J. Ayling ... is doing good work in connection with the spiritual wants of Pitt Town Village settlement. ... many kindly services [have been] performed by Mr. Ayling who, from the first, has taken a keen interest in the temporal as well as spiritual welfare of the settlers. At least once a week he pays the settlement a visit, but more often he is on the ground several times during that period. He visits, in turn, the whole of the families, often in company with his good wife; prescribing for those who are ill, comforting those in distress, providing nourishment and little delicacies for those who are most in need of same, giving kindly advice and offering a cheering word to men and women alike. Mr. Ayling has the welfare of the settlement at heart and he speaks feelingly regarding the evident desire which the men have of making it a success.'[33]

The same article continued with reference to one of Ayling's other interests. He assisted Reverend B. Dinning and R.H. Buttsworth in opening a Good Templars Lodge at the settlement. They held a meeting in a large marquee, where they explained the objects of Good Templary; twenty-seven men remained behind to be initiated. The new Lodge was named 'the Pioneer Settlement Lodge, No. 725', and its meetings were to be held every Friday evening. It was the fourth Good Templar Lodge established within a radius of a few miles in the past two years.[34]

The 'News in Brief' section of the Gazette 10 November 1894 noted 'The Rev. J. Ayling is the only clergyman now visiting the settlement regularly. The

---

[33] 'The Village Settlements.' *Windsor and Richmond Gazette (NSW: 1888–1961)* 27 January 1894: 5.
[34] Ayling, Robert I. *Rev. John Ayling Australian pioneer: the life of Rev. John Ayling clergyman, educator, beekeeper, 1825-1897* Robert I. Ayling Marco Island, Florida, 1999.

Rev. gentleman has given up other work, believing it was his duty to attend to the spiritual wants of the settlers.'[35]

A final reference to Ayling in relation to the Village Settlements reveals his membership on the local Board of Control and the end of the settlement venture.

William Francis Schey – right man for the times?

Different times in a society's evolution demand different styles of leadership. Schey's personality and background seem to have made him an appropriate person of influence for the testing times of the late nineteenth century. Observations by a letter writer and journalist, one Mary Salmon, give an insight into the man. In June 1902 she wrote:

> The services of such a man as Mr. Schey, the Chief Labour Commissioner, have been invaluable in bringing out of chaos some degree of method in dealing with a large proportion of the unemployed. His power of organisation, his genuine interest in the great social problems that confront us daily … and his great gift of being able to turn apparently impracticable theories into workable methods, make him precisely the right man to deal with the matter.[36]

Schey's mode of life may have been to earn the respect and trust of those with whom he came into contact as per the expected behaviour of those, like himself who practiced Freemasonry. As a Mason he was expected 'to treat every man as his brother, to practice temperance and charity.'[37] When needed, and to meet the needs of the time, though, Schey was not averse at practising tough brotherly love.

The Labour Commissioners classified unemployed men by 'the three Rs', but this referred to their value in the state labour market and to their general

---

[35] 'News in Brief.' *Windsor and Richmond Gazette (NSW: 1888–1961)* 10 November 1894: 3.
[36] 'A Government Labour Experiment.' *Australian Town and Country Journal (Sydney, NSW: 1870–1907)* 21 June 1902: 31.
[37] *What is Freemasonry?* Masonic Lodges of Victoria. Pamphlet.

physical conditions. 'An able-bodied man, equally with a paralytic or extremely aged person, would be ineligible for the State Farm [Pitt Town]. ... As often happens, misfortune or other causes so reduce a man's physical frame that for a time being his nerve and will power seem almost gone, and he is utterly unable to forge ahead for himself. "We quite realise", said Mr Schey, "that a man may be in such a condition that State aid in the way of finding employment, and building him up, is necessary. There is also the idle vagrant who will not work. I should like the Government to take an island and place on it men, who, without being criminal, are so lazy and incompetent that they are only a burden to themselves and others. After getting them into good health, we would see that they had plenty of cold water and bread, and a rude bed in which to sleep. This we would give them. It would rest entirely with themselves to get three good meals a day and wages to boot: but they must earn it." At present these cases, and others graded with them, are dealt with either at the Pitt Town Casual Labour Farm, 'or at the Casuals' Home, beyond Kensington.'[38]

Conclusions

The story of the use of the site as the Pitt Town Co-operative Settlement and later as the Casual Labour Farm resonates with the history of the colony of New South Wales as Federation neared in 1901. It was seen as a radical response to social problems experienced by families in the 1890s economic depression. It is a significant example of state intervention in the lives of the unemployed, in the name of welfare. The State had taken a greater direct role in people's lives.

On 15 May 1911, the Pitt Town Co-operative Settlement Post Office officially became known as the Scheyville Post Office. This occurred after the locals of that area petitioned the Post Office bureaucracy, complaining that the title of their post office was too long, and that the area was no longer a labour settlement. After consultation with the former parliamentarian and Labour

---

[38] 'A Government Labour Experiment.' op. cit.

Commissioner, Mr William F. Schey, the change was made to name the place after him, with the justification that he had quite an association with the area.

The naming of the site after Schey also says something about the character and personality of the type of influential person of the time. There is no intention here to argue the case for the 'great man' archetype. The financial trauma of the 1890s and expected gender roles, both reflect the version of 'masculinity' and 'expressions of the feminist movement'[39] of the time. Men were to be the providers, and the hard times meant that many had to cope with the notion of dependency. The site can be thought of as 'masculine' because although women were in residence between 1893 and 1896, there were no women again until the Great War. Then they were only there a few months and the site reverted to an all-male venue till after World War Two. The way the site was run between 1896 and 1910 was modelled on the Leongatha Labour Colony in Victoria, which was exclusively male.

Curiously, the 'experimental' Training Centres to help the most needy unemployed weren't established at the larger country towns, as mentioned above, but experimental agricultural farms were established to help farmers. These were established at Yanco, Glen Innes, Wollongbar (near Lismore) and Cowra.

Measuring outcomes

A lot of press and inquiry of the time concentrated on the failure of the operations at the site when measured by a simple revenue and expenditure method. However, society has always found it harder to measure the indirect benefits of such schemes. They might fail by modern accounting practice terms of cost centre or responsibility accounting, but the following summation, written in 1902 gives a more positive view of the outcome of three months at the state farm:

> In many cases, after three months in the fresh air with regular food, the patient (if we may so term him) has been toned into full working order.

---

[39] Scates, Bruce. *Mobilising Manhood: Gender and the Great Strike in Australia and New Zealand*. Gender and History, Vol. 9 August 1997, pp285-309.

He then no longer needs the Government crutch, but is in trim to face the world again and look out for work for himself.[40]

A quoted keynote of the system was the 'building-up' of individuals. The idea was to eliminate the need for charity idea, but an element of barter existed.

The labourer hoes so many potatoes, and weeds such a patch, in return for his bed, food, the use of a smoking and reading room, and a place for the ablution of himself and his clothing. This being squared, a wage not exceeding five shillings a week is given.[41]

A latter-day authority on communal living, Bill Metcalf wrote that 'These New South Wales co-operative settlements failed as communes, even though many unemployed people were taught agricultural skills, and were helped to survive the severe economic crisis of the 1890s. Pitt Town, with five hundred residents, was the largest communal venture in Australia, larger than any contemporary intentional community.'[42]

The site of Scheyville is significant in terms of the study of communes and intentional communities. It was larger than the 'intentional' or 'alternative communities' or co-operatives, founded in the 1970s. Tuntable Falls in northern NSW had nearly three hundred members. A similar modern-day community, the Kibbutz Givat Brennar; in Israel, has 1,800.[43]

---

[40] 'A Government Labour Experiment.' *Australian Town and Country Journal (Sydney, NSW: 1870–1907)* 21 June 1902: 31.
[41] 'A Government Labour Experiment. op cit.
[42] Metcalf, Bill. *Co-operative Lifestyles in Australia – from Utopian Dreaming to Community Reality*. UNSW Press, Sydney 1993. p 26.
[43] Ibid. p 12.

Dreadnoughts 1909 to 1939
Raising funds for a battleship!

Australia is an island continent. Its inhabitants tend to be wary of foreign naval vessels being in its waters. After all, Russian warships entered the Derwent estuary near Hobart in 1873. Come the early years of the twentieth century there was a scare in Australia over the growing German naval power in the Pacific.

Australians are also a generous lot when it comes to fundraising activities, as reflected in their response to the 2020 Bushfire Relief Appeal. They were no different back in 1909. In that year, the then Lord Mayor of Sydney, Sir Allen Taylor, launched a fund to buy a Dreadnought – a large battleship – for the Royal Navy. The idea was to induce the British to have a greater naval presence in the Pacific and Australia. An amount of £90,000 was raised by public subscription. To work out the equivalent amount in today's dollars would be a guess, but the amount raised was a lot of money.

Five of the wealthiest men in Sydney donated £10,000 ($20,000) each to the fund.

On 2 April 1909, the Sydney Morning Herald carried the story:

The Lord Mayor of Sydney (Alderman Taylor) presided over a meeting of the committee of the Dreadnought fund yesterday. The following names were added to the committee:– Messrs. H. Gorman, R.R. Dangar, Padfield, T.A. Dibbs, A. Paton, E.J. Hill, T.F. Hitchinan. Alderman T.H. Kelly was elected vice-chairman and the following were elected vice-presidents elected:– Messrs. A.A. Dangar, S. Hordern, W.F. Buchanan, Walter Hall, H. Dixson. …

The next thing, said the Lord Mayor, was the question of making an appeal to the Mayors of municipalities and shire councils throughout the State. Mr Dangar: "That is the only way to work it." …

Some of our wealthy citizens have led the way, and I confidently appeal to the people of New South Wales, who never fail in any worthy object, to assist.[1]

---

[1] 'Appeal to Country.' *The Sydney Morning Herald (NSW: 1842–1954)* 2 April 1909: 7

Like a modern-day Easter Good Friday Fundraiser for the Royal Children's Hospital in Melbourne, the populace became involved. The enthusiasm was almost infectious. The article included examples like the following to highlight just a few of the many examples of the population's generosity over the following month. For example, when Mr John Wallace was proposing a toast at the Commercial Travellers' Association banquet, he said that the 'Dreadnought enthusiasm had swept like a wave through the various states showing the loyalty of the citizens.'[2]

The Lord Mayor said that by that afternoon's post he had received 10 letters, nine of which contained subscriptions to the fund ranging from £1 to £100. … A man, apparently a workman, walked into the city treasurer's department and handed him £50.

The Lord Mayor suggested an office be opened at the Royal Easter Show, be well advertised, at which contributions could be received. The Daily Telegraph newspaper announced they would give £1000. The Secretary of the Committee suggested firstly a 'self-denial week', secondly, a race meeting under the auspices of the Australian Jockey Club and thirdly, theatrical matinees. A 'lady teacher' sought the sanction of the Minister for Education for a voluntary subscription of threepence per child in all Public Schools, and that all teachers give one day's pay.

The Sydney Morning Herald of 14 April 1909 announced that 'lady collectors' would take a collection for the fund at a sports day being held in Moore Park'[3] and on 19 April 1909, told of a subscription being opened at the Hawkesbury Agricultural College Old Boys' dinner, and the Clyde Engineering Company's workshops subscribing £150.[4]

In explaining the enthusiasm, let's not forget the country people of New South Wales. A review of newspapers reveals that the Queanbeyan Dreadnought Fund reached £104 quickly, and the Sydney Morning Herald on 26 April 1909 and

---

[2] 'Hands off!' *Sydney Morning Herald.* 2 August 1909: 8.
[3] 'Athletic Display.' *The Sydney Morning Herald (NSW: 1842–1954)* 14 April 1909: 9.
[4] 'Hawkesbury 'Old Boys.'' *The Sydney Morning Herald (NSW: 1842–1954)* 19 April 1909: 7.

14 May 1909 listed country meetings held at Delegate, Dungog, Kyogle, Muswellbrook, Quirindi, Richmond, Tamworth, Temora, Tenterfield, Grenfell, Molong and West Maitland.[5] The Cornishmen's dinner was another chance for loyalty to be shown, and a special 'Dreadnoughts Meeting' was held at Randwick Racecourse on 22 May 1909 with the racing club 'on this occasion donating £1100 towards the Dreadnought Fund … also presenting the winner of the Dreadnought Novice Purse with a handsome silver cup.'[6] The Sydney Morning Herald of 25 May announced that the children of Lindfield Public School had elected 'to forego the usual Empire Day picnic and sports, and devote the money to the Dreadnought Fund'.[7]

The Public Service Association arranged a popular concert at the Town Hall for Empire Day in aid of the fund.

It also appears that if you didn't spontaneously contribute then you would be cajoled into donating, with the Sydney Morning Herald of 27 May 1909 reporting that during a debate on the Dreadnought question, the House of Representatives was informed that 'New South Wales public servants had been forced by superior officers on pain of injuring their prospects to contribute to the Dreadnought fund.'[8]

The above demonstrates the fact that although there were five wealthy businessmen who dipped into their own funds in a big way, these same men had fostered a wave of loyalty and went on to control the money that everybody from engineering factories, school children and travelling salesmen contributed to the Dreadnought Fund.

Within a few months of the setting up of the Dreadnought Fund, a series of events and decisions were made by the Commonwealth Government and at the 1909 Imperial Conference that culminated in the King's approval on 10 July 1911

---

[5] 'Country Meetings.' *The Sydney Morning Herald (NSW: 1842–1954)* 26 April 1909: 7; 'Shire Councils.' *The Sydney Morning Herald (NSW: 1842–1954)* 28 May 1909: 10.
[6] 'Sporting the Turf.' *The Sydney Morning Herald (NSW: 1842–1954)* 17 May 1909: 10.
[7] 'Northern Suburbs.' *The Sydney Morning Herald (NSW: 1842–1954)* 25 May 1909: 7.
[8] 'The Proceedings.' *The Sydney Morning Herald (NSW: 1842–1954)* 27 May 1909: 8.

that the ships of the Commonwealth Naval Forces would be known as the Royal Australian Navy and be designated as His Majesty's Australian Ship. This course of action had been promoted by the Director of Naval Forces, Captain William Creswell and his ally in this matter, Prime Minister Alfred Deakin.

Thus, the money wasn't needed for its original purpose and a meeting of subscribers to the fund was called to decide what was to be done with the money. The meeting decided that approximately half the money should be used to promote and assist the migration of youths from Britain who were willing to become farmworkers in Australia. This fund would be administered by a trust, chaired by Sir Allen Taylor. The other half of the money was allocated to helping to build HMAS Cresswell, the Naval College at Jervis Bay.

How the scheme operated

In the following year, the Dreadnought Trustees negotiated a scheme with the New South Wales Government whereby youths selected in Britain would receive loan money for all or part of the fare to Australia. At that time the fare was about £12, which was to be repaid by the boys over a period once they were earning in Australia. According to William Francis Schey,[9] the Trustees paid the Government £5 for each lad sent to Scheyville.

On arrival, the boys were given a three-month period of farm training under Australian conditions. This was billed as a special feature of the scheme. The training was given at a number of farms, including Yanco, Grafton, Glen Innes, Cowra and Scheyville. More than half the 7500 boys were trained at Scheyville who came between 1910 and 1939. Approximately 5500 went to Scheyville first, and some of these boys went to the other farms after an initial three months at Scheyville.

These were established at Yanco, Glen Innes, Wollongbar (near Lismore) and Cowra. This farm was ready-made for the purpose of training young boys as it had been used in a previous scheme to train city boys to be farm labourers.

---

[9] Schey, William Francis *The Government Training Farm Scheyville* p 3.

Scheyville was run by the New South Wales Department of Labour and Industry. The Dreadnought Trust contributed to the cost of the training and provided each youth with pocket money during training, and a good conduct bonus on completion. A bonus of £2 was paid to the boys, partly while under instruction, and the remainder at the end of their period of tuition, provided they went to employment approved by the Director. Approval was never given to any employment other than on the land. The compulsory period was ten weeks, and the desired period thirteen weeks.[10]

The first twelve Dreadnought Boys arrived on 21 April 1911, followed by twenty-seven others on 15 June. A range of farming operations was already established.

Early in 1915, the scheme was suspended because of the World War. The boys had come at the rate of about twenty a fortnight, and 1738 British youths had come to New South Wales under the Scheme. Of these, 600 received assistance from the Central Unemployed Body in London.[11]

Upon arrival in Australia, 1200 boys passed through Scheyville. This was despite the wish of the New South Wales Agricultural Department to offer more training at the Hawkesbury Agricultural College (founded 1891) and at the Grafton, Glen Innes, Cowra and Wollongbar Experimental Farms.[12] A further link between those who went to Scheyville and those who went to the Northern Rivers Experimental Farms is that of the 800 who came to Scheyville in its first fifteen months, 746 completed the course and the majority of those went on to find employment on farms, especially on the Northern Rivers. This pattern partially explains why the Dreadnought Association has always operated from the Wollongbar, Lismore area. Although the Association wasn't formed till 1974, a nucleus of Dreadnought Boys was on the Northern Rivers, and had stayed there, or returned after World War Two.

---

[10] William Francis Schey *The Government Training Farm Scheyville.* p 25
[11] Sherington, Geoffrey, 'British youth and Empire settlement: the Dreadnought boys in New South Wales' *Journal of the Royal Australian Historical Society* 82, 1996, 1–22.
[12] Report into Scheyville Edds p 35; quoting Sherington, Geoffrey, op cit.

Migration under the Dreadnought Scheme resumed in 1921, with the first postwar Dreadnoughts arriving in October of that year. Between 1921 and 1930, 5585 arrived. This was the time of the main migration. About half of them went to Scheyville, while most of the others were placed on the Experimental Farms, and seven per cent went straight into rural employment.[13]

During the 1920s the financing of the Dreadnought Scheme underwent fundamental change, with the governments of Australia and Great Britain playing a bigger role. By 1925, these two governments were sharing the costs of a direct grant of £22 towards a total fare of £33 for boys over seventeen years of age. The New South Wales Government paid the full cost of the training at Scheyville or the other training farms.

There were also changes in the method of recruitment. Before the World War, boys had been recruited mainly through organisations in London that specialised in placing unemployed people and from some industrial towns. Initially, those selected were not to be under seventeen, nor over twenty- one. The age group was changed however, and the age group targeted became fifteen to eighteen. Australia House played an active part in the postwar recruitment, and the method of recruitment throughout Britain was by means of advertising literature sent to schools, church organisations, youth groups such as Scouts, and to newspapers and magazines.

The boys who, with their parents, were persuaded by the advertising that their prospects in Australia were better, submitted applications with references and letters of support from clergymen and school headmasters. They were required to undergo a medical examination before final acceptance. Those accepted were assembled in batches of fifty or so at Tilbury Dock in London for sailings which took place every month or so. They were transported to Sydney under the care of a supervisor, appointed to maintain order and morale during the voyage.

---

[13] Sherington, Geoffrey, op cit.

Life at Scheyville
The daily grind

The boys were rotated around the various farm sections. They would spend a week in the dairy where they learned to milk, and then worked a period in the piggery, the stables, the orchard and the poultry section. They were also taught to plough, cart and clear the bush. Each boy had to serve a stint in the kitchen and the dormitories. According to Bill Wilson, the literature promised them the chance to 'learn a little about cooking'. He says, 'we spent a week on kitchen duty all right but all we did was peel potatoes, chop wood and wait at table.' Each boy was rostered to empty the pan toilets. This duty was affectionately called 'the strawberry cart'.[14] The farm was run along the lines of a boarding school with hard labour substituted for academic studies. After three months of training the boys were sent to farms in NSW where there was a request for boy labour.

It wasn't just the boys who had tough conditions and long hours.

Let's not forget the staff. They had long hours too! Correspondence from Cochrane, the Accountant, indicates that a forty-eight-hour week was granted on 18 September 1925 to domestic staff. The Minister decided on 15 January 1926 that the hours of these employees were to be reduced to forty-four per week to bring them into line with the domestic staff employed by the Department of Agriculture at the Experimental Farms and Richmond College. A review of the hours and leave arrangements of all staff in June 1930 found that, 'with the exception of the Manager, the Clerk and the Matron, the other members of staff work forty-eight hours per week'. Working hours seemed to be arranged so that each staff member got one day off a week. The Manager, Mr Scully was deemed to be on duty at all times and was entitled to six days per annum in lieu of public holidays and one day a week in lieu of Sundays.

---

[14] Wilson, Bill, *Dreadnought Boy,* 6-7.

Lighter moments, pranks and humour

According to Bill Wilson there was the 'occasional diversion'. Scheyville had a hall equipped with a stage, a piano and a harmonium. A Smith Family concert party staged a very good party there, and on two occasions ladies came out from Windsor to dance with us. An elderly Church of England clergyman visited on occasion.

One disappointment was the swimming pool. Recruiting literature said that Scheyville had a swimming pool. Bill Wilson imagined a pool in a running river where you could dive and swim. He was not prepared for a muddy farm dam.

There were obviously a number who couldn't swim or were not strong swimmers. Newspaper reports record a number of the Dreadnought Boys drowning.[15]

One of the characters of Scheyville was a rogue horse called Battleaxe. As part of their introduction to the farm, boys were met at Mulgrave railway station by some of the 'old boys' driving spring carts and escorted through a big gate with 'Scheyville Training Farm' on it leading to a drive with a lovely line of trees. White crosses had been placed in the ground near some of the trees and these, the new boys were solemnly informed, were in memory of boys killed by a fierce wild horse called 'Battleaxe'. Further they were informed that each boy must learn to catch, bridle and saddle and then ride Battleaxe to bring the cows in as part of his training. 'This dampened our enthusiasm for a while, quite knocked the stuffing out of us they say, until we discovered the crosses were in memory of old boys killed in the war and Battleaxe, although an old rogue, had not killed anyone – not yet.'[16]

According to Donald Mountfort, he later learned that a number of boys had died at Scheyville in the previous year from gastroenteritis due to bad sanitary arrangements. In a letter to his grandmother, he tells of being weighed every week

---

[15] 'Boy's Body Recovered.' *The Sydney Morning Herald (NSW: 1842–1954)* 2 December 1925: 16; 'Drowned in River.' *The Sydney Morning Herald (NSW: 1842–1954)* 27 March 1928: 12.

[16] King, Olwen and King, Gordon and Dreadnought Association. *They passed this way: stories of the dreadnought boys edited by Gordon King and Olwen King* Dreadnought Association Alstonville, N.S.W 2008

at Scheyville and having put on eight-and-a-half pounds in one week, and one stone nine pounds since leaving England. He surmised that 'perhaps our health was of some concern following the deaths of the other boys'.

Sometimes a boy would awake in the morning to find his face blackened by boot-polish, and the unfortunate whose turn it was to ride Battleaxe often found himself pelted with rotten fruit or worse just as he was returning past the stables where the assailants lay in wait.

The playing of pranks was the same at Grafton Experimental Farm. Norman Monsen writes of an initiation gag on his first night at the Grafton Farm. After listening to stories of the dangers of treading on snakes and the like, an atmosphere was created for their benefit and much excitement about a fox hunt that was organised. After dark they were guided in and out of the same two fields a number of times to disorient them, and then, two by two, the new boys were posted and told to be on the lookout for foxes. The old boys beat the undergrowth to beat out the foxes and the new boys were to use clubs to bash the foxes. All that happened was that the perpetrators of the dastardly deed went back to the dormitories to bed, leaving the new boys at their posts.

Indications are that the initiation ceremony for trainees at Scheyville involved being hit with towels, and running a gauntlet on the way to the showers. One trainee, Harry Compton, experienced this and wrote, 'not hit hard and enjoyed being a new member'.[17]

Mary Booth and the Empire Services Club

Support services in the 1920s and 1930s existed for the boys but were of a different nature to our government-sponsored, supervised activities of 2020.

On arrival in Sydney, the Dreadnought Boys were introduced to the Empire Service Club, a voluntary organisation run by Dr Mary Booth. Mary Booth was a British Empire idealist of independent means. She had established her club in a rented two-storey building in George St North, initially to welcome soldiers

---

[17] Notes from Harry Compton given to Mary Ann Hamilton, heritage officer and historian at Heritage NSW.

returning from World War One. Her idea was to provide a place where they could relax in the company of others of their kind without going into a hotel. The club was staffed by a group of helpers she had permission to call 'The Anzac Fellowship of Women'.

After the soldiers had all returned, the Anzac Fellowship of Women began to focus on welcoming young postwar migrants from Britain. As well as welcoming them on arrival, they provided the opportunity for newcomers to meet other migrants when they were down from the country between jobs. Newly arrived Dreadnought Boys were given tea and buns at the Empire Service Club and stayed overnight on the boat. Next day they would catch trains to their various destinations. They would undergo three months of training and then be dispersed to all parts of New South Wales to work on farms. A large number of them were allocated to coastal dairy farms.

Not all Dreadnoughts experienced the Empire Services Club when they first arrived. Donald Mountfort only became aware of its existence through the writings of fellow Dreadnoughts, Bill Wilson and Reverend Brawn in their '1982 Supplement to the History of the Dreadnought Scheme'.[18] Mountfort obviously felt empathy with Dr Mary Booth's work and perceptions. He writes, 'the President, Dr Mary Booth, sounds a great fighter and a most humane and perceptive person, debating with the Primary Producers Union and Dairy Industry leaders on better conditions for boys.' From Brawn and Wilson's report – 'what Booth appeared to have in mind was that the Dairy Industry seemed to be parasitic upon young migrants, it sucked them in and then replaced them with another batch of eager innocents from the training farms.'

Mary Booth also edited a monthly periodical called The Boy Settler, produced by the Empire Services Club at threepence per copy. Editions of this were produced up until 1944, including news of those Dreadnoughts who had enlisted.

---

[18] Brawn, Reverend, and Wilson, Bill. *The Dreadnought Scheme. 1982 Supplement to the History*. Mitchell Library Sydney. IRN: 153054 Location and Citation Number: MLMSS6448. Part of collection comprising 10 boxes of material.

Mountfort feels he can relate to the contents of Dr Booth's report covering 1935–1937. She points out 'that Dreadnought Boys found more difficulty in marrying and settling down than Australian boys, not having parents or homes to help their "social footing".'[19]

To Mountfort this 'did seem true in my case, I always felt barely able to support myself, let alone a wife and family and with my sole assets contained in two suitcases.' Mountfort manages to put a positive spin on his cohort history, saying 'many boys, however, did very well in Australia with a great variety of careers and widespread involvement in community life.'

The working life of a Dreadnought Boy

This story is typical of the experiences of those Dreadnoughts who came between 1921 and 1930. Arthur Powell wrote:[20]

> I am the son of a middle-class English family of the industrial city of Birmingham. After the death of my mother in 1923 I emigrated to Australia at the age of sixteen, with little money and far less knowledge of the hardships of battling for myself, particularly during a world depression when work was hard to get, conditions bad, and wages very poor.
>
> My first impression of Australia when I arrived in Fremantle was disheartening to say the least, for as we – my shipmates and I – stepped ashore, we were greeted by a drunken sailor exclaiming "cripes, more bloody Pommies." It was to be many years before I realised it did not pay to take offence when referred to as a bloody Pommy.
>
> As a boy I had always been keen on farm life. I loved nothing better than to spend a holiday on a farm. It was only natural that I should choose to try my luck on a sheep station in Western New South Wales.

---

[19] Brawn, Reverend, and Wilson, Bill. *The Dreadnought Scheme. 1982 Supplement to the History*. Mitchell Library Sydney. IRN: 153054 Location and Citation Number: MLMSS6448. Part of collection comprising 10 boxes of material.

[20] Samuel (Arthur) Powell. Personal essay. Contributed by his daughter Kate McVea & son-in-law Grier of Hobart Tasmania. Names have been changed in this article.

My first boss was "Alf Ridley", a rough, hard working man who was more commonly known as "Flogger". "Flogger" was the type of man who would race a horse with you in the early hours of the morning when going to work and blow your head off for even raising a slight sweat on a horse when returning to the station at night. He was often heard to say: "The cheapest way to clear a paddock is to get a mob of floggin' pommies, work 'em till they can't hold an axe, sack 'em and get another mob."

As rough and hard as my life was with "Flogger", he taught me many things that go to make a good bushman and stockman. On his property "Alawa" there were no slack periods. After shearing came teamwork – driving the big sixteen-ton wagon loaded with wool to the nearest railway station about thirty-five miles away. I can recall my first trip with the team of eighteen horses hitched to the wagon. Due to my inexperience, I allowed the wagon to overrun my team, and the resultant tangle of chains and my efforts to calm down eighteen kicking horses taught me my first lesson in horsemanship.

After working on "Alawa" for three years, I decided to move on and see what the northern part of the state was like, but to my misfortune I found work even harder to get in this part of the state and I commenced work on a small property in the Tamworth District on a wage of only a few shillings a week and keep. During the forthcoming months I counted myself very lucky if I got my keep, let alone my wages.

Bob Webber ran this property with the aid of Harold – his youngest son – and I often wondered how they were able to make a living from such a small property, until one morning after I had been with the Webbers about three months, Bob, Harold and I set off with a saddle and pack horse each, and after a fifty-mile ride arrived at a property the Webbers leased from the Crown. I had never before seen or imagined a more desolate spot than "Murdered Dogs Swamp" high in the Nundle

Ranges. Old Bob had told me on the ride to the swamp that he ran up to three hundred brood mares on the lease, and a muster was carried out every third year – the young horses draughted out and saddle broken, railed to Sydney, finally placed aboard a freighter and shipped to India as army remounts. I was soon to find that the station hacks I had used on "Alawa" were akin to kiddies' ponies compared with these young horses bred in this wild country and who had never seen a man since birth.

Both the Webbers were expert horsemen and seemed to be more at home in the saddle than walking down a city street. They could work amongst the horses from daylight to dusk and sleep peacefully on the ground with their saddle as a pillow, while I was too tired and stiff to sleep more than an hour or so each night.

The mustering and breaking took nearly two months to complete and except for occasional trips to the nearest town for rations, the work went on without a break, but by the time breaking and shipping was completed I had learnt my second lesson in horsemanship.

On our return trip we called at the "local", as Bob liked his glass of beer, but was apt to get somewhat nasty when he one over the eight. Conversation at the hotel naturally turned to horses and Bob, in his condition, bet all present that he had a horse at home that could run the tail off any horse in the district. His challenge was quickly snapped up by his adjoining neighbour and a wager of twenty pounds was named, the race to be run in one month at the local picnic races which were an annual affair. It was not until he sobered up that Bob realised that we did not have twenty pence between us until the cheque arrived for the sale of the horses, let alone twenty pounds, and there was chaff and oats to be bought if he was to have any chance of winning the race.

Unfortunately for me, I was chosen to obtain the required chaff and oats, as I was the only one small enough to get into the grain silos on the adjoining property. That's right, we stole fodder from the man who had accepted Bob's challenge.

As no weight limits were stipulated in the bet, I was elected to ride the stallion in the race, and I shudder to think what would have happened had I lost the race, for we had been unable to find a way to raise the twenty pound stake.

I recall an amusing incident when the local trooper stayed for lunch and the main course on the menu was kangaroo stew. As kangaroo was out of season at the time, I thought it was very sporting of the trooper to Mrs Bob after lunch: "that was the best meal of oxtail soup I have tasted for years."

For a few years after leaving the Webbers I moved around Australia doing various jobs, such as a shed hand – or as they are more commonly known Blue Tongues – horse breaking, harvesting in the Riverina, and cane-cutting in Queensland, before finally settling in north-western New South Wales on a Company Station as station hand. I joined the Army in 1941.

Despite the hard life on "Alawa" and Bob Webber, I can always look back on those days and the training I received with some gratitude, as I learnt the lesson all new chums must learn before being accepted in the bush – show the Australian bushman that you can work and play as well as he can and you are no longer looked upon as just another bloody Pommy.

Reunions and the Dreadnought Association

On 13 June 1974, twelve former Dreadnoughts met at the Wentworth Hotel in Sydney. This reunion was organised by Roy Moores, a newsagent of Adelong who had arrived on 13 June 1924 as a seventeen-year-old Dreadnought.

The men so assembled decided to form an Association, the purpose of which was to organise annual reunions of former Dreadnought Boys. The Association grew to have a steady membership of some 400, and annual reunions were organised in both Sydney and Lismore. Many of the Dreadnoughts had settled in northern New South Wales, because they had either been working on farms in that area or had trained at Wollongbar, Glen Innes or Grafton Experimental Farms and had been involved with the agricultural industry all their working lives.

In 1979, the Dreadnought Association organised a survey of the lives and experiences of its members. The questionnaire requested information on each man's work history, family, marriage, war service and community involvement. Two-thirds of the members replied – some in detail. There was evidence of widespread involvement in community affairs. Many were given a new start by the Reconstruction Training Scheme for returning soldiers of World War Two, and many were able to take advantage of the relative prosperity of the 1950s and 1960s.

Beyond the agricultural industry, the boys had taken on a wide range of occupations: plumber, policeman, dairy-farmer, dance band leader, master builder, motelier, minister of religion and Member of Parliament. A large number had been involved – some as presidents or committee members – in community organisations such as RSL branches, sporting clubs, bush fire brigades, unions, or shire councils.

Only about fifteen per cent were in rural occupations; some ninety-five per cent of respondents had married, and more than half had seen active service in World War Two. It was not known how many had died in that conflict. Three-quarters of those who had married, had married Australian girls, and it was estimated that over three generations, the number of descendants was seven times the original number. One Dreadnought Boy who contributed to Professor Sherington's 1970s research had arrived in Australia in 1912, and by 1979 had sixty-one descendants in Australia.[21]

---

[21] Sherington, Geoffrey. Mitchell Library Sydney sources as gifted by Professor Sherington: Dreadnought Boys interviewed by Geoffrey Sherington 1983 Library reference: ML OH 426. Papers covering the Dreadnought Boys 1909-1990, Library reference: ML MSS 6449. These papers include his extensive unpublished typescript entitled The Likely Lads.

While some had regrets regarding the experiences of their youth many had come a long way from the £2 they had when they arrived in Australia.

Although this book's focus is on the contribution of the boys who came under the Dreadnought Scheme to be trained in farming skills, it should be remembered that half the money raised for the Dreadnought battleship went towards building the Royal Australian Naval College at Jervis Bay. That College is still producing naval officers, a body of people that continues to contribute to Australia's development. A number of State Governors in Australia have attended HMAS Cresswell.

Women at Scheyville during World War One

On 25 August 1915, the Minister for Labour and Industry, Mr Estelle, announced that 'the Pitt Town Labour farm will be used for training women to go upon the land. This idea of accepting women students will probably be received with enthusiasm by women of all classes and political creeds.' It was reported that Mr Estelle 'had not put forward any exact scheme because much of the success of the scheme will depend on the length of time the trainees will spend at Pitt Town. If a student is a novice, she will not gain a very extensive insight into farming practice in a few months.' The article in the *Sydney Morning Herald*[22] stated that 'it is hoped the Government will refrain from rushing the women through, and turning them out in a half-educated condition. Her physical capacity and her mental endowment for the work she is undertaking must be both at the highest. Another important point will have to be considered is the age of the students.' Youth was seen as desirable for the Dreadnought Boys 'but in the case of women youthfulness would for once seem to be a drawback.' The writer, a woman, wrote that 'some occupations may be described as purely masculine, but farming is emphatically not one of these, and the fact that we women in Australia have not done more tilling of the soil, may, perhaps, be attributed to general prosperity. It is coming home to

---

[22] 'Women Farmers.' *The Sydney Morning Herald (NSW: 1842–1954)* 25 August 1915: p 5.

us that if our men are to enlist in large numbers we must be not only willing to take their places, but fully equipped to do so.'

Another article in the Daily Telegraph on 1 September 1915 was sub-headed 'Opportunity at Pitt Town'. This article was written in a marketing, rouse-them-up style, to stir the women into thinking they should go into farming: 'The nation needs her. She is roused and ready. ... There is danger that energy will run to waste. ... Equip her with better knowledge through a short course at Pitt Town, and she will surpass her record. ... Hawkesbury's two-month winter school has shown a far-flung programme of farm book-keeping, orchard work, gardening, dairying, pigs, poultry, bees and – and even ostriches! This is, in fact, what Pitt Town could do all year round for the woman farmer. ... The town-bred woman of today is readier than ever before to throw early Victorian ideas of mere "niceness" to the winds.'[23]

Following on from that advertising-style article, the Windsor and Richmond Gazette announced on 31 December 1915 that 'the Government enterprise for training women in horticulture, poultry farming, etc at Scheyville, will probably be launched early next year.'[24]

The same publication reported on 25 February 1916 that Mr Estell, the Minister for Mines and Labour was waited upon by members of the Horticultural Society who pointed out that 'women should be trained to do the lighter kinds of agricultural work. ... The board [appointed to run the scheme] consists of seven women members, three being Ministers' wives, and Mr. Frank Brennan, Manager of the Labour Bureau ... as Chairman.'[25]

A month later it was reported: 'The Superintendent of Labor and Industry accompanied by the members of the special commission appointed to inquire into the practicability of the scheme for imparting agricultural knowledge to women,

---

[23] 'Agricultural Training for Women.' *The Daily Telegraph (Sydney, NSW: 1883–1930)* 1 September 1915: and *The Sydney Morning Herald* 10 September 1915
[24] 'Week to Week' *Windsor and Richmond Gazette (NSW: 1888–1961)* 31 December 1915: 5.
[25] 'The Dreadnought Farms' *Windsor and Richmond Gazette (NSW: 1888–1961)* 25 February 1916: 1.

so that they may be afforded an opportunity of earning a living on the land, paid a visit of inspection to the Scheyville Training Farm last week. They were shown over ... the farm. ... They considered the farm an ideal one for carrying out the proposed scheme, and intend to strongly recommend it to the Minister for Agriculture. It is expected that a batch of women, under the charge of a matron, will shortly be sent to the farm to undergo a course of training in the various departments of agriculture which they may choose to learn.'[26]

Little news of the farm appeared for the remainder of the 1916 year, but early in 1917, Mr Beeby (Minister for Labour and Industry) explained that he was very disappointed in the response to the 'experiment'. He said that the experiment of training women for farm work should not be discontinued, but expressed the opinion that it could be more effectively carried on by the Agriculture Department on some of its experimental farms. 'There is no need to centralise in one farm near Sydney, and the women who want to train in those arts, and to acquire the science, will get far better results if they could take their course at the nearest experimental farm in the district in which they live.' The Minister mentioned the work of Bunnerong Farm Randwick, which was run in conjunction with Scheyville, and which had, in recent years shown fair results. 'It keeps and employs about 90 to 100 men, who cannot, on account of age, infirmity, and other reasons, compete in the ordinary labour market. The men on the farm are constantly employed and the value of their labour resulted last year in a revenue of approximately over £11,000. ... The Scheyville farm is, we understand, to be used for the training of returned soldiers who want to go upon the land and are in need of agricultural experience.'[27]

Mr Beeby reconsidered, and decided that even though he was going to close the farm after a trial of seven months, he would go forward with the fair trial. Criticism of the equipment and general conduct of the farm by a Miss E.M. Brace

---

[26] 'Week to Week' *Windsor and Richmond Gazette (NSW: 1888–1961)* 10 March 1916: 3.
[27] 'Female Farmers' *Windsor and Richmond Gazette* 12 January 1917: 10.

in a Sydney daily newspaper stimulated those interested in its promotion to reply with a volley of figures. The chief points of controversy were:

(1) That branches of work most suitable for women to specialise in and listed on the prospectus were not taught, and that facilities for teaching were not provided. (2) That methods and appliances were not up to date and the buildings, accommodation etc., were inconvenient and badly planned.

Miss May Matthews, an active member of the farm's advisory board, contended that 'every movement has difficulties to contend with at the outset: it must pass through stages of development.'

The first students had entered the farm on July 27, 1916. Two were admitted on that date and two more on August 3. There are now 20 students in residence and five others have definitely arranged to enter before the end of this month. …

The subjects taught as per the vocational training pamphlet are: (a) Dairying, including the feeding and care of cows, milking, separating, making, grading and marketing of butter, making ensilage etc, (b) Poultry raising, including the knowledge of how to handle incubators, chicken raising grading and marketing and preserving eggs etc,) (c) Orcharding work including ground preparation, scarifying manuring, free planting, pruning, grafting, picking and marketing of fruit, (d) Pig raising, (e) Market gardening, including ground preparation and manuring, planting and marketing of vegetables, (f) Beekeeping (g) Horticulture, (h) Sericulture, (i) Jam-making, fruit preserving, fruit drying, picking (j) general farming, including grubbing and clearing, ploughing, harrowing, sowing harvesting etc (k) Domestic management with special reference to cooking.

A Mrs. Hassall, who formerly had a farm of her own on the North Coast district was in charge of the dairy section. She was highly recommended by the dairy expert at the Department of Agriculture.

A deputation of members of the advisory committee, which includes Mr Brennan, Chairman, Mesdames Holman, A. Griffith, Estelle, Ashford, Barker-Young and Seery, Misses A. Golding, May Matthews, Moss, and Swain, and Professor Leo Cotton is going shortly to wait on Mr Beeby, asking that a matron be appointed to the Farm.[28]

Mr Greer, manager of the Scheyville farm for thirteen years was quoted as saying 'the boys were the hardest to manage, but could do the most work. The ladies are very pleasant and quite good; doing what they can, but many of them are not strong enough to lift heavy milk cans, or to wheel barrows laden with soil, or to dig trenches and make garden paths. However, they are shaping well and there will be a new profession in the hands of some women if they only persevere.'[29]

After less than a year of training women the 'Newsletter' section of the Windsor and Richmond Gazette of 29 June 1917 carried an article of protest about the possible closure of Scheyville. 'It was a political move to ensure the Labor vote for certain men standing for Parliament, and was the one thing that Government had done exclusively to train women.' The letter writer said that although some members of Parliament may say it is too expensive an experiment for wartime, '…it is wartime that has made it absolutely necessary for what use will untrained women be to the returned soldier who will have to settle on the land?'[30]

A week later, a further protest was printed:

> Members of the Feminist Club sent a resolution to the Minister for Labor and Industry, expressing regret that it had been deemed advisable to close Scheyville Farm to women, without making provision for their further training. They have pointed out to him that the

---

[28] 'Farming for Women' *Windsor and Richmond Gazette (NSW: 1888–1961)* 2 March 1917: 1.
[29] 'Week to Week' *Windsor and Richmond Gazette (NSW: 1888–1961)* 20 April 1917: 4.
[30] 'Scheyville Training Farm' *Windsor and Richmond Gazette (NSW: 1888–1961)* 29 June 1917: 8.

requirements of the time demand that women be equipped as fully as men to enable them to meet present and after the war conditions.[31]

A few days later the Government responded. The Sydney Morning Herald reported:

> We are informed that there is no intention to discontinue the training of women farmers, but it is proposed to make different arrangements. The present proposal is that the Scheyville farm should be utilised for training returned soldiers in farming, a purpose for which it is better suited than for the training of women. There are eighteen women students at the farm at present, and it is expected that arrangements will be made to continue their training elsewhere and under what should be more suitable conditions. The Cowra Experiment Farm has been suggested as a location. The matter is now under consideration, and the students may rely upon receiving a chance to continue their training.[32]

Closure of this 'experiment' was swift with the Windsor and Richmond Gazette reporting on 20 July 1917 that:

> Two women from the Scheyville Training farm left on Monday evening for the Government Experiment Farm at Cowra. They have been sent to report on the alterations that would be necessary there for the accommodation of the women from Scheyville. It is proposed to devote the Cowra Farm exclusively to the training of women, on the same plan as boys are being trained at other experiment schools. In all probability all the women from the Scheyville Farm will be housed there shortly, and Scheyville will be given over to the training of soldiers. It seems it was never intended to use it permanently for the training of women.[33]

---

[31] 'Week to Week' *Windsor and Richmond Gazette (NSW: 1888–1961)* 6 July 1917: 4.
[32] 'Women Farmers.' *The Sydney Morning Herald (NSW: 1842–1954)* 9 July 1917: 5.
[33] 'Week to Week' *Windsor and Richmond Gazette (NSW: 1888–1961)* 20 July 1917: 4.

By 31 August 1917 the last batch of 'lady farmers' had left Scheyville Training Farm for Cowra.

By early October it was reported that:

A successful start has been made in the training of women students at Cowra experiment farm. Some fifteen students, who recently received a preliminary course of instruction at the Scheyville agricultural training farm, were transferred to Cowra about five weeks ago, and it has been shown that this farm is admirably suited for the training required. It has, therefore, been decided to admit an additional number of students over sixteen years of age. The course of instruction includes agriculture, dairying, poultry farming, beekeeping, vegetables and flower gardening, and other suitable subjects. A fee of £5 is charged for the first six months, and a further six months' training will be given free, subject to the student giving satisfaction in the first half year. The fee includes board and lodging and instruction.[34]

It should be noted that the training was free to the boys at Scheyville. However, women had to pay at Cowra!

Perhaps that explains why a Miss Emily Fenn when replying to some letters with a sexist tone from a Mr Lee Snr. from Schofields in an exchange in the Windsor and Richmond Gazette on 8 October, 12 November, and 26 November 1920 explained that she was able to run her own orchard with the help of another ex-student thanks to the training she received at the Cowra Experiment Farm. She stated that 'during the twelve months that the women were in training, [the farm] showed a bigger financial return than ever before in its history.'[35]

Some of those trained at Scheyville passed on their knowledge. More than a decade after the 'experiment' ended, the Windsor and Richmond Gazette

---

[34] 'Week to Week' *Windsor and Richmond Gazette (NSW: 1888–1961)* 5 October 1917: 4.
[35] 'Women Farmers' *Windsor and Richmond Gazette (NSW: 1888–1961)* 8 October 1920: 9; 'Women Farmers' *Windsor and Richmond Gazette (NSW: 1888–1961)* 12 November 1920: 5; 'Women Farmers' *Windsor and Richmond Gazette (NSW: 1888–1961)* 26 November 1920: 2.

reported on 'a 12-acre training farm for women at Glenfield ... as an example of women's efforts to relieve unemployment among their own sex.

> The credit for this venture is given to Mrs. Jessie Street, President of the United Associations, who with a committee, rented the ground. Miss Emily Fenn, who used to delight concert audiences in Windsor some years ago with her singing, and who is a successful farmer trained at Scheyville, is teaching 20 girls – clerks, nurses, domestics, etc. – who have long been unemployed. These get food relief, which they supplement with vegetables grown by themselves.[36]

However, for many of the women who trained at Scheyville during the Great War, their training was largely wasted.

The Dreadnought Boys' opinions

It was a condition of the Dreadnought Scheme that as part of the boy's agreement to receive an assisted passage, that they must work at least two years on farms before they took on any other form of work.

This is similar to a requirement imposed upon the post–World War Two migrants who came from Europe as displaced persons.

According to Bill Wilson, one of the Dreadnoughts who arrived in the 1920s, the Scheme had two serious defects. Firstly, he believes it was unwise, and unfair to target boys of fifteen to eighteen with romanticised accounts of the life and status of an Australian farm labourer. He believes the boys were too young and naïve to be able to make the decision they were persuaded to make. They may have needed a parent's consent, and should have had a parent's advice, but starry-eyed adolescents are difficult to get through to. Parents also were themselves persuaded by the literature, especially as it was Government sponsored.

Secondly, the prospects for a young farmworker in Australia were overestimated. It was implied in the literature put out by Australia House that a

---

[36] 'Week to Week' *Windsor and Richmond Gazette (NSW: 1888–1961)* 2 September 1932: 4.

boy could become the owner of a farm himself in Australia within a few years. All he had to do was work hard, save his money, gain practical experience working for a farmer, and be 'of the right type'. In the 1920s this was unrealistic. In the 1930s, when the Great Depression hit, it became a bad joke. Migration planners couldn't have for-seen the collapse of farm prices in the Depression, but there had been a wind down in the need for farmworkers that had been progressing for a century. Just as there was an increase in the rate of mechanisation of farm processes, and a consolidation of farming land into much larger holdings since the 1950s, there had already been progress in better seeds, the use of fertilisers, improved stock and disease control which had increased productivity in the 1920s. However, increased production put the squeeze on prices and wages so that people had begun to leave the farms because there was no longer a good living in the rural life for large numbers of people. As the Depression deepened, some of the established farmers were driven off the land, and there was a wind down in the need for rural workers.

Many of the boys who came to Australia in the early 1920s did manage to get themselves established in occupations before the Depression struck. However, those who didn't get on their feet early found themselves handicapped by the nature of the Scheme under which they had migrated. They were young when they migrated. They were without family support. All were literate and some had secondary education, but most of them were without the rudiments of any economically worthwhile skill or occupation.

In the 1930s the prospect of finding a wife or a place in the Australian community seemed hopeless for many Dreadnought Boys. Their social status was low, and they worked long hours for debt-ridden farmers who gave food and shelter but no wages. Wages were sometimes promised, but not paid. Lucky ones got a pound a week. The dole was seven shillings and sixpence a week, and paid in the form of grocery coupons. If anyone complained that the dole rations were not enough, the police would advise that there were plenty of rabbits in the bush.

The work of the Dreadnought Trustees, and the New Settlers League 'form one of the best examples of voluntary effort in conjunction with Government aid ensuring that no detail of the Settlement process is neglected'.[37]

Conclusions

Geoffrey Sherington has spent decades researching the history of youth policy in Australia since World War Two. In relating the general experiences of Dreadnought Boys to contemporary concerns of Australia in the 1990s (concerns that are still current in 2020), he concluded that the spectre of unemployment was a dilemma for many young people in Australia[38] For those, including Professor Sherington and this writer, born in the late 1940s or 1950s, the spectre of unemployment was virtually unknown in our youth. However, for earlier generations brought up in the early twentieth century and particularly during the Depression of the 1930s, the difficulty of finding a job is well understood.

Dreadnought Boys were not typical of their generation. In the early part of the twentieth century in both Australia and Great Britain, many young people had found a job of some sort by the age of fourteen or fifteen which was then the standard age for leaving school. Finding a job though, did not necessarily mean that the young immediately became independent of their family. Most young people continued to live at home with their family until they married. One of the few areas where they could leave home to start a career was in becoming a midshipman. The Royal Australian Navy had an entry scheme until the formation of ADFA (the Australian Defence Force Academy) in 1986, whereby boys entered the Naval College at Jervis Bay at the age of fifteen or sixteen and completed their matriculation studies whilst being introduced to Navy life.

The Dreadnoughts however, didn't leave home to go to sea, having earned a university degree and a permanent job in the Senior Service. They left home to

---

[37] Dickey asserts that the high standard of physical, mental and moral fitness demanded in candidates for migration to Australia, together with her distance from Europe reduced after-care problems to a minimum.

[38] Sherington, Geoffrey, 'British youth and Empire settlement: the Dreadnought boys in New South Wales' *Journal of the Royal Australian Historical Society* 82, 1996, 12.

go overseas as young migrants and had set out on their own independent journey. They were showing initiative and were leaving Britain for various reasons. For some it was an opportunity to travel and have an adventure. For some, a chance for promised better prospects abroad. For many, it was simply to find work when Britain in the 1920s already had high levels of unemployment. Only a few had family connections in Australia. The vast majority knew nothing about Australia apart from some rather misleading information provided by the Australia Governments of the time.

More Australians than people of other nationalities make the effort to travel. An oft quoted benefit of this practice is the meeting of people from different regions. On the way out to Australia, the Dreadnoughts had to mix with people from other regional and social backgrounds. With eight lads to a cabin they had to learn to understand each other's dialects, and get along.

But the Dreadnought Boys did come. They came under certain expectations: they were promised training, they were led to believe that in a fairly brief time they could acquire enough money to buy a farm. In a fairly brief time, they were given only marginal instruction in basic farming methods. Moreover, only a tiny proportion ever were able to acquire enough capital to buy a farm before World War Two.

Sherington asserts that the reality was that the Dreadnought Boys were brought to Australia principally to be offered jobs that Australia-born did not want. From the early 1900s to the 1920s Australian Governments embarked on schemes of closer land settlement. The main way that this settlement took place was through dairy farms or small wheat farms, and most of the Dreadnought Boys were sent to work on these sorts of farms – farms and properties where the small landowners were already finding it tough to make a living. No wonder the Dreadnought Boys often found it hard.

To add to their initiative in leaving their birth country to come to Australia they also had to be adaptable. The help they received from the Dreadnought Trustees was negligible. Some were visited by welfare officers during the 1930s

Depression and many remembered the voluntary work of those like Dr Mary Booth. Some found kindness in Australian communities. Undoubtedly some returned to England, but the vast majority stayed in Australia. Over half of those who joined the Dreadnought Association in the 1970s had fought for Australia in World war Two. Most would go on to successful careers after the war in Australia but few stayed on the land.

Although Sherington believes the Dreadnought Boys should be celebrated in respect of their own initiative, adaptability and endurance, he also argues that the Dreadnought Scheme was not a success, that it was ill conceived in its administration and that its aims were unrealistic given the economic and social conditions of Australia before 1939. In the experience of their lives, however, he believes something can be offered to young Australians of the late twentieth century.

There is evidence that, in this early part of the twenty-first century, young Australians are staying at school longer, and living at home till they are much older. As with young people across the western world in the twentieth century, they have experienced an increased dependence on formal education and training. Young people stay at school longer; and there is an argument that this is inevitable as the economy and technology change, and necessary economic and social skills become ever-more complex. Part of the dilemma of today (being the twenty-first century) is to relate training to a rapidly changing economy. A question can be asked though: in the process of trying to manage change have the policy makers neglected some of the initiative and adaptability that youth can demonstrate? As with the Dreadnought Boys, today's young people often find the promises of adults misleading. There were certain difficulties that needed endurance and enthusiasm to be overcome by the Dreadnoughts, and while social and economic circumstances may be different, some human qualities are everlasting.

Attitudes changed. When W.E.K., a Church of England lad from the south of England was seeking work in the 1920s, he had to be mindful of 'the prejudices still common among Protestant Australians in those days'. The Sydney Morning

Herald job advertisements for station hands and domestics included such qualifications as 'Catholics need not apply' or 'Protestants not required'. By 1949, after serving in World War Two, he was no longer the 'cow-cock's boy' and was supervising all aspects of the production, collection and transport of milk for the Sydney and (later) local distribution. He was to be in that job for fifteen years and 'not hear a single reflection upon his origins,' The term, 'Pommy bastard' seemed to disappear from the native vocabulary. 'Others of almost every other imaginable European nationality became the butts for new terms of derogation.'

Just as W.E.K. seemed to feel he was 'generally accepted as Australian by all', another wave of immigrants began to arrive in Australia. The post–World War two European refugees and migrants are the subject of the next chapter.

The Dreadnought memorial plaque at The Rocks says it all: 'Recruited for farm labour, they branched into a wide range of occupations. A number ultimately achieved community leadership and distinction. Despite early adversities we who now survive recall our youthful venture with satisfaction, and here record complete affiliation with our adopted land.'

The collection of short biographies compiled by Olwen and Gordon King and based on Professor Sherington's research is titled *They Passed This Way*.[39] That is what the Dreadnought Boys did. They passed the way of Scheyville for the first eight to thirteen weeks of their life in Australia.

---

[39] King, Olwen & Gordon, *They passed this way: Stories of the Dreadnought boys* Dreadnought Association, 2008

A training farm for Australian boys — Scheyville in the 1930s

There aren't any records of interviews with boys who went to the farm in the 1930s: none of those boys are alive now. So there can be no oral history. The New South Wales State Records Office has voluminous records relating to the training of Canberra lads, but that is official correspondence. Factual but not inspiring.

This situation contrasts with the biographical and autobiographical material available to quote people who came under the Dreadnought Scheme. That was a high profile 'experiment' that had many interested parties comment on Scheyville.

However, newspapers contain human interest stories. Collecting almost every newspaper article for the decade proved to be a worthwhile exercise. It has provided a positive spin on the farm during the greatest financial depression in recent world history.

All newspaper articles from the Sydney Morning Herald and Windsor and Richmond Gazette for the period January 1930 to December 1939 were accessed to tell the story of Scheyville as reported to the world.

Here is a different approach to documenting the difficult 1930s …

On being more involved with the Hawkesbury community

The 1930s saw the farm being more involved with the Hawkesbury community. Prior to this period the local Windsor and Richmond townsfolk regarded the farm with suspicion. Many official deputations visited and inspected the farm, and there were some social functions there, but it never seemed to be accepted as part of the community. An early change appeared in 1927, when a review of the Hawkesbury Show noted that the farm had 'showed good dairy stock'.[1] In 1928, some Jerseys were exhibited and they attracted the judges' attention. Newspaper reports of prizes awarded in various livestock sections from the 1930 through to 1939 shows always included a number of prizes to the farm.

---

[1] 'A Review' *Windsor and Richmond Gazette (NSW: 1888–1961)* 13 May 1927: 6.

Of significance were the Jersey classes and gelding sections. Mr. J. Powell from the farm was a regular winner with the farm's horses. The district had always been noted for the breeding of magnificent horses of all kinds.

The farm was also exhibiting in the Blacktown and District Agricultural Show from 1931.[2]

The farm was also recognised for helping the local hospital and home for the infirm over the winter months by donating firewood.[3] On a lighter note, teams from the farm participated in sporting contests with the community, for example, in soccer against the Ryde and District Soccer team and in Rugby League against Windsor, Richmond and Parramatta.[4] Members of staff also attended the Anzac Ball.

Scheyville's sheep were conveyed to the Windsor cricket oval to keep down the grass.

The farm received another boost when its manager, Mr Scully was elected to the Hawkesbury Agricultural Society's Council, from a field of forty-five nominees contesting forty-two positions.[5] In the same week Scully was also elected as a Councillor of the Hawkesbury District Cricket Association.

The local council also said that it could 'confidently recommend these lads (Scheyville farm lads) to reputable employers in the shire and any inquiries would receive immediate attention and a careful selection made for the employer'.

The place had improved so much that Dr H.W. Harbison paid tribute to the farm in his farewell address when leaving Windsor after ten years in 1934. The 'three outstanding things' he would miss by his departure were the children's night in connection with the Hospital Ball, the bowling green and the Scheyville Training Farm. During his ten years in the district he had travelled seven thousand miles to

---

[2] 'Blacktown Show' *Windsor and Richmond Gazette (NSW: 1888 - 1961)* 6 March 1931: 8.
[3] 'Wood Week' *Windsor and Richmond Gazette (NSW: 1888–1961)* 5 June 1931: 10.
[4] 'Football Notes' *Windsor and Richmond Gazette (NSW: 1888–1961)* 17 July 1931: 12; 'Football Notes' *Windsor and Richmond Gazette (NSW: 1888–1961)* 14 August 1931: 13.
[5] 'Efforts Justified' *Windsor and Richmond Gazette (NSW: 1888–1961)* 5 August 1932: 1.

and from the Farm, and had seen it grow from a ragged place to the 'splendid' institution it was today. The farm had improved so much that he would not now mind sending his own boy there.[6]

Mr Lawrence, manager of the farm in 1937 was sought to be a member of the Show Society Committee, and was elected in August. The farm supplied dogs and sheep for a sheep dog trial and cattle drafting segment at the show. It also supplied poles, labour and transport in preparation for steer riding and camp drafting events.

Mr Lawrence was complimented by the Show Committee for his work. It said, 'He has proved himself a most valuable acquisition to the Council of the Association – is to be congratulated on the initiative he showed in staging this exhibit' (of the 'justly famous Australian kelpie').[7]

Bill Allport, Dreadnought Boy of 1928 with his daughter and the author at the 2011 Scheyville Centenary

---

[6] 'Dr. Harbison' *Windsor and Richmond Gazette (NSW: 1888–1961)* 27 April 1934: 1.
[7] 'Another Achievement!' *Windsor and Richmond Gazette (NSW: 1888 - 1961)* 12 May 1939: 1.

Dreadnought Boys feeding calves.
Permission granted by NSW Records Office, 6 April, 2021

The Blacksmith Shop, Dreadnought era.
Permission granted by NSW Records Office, 6 April, 2021

Scheyville as it was in the Dreadnought days

The Hledik family at the 2011 Scheyville Centenary.

L to R: Stephen (son), Suzanne, the author, Mark (son in law), Georgina (daughter) and Ria and Karina

The Draft-Horse Stable remains of the Dreadnought days

Dreadnought Boys receiving their mail
(Source: NSW Records File NRS5529-1 Scheyville Training Farm, 1926-1946)

Depression gives Australian boys a chance at training

Some 400 to 450 Dreadnought trainees were put through Scheyville in each of the years 1923–1927, with numbers reaching their peak in 1927. From 1928 to 1939 approximately 800 boys in total were trained. Adding to the drop in numbers, the worsening Australian economy was reflected in the Scheyville Farm Profit and Loss Account, where the losses in 1928 (£1280) and 1929 (£1070) more than doubled earlier years' losses of less than £500.[8]

The Great Depression hit in 1929 and all immigration schemes suffered. It wasn't until 1936 that the economy showed strong signs of improvement. Only limited government assistance was available from 1930; in 1931 it was restricted to family reunion cases.[9]

A reduced birthrate following World War One morphed into a lesser number of school leavers in the late 1920s; coupled with tough economic conditions in Britain and fewer employment opportunities in Australia, this meant that there were fewer candidates for youth migration schemes.

Such was the background to the Depression years of the 1930s. While it is true that that the Government reintroduced limited measures from 1936 when economic conditions were improving to attract immigrants such as farm labourers, domestic workers and juveniles for the specific purpose of being trained for farming in Australia, the Scheyville Training Farm was used to train local boys between 1930 and 1939. The only boys to come under the Dreadnought Scheme in the 1930s came in 1939.

The 1930s. Admission of Canberra boys

Percy McNamara was a man of initiative. He organised a meeting of Canberra citizens to help 'desirable youths, quite adaptable to farm life, who are out of employment and stranded owing to their parents not being in a position to maintain

---

[8] NSW Records Office. Item 5/3476.
[9] Langfield, Michele 'Voluntarism, salvation, and rescue: British juvenile migration to Australia and Canada, 1890-1939' *Journal of imperial and commonwealth history*, 32: 2, 2004, 101.

them.' McNamara was described as the Honorary Director of the Local Boys Institute. It was also known as the Australian Youths Settlement League. Canberra citizens resolved:

> That the Commonwealth Government should be asked to make available to Australian youths the agricultural training farms in the various states at present used only for training boys from overseas, and that it be respectfully requested that urgent representation be made to the NSW Premier asking that the boys of the Federal Capital Territory be permitted to make application for the vacancies now existing at Scheyville.[10]

The resolutions were forwarded to the Acting Prime Minister, and a copy to the NSW Premier's Department.

Action was swift, with the Under Secretary, Department of Labour and Industry providing a reply on 15 October. The Minister had 'approved of 200 local lads being admitted to Scheyville Training farm, and arrangements had been made for the first party of 100 lads to proceed in batches of 20 up to the 21st instant.' Approximately 250 applications for those vacancies had already been received with more coming in daily.

On 14 October the Accountant at the Department of Labour and Industry proposed to make the Canberra boys an allowance of one shilling and sixpence per week as pocket money. The Minister pointed out that this was the same as the British boys in training, in order that no distinction in the treatment of the two groups of boys. This pocket money was to be made available from funds for the relief of the unemployed. The Federal Government also provided the boys with free transport and necessary clothing, including boots, leggings and dungarees. In noting arrangements for placing these boys at Scheyville, Grafton and Glen Innes, the Manager, State Labour Exchanges had used his own car in October to visit the

---

[10] State Records of NSW Item no. 5/3476. Correspondence in this file relates to the use of Scheyville to train Canberra lads. Articles appeared in the Sydney Morning Herald 9 October 1930.

South Coast from Batemans Bay to Sydney making enquiries in regard to placing rural workers. He stated that, 'with the exception of two boys who are over 19 years of age, there will be no difficulty in placing them in employment after training.'

The Dunningham Factor

John Montgomery Dunningham used Scheyville in his electioneering during the New South Wales 1932 state elections. 'One of the first problems that will be tackled by the Stevens Ministry if returned to power is to explore all avenues for the provision of employment for the youths who have left school during the past few years', said Mr Dunningham, the Minister for Labour. As well as mentioning the work in the city of a committee of representatives of all sections of industry and its co-opted organisations such as the YMCA, YWCA, Rotarians, Boy Scouts movement, he mentioned the arrangements that had been made for an extension of their work to country districts. 'As a special scheme he (the Minister) was arranging for an extension of the scheme for training boys for farm work. At Scheyville Farm, controlled by the Department of Labour and Industry, more than 100 city boys were trained for and placed in employment every three months. These boys would, without the assistance of the department, be still receiving food relief, but in the new sphere of life they were receiving wages from 15/ per week and keep, and upwards.'[11]

On 13 May 1932 the Windsor and Richmond Gazette advertised a big sale of Jersey dairy cows and heifers on behalf of the farm, and other cattle on account of various owners.[12] Yet in July of that year, a series of newspaper articles were related to announcements that the Jersey herd was to be increased so that the number of boys at Scheyville could be doubled from 100 to 200. Mr Dunningham discussed his ideas with Mr Missingham, a country MLA and 'one of the State's best authorities, who immediately made a gift of two of the best Jerseys from his

---

[11] 'Unemployed Boys.' *The Sydney Morning Herald (NSW: 1842–1954)* 10 June 1932: 13.
[12] 'Advertising' *Windsor and Richmond Gazette (NSW: 1888–1961)* 13 May 1932: 9.

own herd ... the Minister proposes to place his idea of increasing the herd before the Jersey Herd Society.'[13] The Minister gave 'his assurance that whatever cattle were given would be kept as studs'.[14] The idea was 'to stock up with pure-bred jerseys and ... emulate the success of Hawkesbury Agricultural College with this breed'.[15]

Those politicians of the 1930s having a country background and practical farming experience helped the Scheyville Farm. The member for Coogee and Minister for Labour, Mr Dunningham, didn't have any farming experience. He did though, appoint a committee of parliamentarians to advise him on the running of Scheyville.

This was a political masterstroke. Dunningham acknowledged the farm's usefulness as a training centre and was concerned at the cost to Government. The Committee set up to advise him was selected from Members of Parliament. Dunningham 'found six farming legislators, languishing in the effete urban atmosphere of Macquarie-street, and gave them a job dear to their hearts. They are Messrs Bill Missingham (chairman), Harry Bate, Mark Morton, Harry Carter, Alwyn Tonking, and Major Albert Reid.'

Mr Missingham, the member for Byron, in particular took a keen interest. Mr Scully, manager of the Scheyville Farm for a number of years was also the brother of the member for Namoi, another country seat.

Dunningham lauded in January 1933: 'Scheyville is being modernised. For example, the promise is held for it that it will one day have one of the best Jersey herds in the State'.[16]

---

[13] 'Scheyville Training Farm' *Windsor and Richmond Gazette (NSW: 1888–1961)* 8 July 1932: 12.
[14] 'Employment.' *The Sydney Morning Herald (NSW: 1842–1954)* 15 July 1932: 12.
[15] 'Stud Jerseys' *Windsor and Richmond Gazette (NSW: 1888–1961)* 22 July 1932: 2.
[16] 'Scheyville Training Farm.' *Windsor and Richmond Gazette (NSW: 1888–1961)* 13 January 1933: 6.

Scheyville Speaks

The article in the Windsor and Richmond Gazette claimed:

As a farming proposition and nothing more Scheyville is an abject "dud" and always has been. It involves the Government in an annually recurring loss of £6,000 to £7,000, but now, extraordinary to relate, it seems to be in a fair way to being put on a basis of paying its way in the future.

If this result can be achieved it will be a notable agricultural accomplishment, because Scheyville's 27,000 [sic] acres are rated as that class which runs "a bandicoot to the acre". That, of course is an exaggeration, but it is a fact that the farm is mostly poor, hungry land, quite unsuited for intensive mixed farming.

Scheyville, however, fulfils a very useful function. Every year it takes in between 400 and 500 raw city boys and turns them out with a well-grounded knowledge of almost every branch of practical farming. Further than that, jobs are found for them. Former Scheyville boys are to be discovered in every corner of the State "making a do of it", especially as share farmers. Frequently applications are received for new Scheyville "graduates" from ex-Scheyville students.

Thus, there was a good outcome for the State, and for the young men who went there.

Dunningham considered the Scheyville scheme so successful that 'arrangements would probably be made for training boys at the Bathurst and Berry experimental farms.'[17] He made a visit to the Bathurst Farm which comprised 700 acres and had accommodation for only twenty-three trainees. Berry had an area of 403 acres. The following month it was reported that Mr Scully, 'formerly manager

---

[17] 'Unemployed Youths.' *The Sydney Morning Herald (NSW: 1842–1954)* 8 December 1933: 15.

of the Scheyville Training Farm [had] won his appeal to the department and been appointed to the staff of the Bathurst Experimental Farm.'[18]

Dunningham did use Scheyville as political capital. He made sure he was on site when the Wolsely Company presented the farm with new sheep-shearing equipment in 1936.

In August 1937 Mr Dunningham announced 'that 8209 juveniles had been placed in employment by the vocational guidance and juvenile employment section of his department in the year ended 30 June [1937]. ... Of those sent to work during the year, 1711 were placed with farmers, including 428 boys who were admitted to Scheyville Training Farm, controlled by the department, and who were sent to rural employment after completing eight to 12 weeks training.'[19]

Therefore, the Scheyville Farm was responsible for seeing that five per cent of the juvenile workforce were trained and successfully placed in a job.

Not all plain sailing

Schemes such as the Young Australia Settlers' League training scheme which existed to train Australian boys, particularly unemployed boys, at agricultural training schools (including Scheyville) drew the attention of the Australian Workers Union. A deputation was sent to the Acting Prime Minister, Mr Fenton. Its Canberra President, Mr Gardiner said that 'there was no rural workers' award in New South Wales, and he did not favour a plan which might throw boys on the mercy of the people who held a monopoly of land in the Commonwealth. He viewed with suspicion any movement that might produce coolie or cheap labour for the farmers.'[20]

In 1932, the then manager, Mr Scully, had to respond to the Under Secretary in relation to complaints and questions raised with the Minister's office. These included the boys not being able to play sport on Sundays; that the boys

---

[18] 'Personal' *Windsor and Richmond Gazette (NSW: 1888–1961)* 19 January 1934: 12.
[19] 'Youth Employment System.' *The Sydney Morning Herald (NSW: 1842–1954)* 26 August 1937: 11.
[20] 'Farm Training.' *The Sydney Morning Herald (NSW: 1842–1954)* 16 October 1930: 12.

were allowed to have butter only once a day, the surplus milk being sent to market; that the manager has a house boy from the farm and that his children are allowed to be insolent to same; that the matron of the farm, Mrs Scully, is supposed to inspect the boys' quarters, food and bed linen each day, but only does so about once a week; and youths convicted of wrongdoing in Sydney have the choice of going to Gosford Brush Farm or Scheyville Farm.

It is apparent that the Under Secretary's own son had attended Scheyville, as the Under Secretary appears insulted by the claims made by the complainant, a Mr Solomon, MLA. The Under Secretary wrote: 'If the latter is true, Mr Solomon, you must understand what an injustice it would be to the boys who have been sent there with the best of characters as my own son was.'

In reply, the Under Secretary advised that the Department was obliged to take into consideration the religious feeling of the boys in residence when it came to sport, so cricket and football matches were banned on Sundays. Saturday afternoon was the recognised day for sport and that every encouragement was given to visiting teams on that day. This was similar to the Vietnam era when sport was played on Saturday afternoons.

'I may also state that religious services are held on three out of four Sundays and that the Clergyman attends on alternate Sundays during the whole day.'

The manager had utilised the services of one of the trainees. The butter was a case of none at lunch but a double serving allowed at dinner. Mr Solomon was advised by the Minister that periodic and unannounced visits were made by senior officers of the department, and that the meal he himself ate at the farm on a recent visit was similar to that supplied to the boys.[21]

The 1935 report

The Department of Labour and Industry appeared to be proactive in conducting internal investigations by 1935. The then Acting Under Secretary, Mr

---

[21] File 5/3477 Labour and Industry Scheyville Farm 1936 State Records Office

Wallace Wurth, paid an unannounced visit to the Farm on 19 February. This was in response to a total of thirty-two boys leaving Scheyville prior to completion of their course, over the four-week period; 13 January to 9 February 1935. Inquiries indicated that many of the boys left because they had obtained employment; two had been expelled, one had left due to his mother's illness, and one left to return to school. However, no satisfactory explanation had been provided for twelve of the boys. Visits had been made to the homes of some of the boys and interviews conducted in the presence of their mothers.

The 'Reasons Furnished' inquiries were tabulated under the headings of 'Food', 'Work', 'Discipline' and 'Remarks'. The submission to the Minister summarised the complaints as follows: lack of discipline at lectures and elsewhere; a shortage of milk and sugar; bad meat; the absence of sheets and pillow slips on beds; and petty thieving amongst the boys.

The report found that, 'having regard to the nature of the work carried out, no major complaint regarding the farm can be substantiated'. However, immediate action was required to supply every boy with a pillow slip that washing days be fixed as part of the regular routine for the boys. Further, sufficient lockers with duplicate keys be supplied for each boy. Although the Manager 'stated that his experience is that allegations regarding petty thieving eventually, in many cases, turn out to be the action of boys selling their belongings, [the] Department is open to criticism because adequate locker space isn't provided.'[22]

Parental control was still evidenced to the Inspector who noted that 'Mr Busby was present during part of the interview and he told his son to tell the truth only, as they didn't wish to have any trouble with the Authorities from the Farm'. The Government's publicity campaign had also been noticed as 'Mrs Busby stated that she was surprised at the treatment the boys got as the Farm was advertised so

---

[22] File 5/3477A Labour and Industry 1937 State Records of NSW

much and she thought her son would have received an opportunity of learning something there.'[23]

Mrs Raymond said her son 'would like to go back there, he thinks, because he got better food there than I can give him here. We are on the dole and cannot provide lunch.' The Inspector noted: 'the Raymond family would appear to be in poor circumstances.'[24]

When I reviewed the tabulated responses, the most common complaint from every boy that left concerned the 'rough play by other boys'. These were the antics of boys from 'the rough element' in the dormitories, and particularly after lights out. Concern over the character of other boys wasn't universal though. J.H. Dingwall of Ryde said that 'there was a little rough play and a little fun. Every boy is initiated. He was but did not mind it and helped to initiate other boys.' A H. Birch of Lane Cove gave evidence that supports the accusation that hygiene was lacking in the form of there being 'No sheets or pillow slips on beds. Put on Saturday mornings but taken away before night and returned on Sunday for visit or inspection.'

Maraylya residents continue their sniping

Newspaper articles reveal that the only local opposition to the farm came from a small section of the community and the Maraylya Progress Association. Their opposition was ongoing – forthright and vocal until at least till 1936.

In December 1930 they urged that 'the Council to write to the Unemployed Relief Council asking for a further sum of money to be expended in relieving unemployment, the work to consist of clearing scrub off Government land, containing about 600 acres between Scheyville Farm and Pitt Town, pointing out that such land, when cleared, could be selected or sold for any rural industry.'[25] Throughout the 1930s an ongoing campaign to blame the need for road

---

[23] Memorandum to Chief Inspector Department of Labour and Industry 18 February 1935 in File 5/3477A
[24] Memorandum dated 18 February 1935 by G. Askey
[25] 'Windsor Council' *Windsor and Richmond Gazette (NSW: 1888 - 1961)* 26 December 1930: 7.

maintenance between Windsor, the farm and the Maraylya area was blamed on Scheyville farm activity.

The locals again wanted to muscle in on the farm by asking their local member, Mr Ronald Walker, to see the Minister for Agriculture to procure work for 200 unemployed men in the municipality to clear land at the farm which, they claimed, 'is of a productive nature, and which, if cleared, could be used for farming and dairying'.[26] When it suited them. the locals described the land as 'productive'. A deft politician, Mr Walker was able to 'duck-shove' the council request by reporting back to the Council that their request had to go to the Minister for Labor and not the Minister for Agriculture, as Scheyville came under the Labor Minister's control.[27]

The result was an amount being made available 'from the unemployment relief funds for the purpose of constructing wood and fibro buildings, piggeries, cow sheds and bails. ... all labour must be engaged through the nearest State Labour Exchange, and the hours must not exceed 44 per week.'[28]

Interestingly, the locals again wanted a piece of the site. On 27 March 1933 the Sydney Morning Herald reported that the quarterly conference of the Nepean Federation of Progress and Kindred Associations had passed a motion that the Minister be requested to throw open for selection portion of the farm with the object of relieving unemployment. Mr Tribe from Maraylya (a progress association which always maintained an anti-Scheyville stance) said 'that the farm was being run at a heavy loss, and if 1000 acres [of its 2700 acres] were thrown open it would relieve the State of a very heavy burden.'[29]

---

[26] 'Personal' *Windsor and Richmond Gazette (NSW: 1888–1961)* 22 July 1932: 4.
[27] 'Week to Week' *Windsor and Richmond Gazette (NSW: 1888–1961)* 19 August 1932: 4.
[28] 'Windsor Council' *Windsor and Richmond Gazette (NSW: 1888–1961)* 7 October 1932: 6.
[29] 'Scheyville Training Farm.' *The Sydney Morning Herald (NSW: 1842–1954)* 27 March 1933: 7.

Simply throwing the land open to selection wouldn't necessarily obviate unemployment, and the farm was helping the unemployed by successfully training 400 to 500 boys annually and placing them in farming jobs.

The above article illustrates how far the farm had come in a few years. The State, through Mr Bate, responded, arguing that Scheyville was serving a useful purpose.[30]

The Minister silenced the Maraylya Progress Association in June 1933 by writing to it, but also through the press. He wrote:

> In the first instance it is not my intention at the present time to release any portion of the Farm, but in the event of my deciding to do so, in the future, the association's representations will be borne in mind. Secondly, so far as the Farm itself is concerned, it has received very close personal attention from me since I took office, and a great deal has been done already towards placing it on a more efficient and paying basis. ... I appreciate the fact that the work of the institution is favourably considered, and any suggestion to me will receive my earnest consideration.[31]

In January 1934 the Maraylya Progress Association was shown an avenue to get the roads reconstructed that they had sought for so long. It was 'suggested to the Unemployment Relief Council that if there are sufficient men receiving food relief within walking distance of the proposed work, and the funds required could be provided, the department [Public Works] could undertake the necessary reconstruction of the road through Scheyville Farm as an emergency relief measure.'[32]

---

[30] 'Doing Good Work' *Windsor and Richmond Gazette (NSW: 1888–1961)* 31 March 1933: 10.
[31] 'Scheyville Farm' *Windsor and Richmond Gazette (NSW: 1888–1961)* 23 June 1933: 1.
[32] 'Week to Week' *Windsor and Richmond Gazette (NSW: 1888–1961)* 5 January 1934: 4.

The Maraylya Progress Association had a snipe at the farm, stating 'Scheyville Training Farm has not enough boys at the present time to fill its dormitories, so it is apparent the depression must be lifting! The Minister could do worse than give other people a chance of working portion of this large area.'[33]

Meanwhile, approval had been gained to provide unemployment relief to men to perform roadworks at Scheyville Farm.[34] The local Labour Exchange had trouble sourcing enough local men for the Scheyville work as they were receiving employment at Richmond aerodrome, while others were doing pea and tomato picking. Suitable men were to be obtained from the Central Labour Exchanges. In May it was reported that 'quite a little canvas town has sprung up in the bush along the road to the Scheyville Training Farm.'[35]

The Maraylya Progress Association never gave up on trying to have the Scheyville Farm sold to locals. In the Association's Twelfth Annual Report, Secretary Mr A. Wimble wrote 'Scheyville Farm is considered by all to be too large and blocks further progress to the districts surrounding it. There are some who could convert this land into a paying proposition, thereby helping the progress of Windsor and in no way interfering with the projects of the Farm'.

Scheyville as a model for Western Australia

Other prominent people visited the farm in the 1930s. These included the New South Wales Minister for Labour, Mr Baddeley (1931), the South Australian Attorney-General, Mr Jeffreys (1934), and Mr W.A. Woods of Hobart. He visited as part of his 'inquiry into unemployment schemes particularly for juveniles'.[36] The NSW Premier, Mr Stevens, and a parliamentary party attended in October 1934. Mr Gollan, MLA for Parramatta donated the nucleus of a library and undertook the duties of honorary librarian. Reverend R.B. Robinson, General Secretary of the

---

[33] 'Maraylya' *Windsor and Richmond Gazette (NSW: 1888–1961)* 27 July 1934: 3.
[34] 'Work at Scheyville' *Windsor and Richmond Gazette (NSW: 1888–1961)* 1 March 1935: 9.
[35] 'Week to Week' *Windsor and Richmond Gazette (NSW: 1888–1961)* 3 May 1935: 4.
[36] 'Unemployment' *The Mercury (Hobart, Tas.: 1860–1954)* 10 August 1934: 11.

Church of England Home Mission Society, and Leslie Piper, 'world-wide noted evangelistic minister' visited in 1935.[37]

The Western Australian connection

On 20 October 1935, the Western Australian *Sunday Times* carried a story on the success of Bundidup, a farm school in West Australia. In commenting on the gratifying progress made by the trainees at Bundidup, the chairman of the farm committee drew attention to the fact that Queensland and New South Wales had farm schools operating similar policies with the same successful results. St Lucia Farm School (Queensland) and Scheyville were compared. 'Their policy of dealing with unemployed youth of their respective States is on exactly similar lines to Bundidup.'[38]

Interestingly the Chairman of the Bundidup committee mentions that its second officer, Mr T. Morgan, 'first a dreadnought trainee, had a course of training at Scheyville before coming to Western Australia.'

The article refers to the report of the Employment Research Committee established by the New South Wales Government to ascertain the 'means best suitable to deal with the depressed condition of trade, production, unemployment, including youth unemployment.' One subject of the committee's investigations was Scheyville Training Farm. Its finding in this regard was 'that the policy operating at Scheyville was SOUND AND CORRECT' (in capitals). The writer asserts that: 'the correctness of the policy instituted at Bundidup at its inception is confirmed by experienced management, adopting similar policy in the important institution[s] in Queensland and New South Wales. If further confirmation were necessary it is supplied by the findings of the Research Committee dealing with Scheyville's operations. In as much as extension for accommodation was necessary at Scheyville with the appointments for extended operations, it is equally necessary

---

[37] 'The Scheyville Farm' *Windsor and Richmond Gazette (NSW: 1888–1961)* 11 October 1935: 10.
[38] 'The Success of Bundidup' *Sunday Times (Perth, WA: 1902–1954)* 20 October 1935: 15.

at Bundidup, and on past results is justified.' Thus, the success of the overhaul of Scheyville's operations, particularly under Minister Dunningham in the 1930s, led to a similar policy being adopted in Western Australia. Scheyville was for once a model.

On farm routine and being a 'masculine place'

An internal memo from the Farm Accountant C.B. Cochrane, suggests 'that it could be more economical for the boys to take a meal out with them, and nose bags for the horses' rather than returning for lunch. He had noticed that by the time boys working in the far paddock came back for dinner, it was 1.16pm before they returned to ploughing.[39] Stopwatch management was being practised in an attempt to improve productivity.

In April 1934 about 130 members of the Young Citizens' Association hiked to Scheyville farm to see what farm life involved. They were accompanied by Mr Waterworth of the State Labour Exchange and Mr McNamara; General Secretary of their Association. The new manager of the farm, Mr C.D. Lawrence explained the various activities.

> The course is divided into six sections of three weeks each – general farming, dairy, pigs and poultry, vegetable garden and orchard, domestic work, and a final spell of general farming again. ... The trainees do everything for themselves except cooking. They wash their clothes, scrub their dormitories, and help in the kitchen. According to the lads, the food is excellent. There is plenty of it. Every item on their menu, with the exception of items as bread, tea and sugar, is grown on the farm – honey from the beehives, butter and milk from the dairy, meat from the killing yards, vegetables and fruit from the gardens.
>
> Disciplinary measures are moderate, and generally consist of the docking of pocket money ... Every day seventy gallons of milk is sent to the

---

[39] State Records Office Item No. 5/3477 Labour and Industry Scheyville Farm 1936. File ref 279949 memo dated 24 April 1930.

Mental Hospital, Parramatta, and 28 dozen eggs a week to the Coast Hospital. One hundred and fifty tons of potatoes were sold from the last crop. ... there is about 145 tons of ensilage in the silos.[40]

In August 1934 it was noted by Mr Dunningham that the boys 'rise at times varying from 4.30 am to 6.00 am according to their duties. Breakfast is taken at 6.30 and then out to work. Dinner at midday, work again, then tea at 5.15 pm and the day's work is completed. A lecture is given every week night from 7 to 8 and lights are put out at 9.'[41] A 1936 article noted that the hens laid 140 dozen eggs a week.[42]

This routine was similar to that of the Officer Cadets training for the Vietnam War: training and work during the day with night lectures.

The boys' mental and personal development needs were also catered for. From 1933, Mr Kenny, Director of the Father and Son Welfare Movement, paid regular visits which were regularly written up in the local paper. He first visited at the request of Archdeacon Charlton, the Anglican priest. An article from 1936 reports that he visited 'about 16 times a year, to render any service possible to the unemployed youths undergoing training.' The visit included a service including a screening of the film The Life of Christ, followed by a lecture on 'Problems of Young Manhood' and additional films How to Live Long and Well and Personal Hygiene for Young Men. Boys completing their Scheyville course received a copy of the booklet 'The Guide to Virile Manhood', produced by the Father and Son Welfare Movement and recommended by prominent medical men such as the Director-General of Public Health.[43]

---

[40] 'Scheyville Farm.' *The Sydney Morning Herald (NSW: 1842–1954)* 9 April 1934: 6.
[41] 'Scheyville Farm' *Windsor and Richmond Gazette (NSW: 1888 - 1961)* 10 August 1934: 5.
[42] 'Scheyville Farm' *Windsor and Richmond Gazette (NSW: 1888 - 1961)* 2 October 1936: 5.
[43] 'A Scheyville Sunday' *Windsor and Richmond Gazette (NSW: 1888–1961)* 26 June 1936: 4.

He also delivered lectures on 'The Science of Life' and 'Sex and the Relationship of Strong Young Manhood'. Thus, Mr Kenny delivered sex education to the boys.

Another individual who helped with the boys' spiritual and personal development in the late 1920s to early 1930s was Reverend Phillip Cuthbert Anderson, who had been Chaplain at the farm. Unfortunately, he died in December 1932. In his obituary it was noted that 'as a result of Mr Anderson's visits to the farm, several young men who came from England to settle on the land had entered the ministry of the Church of England'.[44] These included Dreadnought Boys such as Archdeacon Robinson, who later joined other Dreadnoughts in settling on the far North Coast of NSW, and was my Minister when I was growing up.

An article in the Gazette reflects a number of themes. The heading is 'Scheyville Training Farm' with subtitles 'How Street Waifs are Made into Men' and 'Our Pioneers of Tomorrow'. It tells how 'waifs and delinquents from the streets are being moulded in the mould of men. They are being made into efficient farmers – an economic as well as a social benefit to the State.'[45] Thus, we have phrases and sayings that portray the site as having masculine gender.

A letter to the editor of the Windsor and Richmond Gazette extolling the virtues of the Scheyville boys was written by Jessie Buchanan who must have worked at the farm: 'we see ... Youth, whose parents having for years lived on the dole, wishing to make better provision for their future than they themselves enjoy. ... These lads are destined to become the manhood of Australia to whom we must throw the torch to carry on the traditions made glorious by the pioneers. ... We are proud of our Scheyville boys and we have cause to be. No local lad can plough a straighter furrow, grow a finer crop of oats or maize, be handier in the milking yard, garden or orchard, or work or play harder ...'[46]

---

[44] 'Obituary. Rev. P. C. Anderson' *The Sydney Morning Herald (NSW: 1842 - 1954)* 27 December 1932: 6.
[45] 'Scheyville Training Farm' *Windsor and Richmond Gazette (NSW: 1888 - 1961)* 13 January 1933: 6.
[46] 'Scheyville Farm' *Windsor and Richmond Gazette (NSW: 1888 - 1961)* 7 April 1933: 9.

In March 1933 Mr B.W. Daley succeeded Mr Scully as Superintendent. He had an imposing record and was an ex-officer of the Royal Air Force. Whereas Scully had farming experience, this man had none. He did attend Church and appears to have taken an interest in seeing the boys become confirmed as Church of England members.

The replacing of Scully as manager may have been influenced by the fact that he was investigated in 1933 for his 'habit of lending boys of the farm to friends of his and that the boys in question did not receive any pay for their services.'[47] In April 1933, Mr Daley, who was Acting Superintendent at the time reported that there was indisputable evidence was found of at least four boys being lent.

In December 1937 the farm had a herd of ninety-seven cows, poultry, pigs and a flock of approximately one hundred Corriedale sheep. Thus, the boys received experience in the dairy, elementary instruction in sheep, wool and butchering. There was work in the orchard, vegetable garden and field depending on the time of the year. Some learned harvesting, others ploughing. Brief training was given in rough carpentry, blacksmithing and fencing. Under supervision, trainees had built stables and sheds from timber cut on the farm, and metal fittings have been largely improvised from metal taken from the scrap heap. So far as possible, farm produce was used for the trainees. Meat, fruit and vegetables were almost entirely provided by the farm, and butter, eggs and milk never needed to be bought.

The boys were accommodated in large, airy dormitories, and each provided with a locker for his personal possessions. Tobacco, sweets and other small luxuries could be bought at the farm canteen. There was a swimming pool, a football ground, and a tennis court on the farm. As a result of Mr Dunningham's personal interest in the farm, there was a library, a wireless set and a motion picture projector available.

---

[47] Letter dated 5/8/1932 to Mr Solomon MLA. In State Records NSW Item No. 5/3477. Labour & Industry Scheyville 1936.

Mr Dunningham was receiving all the praise but other individuals had helped too; Mr Gollan, the member for Parramatta had donated the library in 1934. The 'swimming pool' was a bit of an exaggeration, according to former Dreadnought Bill Wilson. For him it was a dam that sometimes had water in it. What a change from earlier press it received, when the condition of the dormitories and bedding was commented on unfavourably, to have the buildings described as large and airy! And the boys having their own locker! Earlier press wrote of the petty thieving. No mention of it in the 1930s.

Signs of improvement in 1937 and towards war, again!

Signs of prosperity were becoming evident in late 1937. In August that year Mr Dunningham announced that the period of training had been shortened (at Scheyville) because there was such a strong demand from farmers for the boys' services, but he was prepared to have the period increased again when that demand had been met.

In October 1937 Mr Dunningham replied to complaints from employers that his Department had placed recruitment notices in the Sydney Morning Herald for girls between fourteen and eighteen years of age in about twenty trades at wages in excess of the award. Dunningham said 'It is not only my duty, but my pleasure to advertise jobs at more than the award rates. ... The award rate is the legal minimum, not the maximum. Premiums on award rates indicate our growing prosperity. ... Another sign of the returning prosperity is that, although during the depression we had constantly 100 or more boys in training at the Scheyville farm, today there are only 35. Boys today can get employment without our assistance.'[48]

The first sign of the British coming again was early 1938.

The Overseas League to London announced that it expected 200 British boy migrants would leave London for NSW. The boys would come to Sydney in groups of 25, the first group arriving in May 1938. 'Before being sent to farms, they would undergo eight weeks training at Scheyville. ... the Overseas Lead had

---

[48] 'Skilled Labour Shortage' *The Sydney Morning Herald (NSW: 1842 - 1954)* 23 October 1937: 17.

done great work in gathering boys from the depressed areas in Britain ... the boys ... would be the charge of the aftercare committee, of the British Settlers' Welfare Committee, on which the Overseas League would have a representative.'[49] Unfortunately, Dunningham, the man who had championed The Scheyville Farm for a decade, passed away in May 1938. The trainees stood in silence as a tribute to him at a service held under the auspices of the Anglican Home Mission. Mr Kenny, the boys' mentor, Mr Lawrence, the farm manager and Mr Bellemore, the Under Secretary of Labour, all spoke in glowing terms of the progress of the institution under Dunningham.

In August 1938 the first batch of sixteen boys under the revived Church of England Scheme arrived on the Otranto to commence training at Scheyville.[50]

In January 1939 the SMH announced:

> With the arrival in Sydney tomorrow by the *Strathaird* of 85 youths and young women for farm work and domestic service in New South Wales respectively, the migration schemes of the organisations bringing young people to Australia will be in full swing for 1939. Plans provide for the migration to New South Wales this year of more than 1,000 people between the ages of six and 21. ... the Church of England Migration Council stated yesterday that this year a minimum of 200 farm trainees and 200 domestic servants, who would be selected by the Church of England Advisory Council of Empire Settlement in London, would come to Australia. ... When the youths under this scheme arrive here, they undergo a period of training at the Migration Council's training farm at Scheyville. ... The Salvation Army plans to bring 600 young men and

---

[49] 'Boy Migrants.' *The Sydney Morning Herald (NSW: 1842 - 1954)* 22 February 1938: 12.
[50] 'Young Settlers.' *The Sydney Morning Herald (NSW: 1842 - 1954)* 25 August 1938: 17.

women to New South Wales and Queensland this year. A total of 102 have already arrived.[51]

The first Dreadnoughts arrived in nine years arrived in February 1939. It was a party of twenty-one boys on the Largs Bay.[52]

The influx of young migrants was well under way with twenty-one arriving under the auspices of the Big Brother Movement aboard the Strathallan. They reportedly also went to Scheyville.[53] The *Mooltan* bought fifteen more young men from the Church of England Scheme in the same month. Another contingent was due a fortnight after that.[54] Mr Kenny (Director of the Father and Son Welfare Committee Sydney) wrote to the editor of the Herald commenting that 'in addition to a number of our own Australian youths there were many nominees of the Anglican Church, Little Brothers and Dreadnought Boys all living and working amicably' at Scheyville.[55]

It was also reported that twelve non-Aryan Christian refugees would be leaving on the *Orama* and going to Scheyville. These were sponsored by the Society of Friends (Quakers).[56] The Overseas League also sent twenty-five boys in May 1939. These were the first of an anticipated one hundred annually: they too to go to the Scheyville farm.[57]

These young people were being young people, they got up to mischief. The papers also wrote of the pranks on board the vessels. The *Sydney Morning Herald*, reporting on one ship's approach to Sydney in June 1939, wrote:

---

[51] 'Young Migrants for N.S.W.' *The Sydney Morning Herald (NSW: 1842 - 1954)* 18 January 1939: 10.
[52] 'Farm Migrants Arrive.' *The Sydney Morning Herald (NSW: 1842 - 1954)* 11 February 1939: 7.
[53] 'Little Brothers.' *The Sydney Morning Herald (NSW: 1842 - 1954)* 2 March 1939: 10.
[54] 'English Youths for Farms.' *The Sydney Morning Herald (NSW: 1842 - 1954)* 17 March 1939: 10.
[55] 'Aid for Unemployed Youth' *The Sydney Morning Herald (NSW: 1842 - 1954)* 11 May 1939: 4.
[56] 'Christian Refugees for Sydney.' *The Sydney Morning Herald (NSW: 1842 - 1954)* 15 May 1939: 12.
[57] 'Overseas League Proposal.' *The Sydney Morning Herald (NSW: 1842 - 1954)* 30 May 1939: 10.

Thirty-six hours to go. On the last night before reaching Sydney suppressed excitement found outlet in a raid on the welfare officer's cabin. The electric light bulb was removed and the bunk stripped of its mattress. There were also raids on each other's cabins, compulsory baths with or without clothing according to the preferences of the victims. There were explorations of private portions of the ship. But the welfare officer did not notice anything that night.[58]

All this frivolity had disappeared by October 1940 when it was announced:

The State training farm at Scheyville will be taken over by the Commonwealth on Monday for the duration of the war. It will be used as a military school in artillery and anti-tank warfare.

The Minister for Labour and Industry, Mr Gollan, said last night that the Army would take over the administrative block of offices, four dormitories, dining room and kitchen and other buildings.

Work on the farm, which included a dairy and piggery, would be continued by a small staff. Most of the boys who were now receiving training there would be given employment elsewhere but some would be retained to help with the work of the farm.

Mr Gollan said that the decision to transfer the farm to the Army had been influenced by the fact that boys were not now available in sufficient numbers to justify its continuance as a training centre. Normally about 400 boys a year are trained at Scheyville to become farm workers.[59]

During World War Two the site would become the training home of Searchlight Units and later, the first Australian Parachute Battalion.

---

[58] 'Modern Boy Voyagers.' *The Sydney Morning Herald (NSW: 1842 - 1954)* 3 June 1939: 13.
[59] 'Army School at State Farm.' *The Sydney Morning Herald (NSW: 1842 - 1954)* 11 October 1940: 9.

Conclusions

The life pattern for the Australian boys who went to Scheyville in the 1930s differed from that of the Dreadnought Boys, post–World War Two migrants and Officer Training Unit graduates. They reached adulthood in a world wrung with financial misery and low expectations of anything exciting to look forward to. Due to their age group, it was highly likely that many went on to serve in World War Two. Undoubtedly there would have been casualties amongst their number. There doesn't appear to have been any link to bond this group of men. The Dreadnoughts shared a sea voyage and an adventure to the other side of the world. The postwar migrants came as families and also shared the ups and downs of an adventure to a new country. Those who were conscripted for the unpopular war in Vietnam shared a purpose and have enjoyed lifelong friendships. The Dreadnoughts and the officer cadets have had strong associations. The migrants have had access to a range of organisations to help them settle in this country and most nationalities have their own societies and associations.

All of this contrasts with the Scheyvillians of the 1930s. As far as history is concerned, they are virtually faceless. Few, if any, personal stories survive.

Thankfully, the newspapers offer a record of them having slightly more comfortable living and working conditions than those who frequented Scheyville from 1890 to 1930!

And that the local communities made them welcome.

White fingers and red berets

The Red Beret

(by J.T Hamilton)[1]

Paratroopers from the sky
Men who drop and don't ask why
Fearless men of courage strong
The Red Berets to them belong.

Weapons strapped across their chest
These are men Australia's best
Many a man will jump today
Landing hard on the jungle clay.

Pale blue wings upon their sleeves
Floating down in the strongest breeze
These are men of the Red Beret
Trained before for such a day.

Physically fit to take the fall
Trained in combat one and all
Selected men best of our day
Proud to wear the Red Beret.

Some of these men may meet their fate
Back at base their buddies wait
For they are on the list today
To follow their mates of the Red Beret.

---

[1] J.T. Hamilton, ex paratrooper. Roneoed copy of poem in Correspondence to the ADFA Academy Library, 1985 from Michael Derek Fleming. ADFA Library Reference: MS200.

Searchlights and 'Universal Trainees'

Those who were at Scheyville during World War Two went to war to defend Australia when the nation was under attack from the Japanese. The Anzac spirit may have been forged at Gallipoli but these were real Anzacs, defending Australia. They were protecting our version of civilisation and upholding one set of ideals over another in shaping Australia. Darwin was bombed and the Japanese were in Papua New Guinea.

Scheyville thus became important for Defence training activities. Scheyville again became a site of initiation. This time initiating young men into army life. It was still a site of State initiated control over people's lives. Men received an introduction to the Army way of life that fostered values of loyalty, courage, kinship, mateship and sacrifice. The tradition of those residing at Scheyville as temporary residents continued.

During World War Two, conscripts were called 'Universal Trainees'. From 20 October 1939, all unmarried men aged twenty-one were to be called up for three months militia training. These men could serve only in Australia or its territories.[2] Conscription was effectively introduced in mid-1942, when all men aged eighteen to thirty-five, and single men aged thirty-five to forty-five, were required to join the Citizens Military Forces (CMF).

The Papuan campaign of 1942 led to a significant reform in the composition of the Australian Army. During the campaign, the restriction banning CMF personnel from serving outside Australian territory hampered military planning and caused tensions between the AIF and CMF. In late 1942 and early 1943 Prime Minister John Curtin overcame opposition within the Australian Labor Party to extending the geographic boundaries in which 'Universal Trainees' could serve to include most of the South-West Pacific. The necessary legislation was passed in January 1943.[3]

---

[2] 'Compulsory Training Reintroduced.' *The Sydney Morning Herald (NSW: 1842–1954)* 21 October 1939: 15.
[3] Beaumont, Joan. *Australia's War: 1939-1945*. Allen & Unwin. Sydney 1996. pp41–42.

The role of Search Light units

History is filled with accounts of infantry and light-horse soldiers; by comparison, the Search Light Batteries, which played an important role in the Royal Regiment of Australian Artillery, have been largely forgotten. Scheyville was first occupied by Anti-Aircraft Search Light (AASL) units on 15 September 1942 on transfer from Clarendon Racecourse where Universal Training had first begun in early 1940. It was named the AASL Training Battalion and supplied reinforcements to all Search Light units. All AASL units were transferred to the Royal Australian Artillery from the Royal Australian Engineers (RAE) on 1 May 1943. The searchlight itself – the article of equipment which emitted the 'long white finger of light' into the sky – was called the projector. Briefly and fundamentally, Searchlight Control (radar) was a method of picking up aircraft in the sky by transmitting radio signals and receiving reflected signals. A 90-centimetre projector was fitted with transmitting and receiving aerials and a control panel with screen assembled inside a small canopy fixed to the back of the projector.[4]

Joining up and recruiting the 'Universal Trainees'

By the time of the Scheyville Centenary in 2011, only two of the surviving eleven men who had trained in Search Light units were able to attend the celebrations. Of those, Don Roberts was interviewed in May 2004 for the Australians at War Film Archive – quotes in this section are taken from that interview.[5]

There was a certain amount of pressure on young men to join up. According to Don Roberts, the girls on the street would hold up a slouch hat and say, 'here Mister, here's your hat'. His mother wouldn't let him volunteer for the

---

[4] Hill, Noel Francis, *Expose! a history of searchlights in WWII* Boolarong Publications 1993. p 9.
[5] 'Donald Roberts' Australians at War Film Archive, http://australiansatwarfilmarchive.unsw.edu.au/archive/1983-donald-roberts, 2004. Archive number 1983.

AIF so he joined the Army to get used to full-time duties. His initial training was at North Head, Sydney. At five foot four-and-a-half inches tall and of a light build he was well below the required height of five foot nine inches to be allowed into his preferred artillery gun training. The Sergeant Major called those for artillery training to one side and those for Search Light training to the other side. Recalls Roberts, 'those blokes that I went through basic training with went to Darwin and were there when the Japs attacked in February 1942'. Roberts subsequently did his Corporal's training and then went to Clarendon to do Search Light training. The Government didn't think there were enough volunteers so Roberts was one of those tasked with bringing in more people. He went by train to country New South Wales areas such as Coonamble to 'recruit' these 'Universal Trainees'. Each Search Light Unit had approximately 250 trainees, who stayed six weeks.

Once trained at Scheyville they were sent as reinforcements to 57 and 63 Search Light Batteries (SLB) at Port Kembla, as well as 61 SLB on the north side of Sydney, 62 SLB on the south side and 'those older fellows in the Fifty-Second' in western Sydney.

70 SLB trained behind 73 and then went to Darwin. 82 and 83 SLB were also formed at Scheyville and later went to New Guinea.

Roberts himself was posted to 73 Mobile SLB, the first Search Light Unit to go overseas. According to Roberts, 'there was no equipment at Scheyville, it was only physical training, marching, drill and route marches to get us into some sort of physical condition'.

Search Light training and operations

Don and his mate Blackley's recollections of Scheyville include dirt roads, lots of route marches and living in tents while the officers and NCOs were accommodated in the buildings. Happy memories include raiding each other's unit's camp and stealing rifles, and being ordered to strip off and cross a swollen river in pouring rain. Says Blackley, 'the sight of two hundred and forty nude blokes made the local ladies laugh'.

Not so much fun is the memory of the tent at 'gas school' at Cattai, near Scheyville. After leaving their respirators on for a few minutes they had to breathe tear gas for two or three minutes without the protection – 'vomiting often'. Blackley sees the positives of Scheyville training as 'getting fit, after going soft sitting around Sydney for many months'.

Daily routine in a unit within Australia would involve 'getting up about seven o'clock or so because they were up half the night. Wash. Shave. Wake the cook. Have breakfast about eight. Be on parade with rifles about nine. Make sure palliasses and blankets folded the right way, clean the dixies by eleven thirty. Make sure the telephone was manned twenty-four hours a day and that the equipment was guarded. Rest in the afternoon till about three thirty. Manning drills were practised from about six thirty pm to about nine thirty.

Actual training on the equipment involved: First up '... was learning about a searchlight which was a ninety centimetre projector that had a carbon arc. This was driven by a mobile generator that produces 75 volts and 150 amps. The carbon arc is very similar to the one in a picture theatre. But the reflected candle power from a paraboloid reflector shot the beam up in the sky. We had to learn about the generator, aircraft identification, drill, how to light the lamp and "expose" into the sky. A detachment of nine men operated each searchlight.'

'You lived under canvas; you'd be out in the scrub a week or so at a time. Rations came every second day or so. Of course, half the blokes had no idea how to cook, but one had to take a turn at cooking. So, the food was pretty awful as you can imagine. You had to man your searchlight at night for an hour or two.'

As an NCO, one of Don Roberts' duties was to read letters from home to the soldiers as a lot of the country blokes couldn't read or write!

It wasn't until they were told to dye all their khaki gear jungle green after having been in Brisbane a few weeks that the penny dropped that they were going to the islands and not the Middle East.

Roberts' unit proceeded from Scheyville to Brisbane and then to Townsville before sailing to New Guinea. They spent eight months at the village of Vabukori, just outside Port Moresby. Once they had dug in, the daily routine for a detachment was similar to that they had been used to in Sydney.

Dysentery and the constant threat of contracting malaria were problems in the tropical climate. An air raid in New Guinea for Don's unit usually involved three Japanese planes at a time flying over. Sometimes one or two but usually three. The Japanese aircraft had a different engine sound to the American, English and Australian craft. The engines were usually unsynchronised and of a higher pitch. 'Ours were like a deeper sound and your ears soon get used to knowing what's what.'

After Port Moresby it was on to Lae in November 1943. That 'was a bit of a dead end for us, after being there just a couple of months all they did after we serviced our equipment and did the camp chores every morning, they took us to working parties, to work at the hospital digging drains or unloading ammunition, unloading food from the ships or in the stores, or things like that, so we were just acting like labourers for two or three months … and that was a dead loss of time really.'

After seventeen months' duty they were brought home in June 1944. When asked for something to say to the people of Australia over the fifty to one hundred years the Archive will be kept, Roberts recommended that we should enjoy every day as it comes, realise every day's a bonus, be friendly to our neighbours and realise what a marvellous country we have. 'And the beauty of it [Australia] is that we're an island and we haven't got bloody neighbours to argue and fight with … Australia is the best place in the world', so our children should be taught to understand and appreciate it.

Secrets of the obelisk at Scheyville

When Don Roberts was on the committee of the Searchlight Association, he organised the erection of the obelisk at Scheyville. Don located the stones to be used, then his stonemason friend, Ron McMahon, together with his bricklayer son, came voluntarily to lay the concrete foundation and build the memorial. The obelisk contains a casket containing the narrative history of their Search Light

Units, local newspapers and several rolls of other items from members. According to Les Blackley and Roberts there had been intermittent reunions of their members, though they only went back to Scheyville every five or six years. The objective of the Searchlight Association 'in placing this memorabilia in the obelisk we are informing people in a hundred years of the unit's history when the memorial falls, or is knocked down', said Roberts.

It is a recurring fact that people who inhabited Scheyville at a particular time know little of what went on during other people's time there. Although both men had spent time training for war, Roberts only had contact with Colonel Overall, the Commanding Officer of 1 Parachute Battalion, when erecting the plaque at Scheyville. Roberts knew about the debacle of Sandakan and the story of why the Parachute Battalion wasn't used to rescue those men.

The creation of a paratroop unit in Australia

Whilst the Searchlights, as part of the Artillery, have a link to military pasts, the parachutists heralded a new element in the fighting Corps. It was an important part of the journey of parachuting in Australia, and signalled the beginning of the Red Berets. The banner and colours of the 1st Parachute Battalion are cared for by troops of 3 Battalion RAR (Royal Australian Regiment). Unlike those who joined the SLUs the paratroopers were an elite group drawn from existing soldiers who had been to war in the Middle East, ten of whom had gallantry awards including the Military Cross. Despite this, the 1st Parachute Battalion didn't get to go to war.

The Australian War Cabinet, at its meeting on 10 June 1941, recorded the following decision:

> The Minister for the Army asked whether any consideration had been given to the training of parachute troops in Australia. The Chief of the Air Staff stated that, while training of these troops was not beyond our capacity, the only type of aircraft in Australia suitable for the purpose were Hudsons, and these were being used to full capacity on general

reconnaissance work. The Minister for the Army asked whether there was not a preliminary stage of training such as jumping from heights, which might be undertaken without aircraft. The Chief of the General Staff said that paramilitary troops at present undergoing special training were the type that could be appropriately trained in parachute work. It was directed that the Chiefs of Staff should consider the question of training parachute troops.[6]

The Defence Committee, consisting of Vice-Admiral Sir Guy C.C. Royle, Chief of the Naval Staff, Lieutenant-General V.A.H. Sturdee, Chief of the General Staff, and Air Commodore W.D. Bostock, Deputy Chief of the Air Staff, considered the matter on the basis of the views of the Chief of the Air Staff and the Chief of the General Staff.

At its meeting on 24 July 1941, the Committee recommended that elementary ground training in parachute work be given to paramilitary troops at No 7 Infantry Training Centre (Yanakie) by attaching suitable RAAF personnel.

The Committee pointed out that aircraft could not be provided at the moment to enable 'live descents' to be made, but the possibility of making available a suitable aircraft in the future would be investigated by the RAAF. The training of parachute troops would be further reviewed by the Chief of the General Staff in the light of developments in the United Kingdom.

The proposal to create a paratroop unit, promoted by the Deputy Prime Minister and Minister for the Army, Frank Forde, does not seem to have been welcomed by senior military officers and it was to be some time before his proposal was implemented.

On 30 December 1942, the Commander-in-Chief, Australian Military Forces, General Blamey, wrote from Allied Land Forces Advanced Headquarters in New Guinea to the Chief of the General Staff as follows:

---

[6] Australian War Memorial archives., War Cabinet Minute 1136 para. C(iii), 729/6

With reference to the scale of airborne troops, I do not propose to increase the number of Australian parachute troops beyond that already approved, one Independent Parachute Company, which is now in process of formation.[7]

Timeline to a battalion

A composite parachute training unit was formed at Laverton, Victoria, on 3 November 1942, then moved to Tocumwal, New South Wales, on 16 November 1942. Limited recruiting for men to be trained as parachutists took place in October 1942 but it was not until early December 1942 that approximately forty personnel, mainly recruited from an Independent Company Training Depot, assembled at Tocumwal Aerodrome.

The establishment of the training unit was made up of Wing Commander Glasscock as Commanding Officer, two Squadron Leaders – one as Administration Officer, the other as pilot, with Pilot Officer Jack Milne (former exhibition parachutist) as co-pilot, and a Flight Officer in charge of female staff including parachute packers, as well as physical training staff. The Army personnel consisted of Captains as Chief Instructor, Adjutant, Officer Commanding Training and Quartermaster, with Sergeants to be trained as instructors and jumpmasters.

By the end of January 1943, the first intake had completed the initial course of four jumps each. At this stage all personnel packed the parachutes with which they jumped. A course of parachute jumping consisted of: (a) an initial solo jump from 2000 feet (b) two solo jumps from 1000 feet, and (c) a final stick jump with ten men from 500 feet.

The unit suffered its first fatality in early March 1943 when one man had his canopy apex caught in the tail plane of the aircraft. His subsequent release over Lake Yarrawonga resulted in his death.

---

[7] National Archives Australia. Series MP 729/6.

During March 1943 experiments in water jumping into the Swan Hill lakes were undertaken by the Commanding Officer, Wing Commander Glasscock, Flying Officer Milne and Captains White and Smith.

By this time, three groups had finished their jump courses and three more were undergoing training. Those who had completed the jump courses were making endurance marches and testing rubber jump boots.

From 6 April 1943, the unit was commanded by Wing Commander W.H. Wetton, RAF. Wing Commander Wetton had been seconded from the British airborne forces at the request of the Australian Government. Also seconded was Major H. Roberts, who joined the unit as Chief Instructor. These appointments were not welcomed by everyone in the Parachute Training Unit as it was considered that the Australian members of the unit had demonstrated a capacity to develop the training program without the inclusion of personnel from outside Australia.

On the recommendation of Wing Commander Wetton and Major Roberts, the Chief of Air Staff decided to move the Parachute Training Unit from Tocumwal to Richmond RAAF Station, near Sydney. This decision was based on weather conditions and the limited training facilities at Tocumwal. Another consideration might have been Richmond's proximity to Sydney.

The transfer was completed on 13 April 1943. Training from then on was based on airborne training in England.

On 19 April 1943, A Company of 1 Parachute Battalion was formed at Richmond RAAF Station, New South Wales, from personnel trained by the Parachute Training Unit. It consisted of Company Headquarters, three platoons and a mortar section, with Captain I.L. Smith in charge. The new unit was called Group 244 RAAF – Army.

B Flight 36 Squadron, flying DC-2s, was the RAAF Squadron attached to provide the aircraft support for parachute descents.

At Richmond the students worked most of the first two weeks of the four week, seven-descent qualifying course doing physical training and skills required for the actual drop which consisted of one solo, one slow and one fast pairs, one stick of slow and one stick of fast fives and finally two stick jumps from approximately 700 feet of fifteen to twenty-one jumpers. All were fitted with a statichute only, exiting with either the .303 rifle held with its butt against their cheek, a sten gun carried horizontally inside the front of the harness, or a Bren gun encased in a felt sheath which was lowered to the ground by a cord prior to landing.

At this time a Parachute Training Centre was formed under the command of Captain R.S. Freeman to receive recruits for the Parachute Battalion and other special forces, train them as qualified parachutists and so build up a reserve of trained personnel for other companies as they were formed.

The first operational training jump was made by 1 and 2 Platoons at Yarramundi drop-zone.

Parachute jumping into water at Cataract Dam began in July 1943 but was discontinued after the death by drowning of Captain Dossiter on 23 August 1943. During this period the company also carried out night jumps, water jumps and jumps at the Jungle Warfare School, Canungra, Queensland.

On 9 August 1943 B Company was formed with Captain J.F. White as OC.

On 15 August 1943, 1 Parachute Battalion was formed with Major Overall as CO.

On 21 September 1943 an advance party of the battalion moved to Scheyville, to be followed on 24 September by the main body of the battalion.

By mid-January 1944 the battalion was at full strength, consisting of Headquarters Company, A, B and C Companies, Battalion Headquarters and a troop of engineers.

On 31 May 1944 an advance party of the battalion arrived at Mareeba on the Atherton Tableland in Queensland. Following company and battalion-level exercises the 1st Parachute Battalion was declared ready for operations in May 1944. A fourth rifle company was formed in June 1944 and the Battalion was joined by the parachute-qualified 1st Mountain Battery, equipped with short 25-pounder guns, in September 1944.[8]

Media exposure

A 1945 article by 'A War Correspondent' painted a picture of the Australian parachutist as heroic and daring:[9]

> At this service school they breed the Army's toughest, fiercest soldiers, for the parachutist must be brave as a lion, strong as a bear, cunning as a fox, and ruthless as a tiger.
>
> Every man is a volunteer, aware of the rigours he must face and the risks he must run. …
>
> Every man is hand-picked for physique and intelligence. There is a minimum age limit of 22 and a maximum of 32. Recruits must not be less than 5ft 6in nor more than 6ft, and their weight must not exceed 186lb.
>
> … squeamishness has no place in the curriculum. You must be willing to jump out of a plane flying at a low altitude and land safely in a few seconds. You must be able to crawl through miles of wet jungle at night, guiding yourself by the stars or by compass to the heart of the enemy's encampment. …
>
> Some of Australia's best athletes, boxers, wrestlers, and exponents of unarmed combat are employed at the school to build brawn and muscle. Day after day the men are put through a rough and tumble course of physical training, gymnastics, medicine ball, basket- ball, climbing, jumping, hurdling, obstacle racing and free-for-all fighting with fists,

---

[8] Item AWM 52 Barcode 1138444 containing the War Diaries of the Unit were consulted.
[9] 'How Our Paratroops are Trained to be Tough' *The Sydney Morning Herald (NSW: 1842–1954)* 24 July 1945: 2.

boots, knives, and clubs. By the time they are ready for action they will have succeeded in dragging to the surface all the more primitive characteristics of their caveman ancestry. …

… the time arrives when the paratroop man must make his first parachute descent. He boards a transport plane with his companions and attaches his parachute to a static line, a device which automatically opens the parachute a moment after he leaves the plane. It enables descents to be made from extremely low levels and mass landings to be effected speedily.

As the plane approaches the landing field a small red light is switched on in the cabin as a signal for every man to stand up and take action stations. When the light changes to green they jump, one by one, at intervals of only a second, through the open door.

With the equipment they carry the parachutists are ready to go into action the moment they land. … To increase their firepower and fighting efficiency, additional Australian-made arms, supplies and equipment are dropped with them in containers attached to separate parachutes.

Quite a picture of individuals who are not to be messed with!

First jump memories

The following is an account of one of the first jumps and its background, taken from the diary of Captain Syd H. Buckler of Coffs Harbour, New South Wales, as quoted by Frank Mines in his history of parachuting in Australia.[10]

---

[10] Mines, Frank. *A Draft history of parachuting in Australia up to the foundation of sport parachuting in 1958*. Website of The Australian Parachuting Federation. Permission granted by the CEO of the APF in an email dated 1 December 2020.

Sunday 17 January 1943. Yesterday I packed my own parachute in preparation for my first jump. At this school my section of sixteen men will be the first to jump. Flying Officer Milne who is an instructor here – ex-professional parachutist of approximately 150 jumps will be first out of the plane. I will be next so that will give me the honour of being the first Australian Army man to parachute.

Almost five weeks ago, I arrived at Tocumwal to commence this first course; – mainly consisted of intense physical training, wrestling, tumbling, jumping and boxing – during the first week we were all very tired as the course was severe and weather hot, Instructors are found from professional P.T. men, boxers, wrestlers and gymnasium attendants. Well, we are perfectly fit for the jump and have no worries that the chutes won't open as we have seen them dropped with 300-pound dummies attached to them. Besides each man has packed his own chute with an instructor standing by. In addition to the big statischute 32 feet canopy which is harnessed to the back, there is a 24 feet canopy attached to the chest – this will give an auxiliary just in case. Instructors packed these whilst we looked on.

Monday 18 January 1943. Disappointing day – wind had been too strong to allow droppings to take place, perhaps first thing in the morning, The Chief Instructor took up three dummies to drop, very pretty seeing the chutes come down through the red and purple bands of the late evening sky. From this point of view one chute at 2000 feet appeared to pass by a large star.

Thursday 21 January 1943. On Tuesday 19 January 1943 I made my first jump from the plane. Took about fifteen minutes in the DC2 to obtain 2000 feet and arrive over the correct dropping place. During this time the nine students in the plane talked and smoked and speculated on results of first jump, all were in good humour.

A red light went on to indicate approaching dropping area, moved to the doorway with parachute or statischute, static cord attached to the static line within the plane – stood in the doorway crouched ready to jump. Wing Commander Glasscock tapped me on the backside and I was into space before I knew it. I can remember saying to myself 'Oh Christ', soon after looked upwards and saw the white silk had developed above me. From time of leaving plane until chute had fully developed took three seconds, so one hasn't very long to worry. Oscillated freely but could only tell this by looking up at the silk. The descent from 2000 feet took 2 minutes 8-2/5ths seconds. I landed with a slight jar much less than anticipated fell over on to one cheek of my backside and then rolled forward, caught the rigging lines and deflated the canopy. There is no difficulty in parachuting, a mental strain for a few minutes is apparent whilst waiting the turn to jump. The three seconds whilst the canopy develops may worry troops but is only a short space of time. Amongst my section of sixteen everyone jumped without hesitation. Injuries were one ankle tendon and one bad knee; both will be unable to jump again for a week.

The feelings of troops on first jump taken convey those emotions that relatively few experiences. In notes of the individuals commenting immediately upon landing:

Q.X. 5748 L/Sergeant K.P. Kane 24 1/2 years (civilian life, derrick man on oil wells). In plane before jump, filled in time by talking and watching others go out.

On leaving plane first jump, felt alone, nothing to hang on to, no sensation as chute opened. Felt alright once I got away from plane. Great feeling, hard to stop oscillation. No difficulty in landing.

A general observation of all troops on first jump, apprehensive whilst in plane waiting turn to jump, control their feelings by smoking, talking, laughing and cracking jokes about probability of others not having successful jumps, but confident that theirs will be O.K.; or they try to give outward signs of that confidence. Numerous thoughts pass through mind whilst standing at doorway ready to go out. No one could quite express their feelings on casting themselves into space but all expressed relief on looking up and seeing the canopy had developed. No one felt a jerk as the chutes opened, just a slight pressure on shoulders; ground did not appear to rush up, landing jar was lighter than expected.

I have the honour of being the first member of the Australian Army to have made the statischute jump and the third person in Australia to use the "Statischute." Two went before me, an ex-professional parachutist Flying Officer Milne and the chief instructor, Wing Commander Glasscock, both of the RAAF. The former stated that it was his 147th jump and was the smoothest chute opening he had experienced, with an exceptionally slow landing. Said it was just like stepping off a tram.

Headquarters of 1 Parachute Battalion

Members of the Parachute Battalion training for war

These photographs by courtesy of Tim Overall, the son of Colonel Overall

Members of the Parachute Battalion training for war

Lord Gowrie and Lt Col John Overall inspect troops of 1 Parachute Battalion
Scheyville October 1943

Practice jump with cover of a smoke screen

Search light, low-resolution

The Overall family at Scheyville

On 4 August 1943 Major J.W. Overall arrived at Richmond as 2IC and Commander elect. The War Diaries indicate that formal formation of the Battalion Headquarters was not made until 15 August 1943.[11]

Overall's arrival heralded a connection with Scheyville that lasted through till the Vietnam War. John Overall's son Timothy was to graduate from OTU (Officer Training Unit) Scheyville in 1968. His brother Andrew was a graduate of RMC (Royal Military College) Duntroon, and following a tour of duty in Vietnam, was a member of the Directing Staff at OTU in 1970–71.

As recalled by Lieutenant Colonel John Overall (in his personal memoirs supplied by his son Tim):

> After being wounded in Tobruk there was about three months hospitalisation and convalescing in Cairo with plenty of golf and tennis and good living on the Houseboat on the Nile. Then came Syria, Lebanon, Egypt and Alamein. There was a fair amount of active service in those two-and-a-half years and some interesting times. The 9th Division returned to Australia in 1943.
>
> The 9th Division re-assembled in North Queensland and shortly afterwards I was told to report to a meeting between General Morshead, the Corps Commander, and Field Marshal Blamey, the Commander-in-Chief. I had no idea what it was about, but out of it came an invitation to join a new Unit, the 1st Australian Parachute Battalion, with an engineer Unit and an Air Force Unit attached – as Commanding Officer. This came out of the blue and without any prior warning. I was appointed as CO with the job of developing it into an independent force. Rapid promotion (from the rank of Major) and accelerated parachute training followed with the US 503 Parachute Regiment. I was

---

[11] Item AWM 52 Barcode 1138444 containing the War Diaries of the Unit were consulted.

given more parachute training and jumps in two weeks than others had in a year. Then came a general officers tactical training school for six weeks before getting down to the job with the Battalion.... of the 2000 men ultimately involved, I was the only non-volunteer. We had 60 or so officers including ten Duntroon graduates. Our pay was supplemented with a special allowance. The Unit had high morale which is still evident.

The paratroopers' role in the war

According to John Overall:

There were a number of operations arranged for us. The first was to take a major role in the initial assault on Balikpapan in 1944, the second, early in 1945, was to undertake the rescue of 2500 Australian POWs at Sandakan, North Borneo. These were the remnants of 3500 POWs (#Reference Book "Kingfisher" by Judge Athol Moffit)). Both operations were aborted because the Americans would not, or could not, let us have the transport planes required. The Australian High command and General Morshead had sought planes for both from General MacArthur. It is now known there were problems with co-operation between General MacArthur and General Blamey. It was a tragedy that Kingfisher was aborted as only six of the original POWs survived the subsequent death march.

A third operation was to take part in the relief of Singapore in 1945. We were to be part of an Australian group consisting of an Armoured Regiment and the Parachute Battalion which were to be placed under Mountbatten's British command. This also was aborted at the very last moment – our planes were ready for boarding – and just before "take-off" the atom bombs were dropped in Japan.

There were regrets that the Battalion did not see action. Perhaps it was fortunate as inevitably there would have been casualties.[12]

The following excerpts from *"Sandakan: A Conspiracy of Silence"* paint a different picture of the scenarios that unfolded in those dark days of World War Two.[13]

A proposal to use the battalion to rescue Australian prisoners of war in Borneo in the closing stages of the war, 'Operation Kingfisher', was cancelled by General Blamey, the commander of the Australian Army. The proposal had the support of General Macarthur and more than enough aircraft and naval support were available. Australian troops had already landed in Borneo and Australian Special Forces Units were operating in the interior. The operation effectively ended when General Blamey personally ordered 1 Parachute Battalion, which had been on standby for the operation, to go on two weeks leave. In the event the Australian prisoners of war were massacred by Japanese troops during the Sandakan death march. An order had gone out from the Japanese military headquarters in Tokyo that all Allied prisoners of war were to be killed before the termination of hostilities. Borneo was the only location where this order was carried out. In the case of Japanese-controlled prisoner-of-war camps in Malaya and Thailand, the British military authorities had sent in paratroops to watch the camps with a view to forestalling any attempted massacre of the prisoners. In the case of Thailand, they had the co-operation of members of the Royal family.

On 23 August 1945 the Battalion was notified of a move to Singapore under the command of Major Clarke.

---

[12] Overall, John. In correspondence supplied by his son TimOverall.
[13] Silver, Lynette Ramsay. *Sandakan: a conspiracy of silence* Sally Milner Publishing, Binda, N.S.W, 1999

On 26 August 1945, 120 troops left Cairns by air and after a stay of nine days in Labuan arrived in Singapore on 9 September.

The move of the rest of the battalion was cancelled but a further 75 all ranks arrived in October.

The members of the battalion participated in the Singapore surrender on 12 September and afterwards carried out many duties. These included disarming and concentrating the Japanese troops, guarding dumps and guarding Army headquarters.

The battalion elements left Singapore on 10 January 1946 by boat and arrived at Sydney on 27 January. They moved to Ingleburn Camp where the unit was disbanded in February 1946.

The first steps had been taken towards the formation of a second parachute battalion when the end of the war made it unnecessary.[14]

The role of female parachute riggers

Parachute Riggers can trace their origins back to the 1920s, when parachutes were first introduced into the RAAF. These parachutes were maintained by Carpenter-Riggers. A new mustering of fabric worker was formed later, who took on the responsibility for parachute maintenance. In World War Two the fabric workers – predominantly female – packed parachutes for the first Australian parachute battalion. The Army's first recorded involvement in parachute maintenance was in 1943, when the 1st and 2nd Australian Parachute Refolding Platoons (APRB) were raised.

Riggers ensured that all parachutes were hung and dried in a heated drying tower, inspected, repaired and packed, just as today's riggers do. At the end of World War Two, the Parachute Refolding Platoons were disbanded; parachute maintenance remained with the RAAF until the 1960s.[15]

---

[14] National Archives Office Australia Box B6390. Item AWM 52 Barcode 1138444 containing the War Diaries of the Unit were consulted.

[15] Thamm, WO1 Phil . Extracted from articles written by WO Thamm for the Ordnance Journal. June 2006 edition Defence.gov.au/armyweb/sites/parariggers.

Fallow memory meadows

The Army made use of Scheyville on an itinerant, sporadic basis during World War Two.

In May 1941 the Maraylya representatives at the Hawkesbury District Conference of the Fruitgrowers' Federation advocated the cutting up of 1000 acres of Scheyville with soldier-settlement blocks. Mr A. Wimble stated that that portion of the land was merely used for running cattle and 'horses for the Government week-enders to ride'.[16]

It was really only for a matter of months in 1942 that the Search Light units used the site. The parachute battalion was only there from September 1943 to September 1944.

The site was left in a run-down state by the military. This was followed by years of inactivity postwar.

Finally, on 5 April 1949, Windsor Aldermen were advised that the site was going to be used as a migrant Holding Centre. The place was then constantly populated and phenomenally busy until 1973.

---

[16] 'Soldiers' Blocks' *Windsor and Richmond Gazette (NSW: 1888–1961)* 30 May 1941: 11.

A memory meadow is foreshadowed

Scheyville played a significant role in a major period of nation building after World War Two, due to its role as a Migrant Holding Centre. Conservatively 30,000 – possibly 50,000 – people may have resided in Scheyville during the migrant era. Records indicate that between 800 and 1200 people were in residence at any one time over the fifteen years the site functioned as a Migrant Holding Centre. Some stayed a month or so – others a few years. It was one of many sites used to house migrants during the postwar surge of new settlers. Most sites were former Defence establishments. Different sites had different roles – Reception Centre, Hostel or Holding Centre. Reception Centres such as Bonegilla, in Victoria, processed large numbers by providing medical examinations, x-rays, employment assessment, rudimentary English instruction and a basic introduction to the 'Australian way of life'. Bonegilla could accommodate up to 7700 people and in some periods of its operating history had about 1,000 people arrive each week. A bit like a factory: in you come, we'll process you, and out you go! Hostels such as Marrickville, Sydney, were used to accommodate people who had been assessed and required accommodation close to their work.

The role of Holding Centres like Cowra, Bathurst, Greta and Scheyville was to accommodate family units together. Usually women and children were sent to Holding Centres. A common feature of their existence was that the men were sent to places of employment such as Port Kembla steel works and were allowed to visit on weekends or monthly. Family separation wasn't popular, but was tolerated.

On 5 April 1949 the Windsor aldermen were informed by the Commonwealth Government that Scheyville was going to be used as a Reception Centre for migrants.

'Calwell's Beautiful Balts' arrive

In December 1949 Scheyville received its first intake of migrants. These were some of what became known as 'Calwell's Beautiful Balts' – Latvians, Estonians and Lithuanians!

This was 'a period when citizens from the wider world were invited to become Australian'.[1] The 'wider world' meant non-British Europeans. There were 'strings attached' to the 'invitation' to become Australian. Migrants were bound by an undertaking to work anywhere in the country doing any work deemed suitable for two years. Concerns about the health of newcomers also impacted harshly on some families. John Bulmanis's eldest sister for example, was left in Germany because she was not initially accepted for migration: she had tuberculosis.[2] When she was cleared to come to Australia, her parents had to pay for her air ticket and to guarantee that she would never be a burden to the Australian Government. It was a time when the State and the Church played a direct role in people's lives.

In a speech to the Fifth Australian Citizenship Convention on 27 January 1954, Harold Holt, Minister for Immigration, cited the reasons for migrants coming to Australia as including: 'the chance to improve their position economically and take advantage of wider opportunities, some to gain greater security, some to escape religious persecution'.[3] Political persecution drove hundreds of thousands to seek a happier homeland and this was propitious from Australia's point of view. With a 'populate or perish' mentality remaining from the fear of the country almost being taken over during the war, Australians warmed to

---

[1] Pickett, Charles & Williams, Anna, *Fields of Memories: the Scheyville Training Farm and Migrant Accommodation Centre 1911-1964.* Pamphlet of the Migration Heritage Centre NSW, Powerhouse Museum Sydney NSW.
[2] Blumanis, Rita. Oral Interview and email correspondence with Roger Donnelly 16 November 2008.
[3] National Archives of Australia File 663/27. Speech by the Ho. H.E. Holt, the then Minister for Immigration at the Fifth Australian Citizenship Convention titled 'An outline of Australia's Immigration Policy and Programs'.

changing the White Australia Policy and to the cultural changes that the newcomers brought.

As the agent of the State, Mr Holt may have outlined some of the benefits that the State could provide for the migrants, but the State wanted plenty from them. Australia wanted a mobile workforce to build infrastructure such as the Snowy Mountains Scheme and Warragamba Dam. That's what she got.

The Canberra bureaucracy awakens

A memo from the Surveyor-General dated 24 January 1949 states: 'in view of the excellent situation of this property [Scheyville] and the farming development that has taken place it would appear to be a good proposition for the employment of immigration labour for agricultural and pastoral pursuits'. The main objections to use the site as a migrant Centre were to do with distance from shopping centres and the railway. 'Trains run from Sydney to Windsor and take one and a half hours for the 34-mile journey. The timetable is deemed adequate to meet the needs of visiting husbands on Fridays and Saturdays.'[4]

In a series of letters between the Commonwealth Department of the Interior and the New South Wales Department of Labour and Industry and Social Welfare (owners of the property after World War Two) indicate that the latter's representative, a Mr Bellemore, disliked putting negotiations in writing and verbally agreed to sell the property to the Commonwealth for £25,000, but the New South Wales Valuer-General placed a price on the property of £39,000. Mr Bellemore died during the course of the negotiations. Apart from the purchase price, the cost of converting the existing buildings and constructing new ones including building works, provision of electric light and power, mechanical engineering services, water, sewerage and drainage, came to £170,000 ($340,000). Property damage was reported as having been done by the Army.

A memo dated 1 March 1949 from R.H Wheeler to the Immigration Department Secretary outlines 'a proposal to accommodate up to 1,000 women and

---

[4] National Archives Australia Series C3939/2 Correspondence File N1955/25/75704

children plus staff. Construction of twenty buildings was needed each containing 25 rooms for sleeping quarters for Displaced Persons. Buildings are to be constructed from light timber framing, sheeted and roofed with malthoid. Other community buildings such as kitchens, mess rooms, recreation rooms, a school, church and cinema are to be constructed from Quonset Huts from Manus Island.'[5]

The building work required for the migrant camp to open included: 'In each of the dormitories 18 cubicles, each twelve feet nine and a half x nine feet one and a half, for two persons and six cubicles, each eight feet four inches x nine feet one and a half for one person will be provided, as well as lavatories, bathrooms etc. These will be for staff, including teachers.'[6] Accommodation blocks consisted of twenty-four rooms, and these were allotted to families according to the number and age of their children.

The importance of the huts

Some refer to them as Quonset, others Nissen, and yet they were SAAR huts![7] They had to be in place for the centre to open. Having been sourced from Manus Island,[8] initially going to South Australia and then sent by train to Scheyville, these huts provided a communal service hub. They were used for recreational and communal dining purposes. I have been unable to determine what the individual letters refer to in the term SAAR. Iain Stuart surmises that the buildings that came to Australia were often called Elephant Houses, but in Australia they attracted the term SAAR, which is possibly a corruption of Stran Steel Arched Rib hut. The Stran Steel Division of the Great Lakes Steel

---

[5] National Archives Australia Series C3939/2 Correspondence File N1955/25/75704. Letter notated as N49/5/206.
[6] NSW Records file 14/7837 letter dated 11 May 1949
[7] Information for this section is as per an email dated 30 June 2020 from Stuart, Dr Iain, CHS Newsletter No.85 'Of the Hut I Bolted: A preliminary account of prefabricated semi-circular huts in Australia.' *Historic Environment,* 2005. As per p235 of the Draft Conservation Plan for Scheyville National Park 2006 sources researched in trying to identify the meaning of SAAR huts it is possible that as it was South Australia which imported 30 SAAR huts from Manus Island it may be a South Australian term.
[8] National Archives of Australia. Item D156/122, 1955/277. Letter from the Director General of Works to the Secretary of the Navy.

Corporation produced about 120,000 huts. However, the common term for semicircular, prefabricated huts used on military bases, hospitals and migrant Centres is the Nissen Hut. SAAR huts were identified at Villawood Detention Centre, the former East Hills Migrant Barracks (demolished in 2001), Mayfield Migrant Centre, a migrant centre in Adelaide and the East Campus of the University of Wollongong. Scheyville contains two intact examples of the SAAR huts located in their original position, and with their original kitchen extensions. These huts are rare examples of the SAAR huts made mid-twentieth century. The size and volume of the huts as well as their location in the centre of the site demonstrates the importance of the huts in housing the communal dining and recreational facilities for the migrants. Unlike SAAR huts in other locations, the Scheyville huts are not subject to development pressures, now being part of a National Park. The huts are significant for their memory value to the former migrants in addition to their physical heritage.

Journeys from afar and first experiences

Val Dollin is one of a minority of former child migrants whose mother told the story of the family's journey from a migration camp in Europe to Scheyville. Her family was in a migration camp in Germany and 'wished to migrate to any other country rather than go back to war-torn Ukraine ... My parents initially wanted to migrate to Canada but decided on Australia.'[9]

Val was five years old and her brother one when the family boarded the MS *Nelly* in the German port of Bremerhaven for the voyage to Australia on 28 May 1950. The usual departure point was in Italy, but this port was closed due to an outbreak of cholera. Her mother spoke of the hardships she had experienced during the war, the poverty, the many people who lost partners and remarried with members of cultures other than their own. On the trip, the ship crashed into the walls of the Suez Canal. On arrival in Melbourne in July 1950, all the migrants were sent by train to Albury and transferred to nearby Bonegilla Migrant Reception

---

[9] Dollin, Val. Oral interview 23 July 2009 with Roger Donnelly and typed notes supplied by Val.

Centre. On a visit to Bonegilla many years later Val used a tape measure to determine that the room her family lived in was three metres by three metres. Her mother's account of Bonegilla was alarming: 'our room had a 30 centimetre opening across one wall. We were told the possums would not harm us if we placed a piece of bread in the opening. This was so, but this did not keep the rats away. Our greatest fear was that one of us would be bitten while we slept.'

From Bonegilla the family moved to Cowra Migrant Centre NSW. Memories of Cowra are better: 'I remember it being hot and told to wear a hat at all times.' Although the Migrant Centre was a few miles from the Cowra town centre, Val remembers 'the primary school being set in a magic place with large trees and beautiful buildings. I have fond memories of that school and I mixed with a lot of the local children. Yet it did not occur to me that I or my peers were different or that I was unhappy until much later on in the beginning of my high-school year.'

For Stefania McDonald (Latka), Scheyville was the second migrant camp she lived in before her first birthday. Stefania was born at Bonegilla to Polish and Ukrainian parents: 'Dad was a Roman Catholic and Mum a Greek Catholic.' They had married in Germany and boarded a ship in Naples, Italy to come to Australia. Her mum remembers the men and women being separated on board the ship. Once in Australia the family was still split. 'Dad stayed at Bonegilla and Mum went to Cowra.'[10] Although she was only three when she moved from Scheyville, Stefania's family retained strong links to other migrant families and about twenty-four ex-Scheyville people attended her wedding.

Gerald Sinsig came from Czechoslovakia aged eleven, having found the sea voyage to Australia 'immensely exciting'. His war-widowed mother remarried in Germany. The family arrived in Sydney on 24 November 1949 and was sent to Bathurst initially, then transferred to Scheyville a few weeks later. The conversion into a migrant camp was still under way when they arrived in December 1949. He

---

[10] McDonald, Stefania. Oral interview with Roger Donnelly Melbourne 29 November 2010.

found that 'petty jealousies surfaced at times when members of one nationality felt they were being discriminated against relative to members of some other nationality. On the whole though, people got on well. A few of my friends were Yugoslavs. I never found out if they were Serbs or Croats, didn't seem to matter – unlike the unfortunate situation today. Because both my parents had obtained staff jobs at Scheyville, we stayed there longer than most migrants. I was the first of the family to move when I secured an engineering cadetship with de Havilland Aircraft in Bankstown.'[11]

The Post Office – a lifeline to the world

The post office provided necessary and much appreciated service to the migrants. In an internal postal service letter of July 1962 mention was made of the postmaster, Mr Dale, fitting in very well with unusual conditions. This particular period saw some 100 of the 800 migrants out of work for several months.

The post office opened till noon on Saturdays. An analysis of Post Office Statement of Business Transacted Returns covering 1951, 1955–56 and 1961–62 shines a light on some facets of people's daily lives at the time. The mail was important, with between 28,000 to 33,000 letters posted, as well as hundreds of parcels and 467 registered items (many posting items to overseas relatives). Residents also relied increasingly on trunk (phone) calls and telegrams. The transactions also reflect the number of children in the camp with over 3000 child endowment payments being collected at the post office. With between 767 and 1123 savings accounts being used, the migrants were good savers. As a child, Val Dollin, remembers Mr Dale helping the migrants open their bank accounts. The taxation regime of the time is also reflected in the forty-three wireless licences and twelve television licences being issued in 1962.[12]

---

[11] Sinsig, Gerald. Transcript of oral interview. Unable to identify time or place of interview. Transcript states Gerald is living in Canada. Contact attempted by Gerald's friend Margaret Ginnings. Did not hear from him despite her efforts.
[12] National Archives of Australia. Information on Scheyville Post Office extracted from Series SP459/2, Item 42/911. Series 105/1 Item Ga 2068. Item 1955/1956

Hungarian Barbara Albury made friends with Margaret Ginnings, the Post Office Manager's daughter and regularly stayed overnight at the Dale's place in Windsor. At Mr Dale's funeral Barbara recounted her memories of him:

> He was our first real contact with our adopted land and became the source of our information, our translator, adviser, confidant. Our lifeline. He was fascinated by the migrants and saw them as an entry into a new world, often strange and unsettling, but he didn't see us as trouble. This was the fifties and Windsor was just a sleepy village. This was a time when pubs closed at six, when women were only allowed in the ladies' lounge and the kids could still buy jumping jack crackers for Empire Day celebrations. People went to Church, cappuccino was a strange foreign froth and cows would wander across George St to nibble the roses. Back gardens had vegetable gardens, chooks and tyres hanging from a tree to make a swing for the children. It was like a hermetically sealed life in Windsor. A train ride to Parramatta was exciting, and to go overseas was the grandest of adventures.[13]

According to Mr Dale's wife and family, being one of the few Australians providing daily front-counter service to migrants gave the Dales an insight to the migrants' emotions and thoughts. There was boredom for the women who had older children, and were stuck at the camp with just the company of other women. Depression affected some of the residents and Mr Dale remembered 'one chap who disappeared and was found hanging from a tree not far from the camp. Many were inventive with their knitting, embroidery and leatherwork.' Mr Dale said that 'the residents would buy clothing and other items to send back to Europe. To do the customs declaration, sign language was used in conjunction with simple written instructions.' According to the Dale family, their husband and father was aware

---

[13] Albury, Barbara. Transcript of obituary read at Mr Dale's funeral. Also paraphrased from phone interview 8 July 2009 with Roger Donnelly, and article in Hawkesbury Gazette Wednesday August 20, 2003.

that the post office was a lifeline to the rest of the world and he would help his customers fill out the various forms. During the 1950s and sixties, a series of floods cut Scheyville off and Mr Dale would have to commute by boat. One of the main images in daughter Margaret's memory of the Scheyville site is the feeling of isolation. The average person in Windsor didn't know much about what went on at Scheyville.

Margaret was eight years old when her dad went to work at Scheyville Post Office. Her father enjoyed working with the migrants. Margaret accompanied her father to Scheyville and formed a number of friendships playing with other children at the camp. She remembers a change in the make-up of the migrant population from the 'Reffo Balts' who came as Displaced Persons, to the Hungarian refugees of 1956, the Dutch who came as economic migrants, and later, the Finns and Swedes who came because they were tired of the socialist governments in their country.[14]

Child's play

Val Dollin's family moved to Scheyville mid-1954.

> I have happy memories of Scheyville, which is a lot different to what my parents thought of the place. It wasn't set in a nice place like Cowra, yet I had lots of friends and the space around us was to be explored and enjoyed. Most of us were bilingual at that time and we mixed with a lot of different cultures: Poles, German, Swedish and Finnish. Quite a few of my close friends had step-fathers or no father. I particularly remember the Plahotnichenko family. It was a mixed marriage and Mrs P used to play the gramophone. Yes, she had one and played nice German music. I liked using the silos as a slippery dip, climbing and exploring huge old farm buildings, learning to swim in the ponds; and playing with countless amounts of friends. While our rooms

---

[14] Ginnings, Margaret, Dale, Norm, & Dale, Mrs James. Oral interview at Dales' family home Windsor 23 July 2009 with Roger Donnelly.

were the same size as Bonegilla and Cowra, we all enjoyed the freedom of playing outside. We either didn't have any toys or a minimal number. Nor did we feel that we missed not having toys. Our toys were organically made if anything.[15]

Similar sentiments have been expressed by Gerald Sinsig:

Not an ideal place for adults but idyllic for children, a wonderful environment to grow up in. Surrounded by bushland where kids could explore for hours, play hide-and-seek, swim in numerous ponds, climb trees. Plenty of companions to share such activities. I developed a love of the outdoors, and for the Australian bush, and made some lifelong friends.[16]

Gerald Sinsig was up to many mischievous boyish pranks with his mates. These included climbing the water tank, 100 feet above ground, at dusk and throwing pebbles onto the corrugated iron roofs below; and being chased by a security guard after he and a friend rang the fire bell at midnight. His favourite prank, however, was perpetrated in the communal bathhouse. To his devilish delight he found that he could divert high pressure cold water from the elevated tanks he climbed into the low-pressure hot water systems (small boiler-heated tanks located beside each bathhouse) simply by pressing his hand over the shower head outlet to block the outlet.

---

[15] Dollin, Val. op. cit.
[16] Sinsig, Gerald. op. cit.

Luba Borysko and Kazi Bileski preparing food in the Camp kitchen

Rozalia Borysko playing a gypsy, Maria Wenc playing a princess and Janine Makaruk playing a princess

Alexandra Bilokur and Kazi Bilecki serving meals in the Camp kitchen

Residents could buy necessities such as toothpaste, ice-cream, lollies, etc.

Mushroom farm, Maraylya.

L to R: Michael Jacek, Nick Borysko and four friends

The choir won the Eistedford and went to Canberra

Nick Borysko was an indentured worker for for the Water Board in 1951

Val Dollin and Rozalia Good outside the hut where the nuns held craft activities for the children

Primary School Teachers. Back L to R: Mr Cole, Mr Robb, Mr Yapp, Mr Baltins. Front L to R: Mr Lippiat, Mrs Lippiat…Miss Tchaikovski at end

Scheyville Netball Team

Mr Lippiat and baseball team

Scheyville School Play, 1958

The Scheyville Choir with Mr Yapp, 1957

Social aspects of camp life

The arts were important to Val Dollin's parents and she was encouraged to learn music by playing a balalaika first, then the mandolin and finally the piano. She had talent playing the piano and it was recommended to her parents that she take exams at the nearby Windsor High School. It didn't occur to Val that her parents had to pay for these lessons until much later on. Back in their country (the Ukraine) anyone who had musical talent received free tuition.

'Films were shown three nights a week in the Cinema Hall, which was also used for meetings and concerts,' reports Betty Eady.[17]

Meal time was a most important part of the daily routine. Meals were eaten in two large communal messes. There was a huge kitchen where all meals were prepared and cooked by steam or electricity and each family had its own tables and chairs. Three block supervisors were on duty to see to people's needs and welfare. Each family had a table in the dining room. In 1949 concrete footpaths were yet to be built so it wasn't much fun going between buildings on wet days.

For Australian-born staff member Betty Eady, the red cabbage soup conjures up 'yuk tastebud memories' even at ninety years of age. Likewise, Suzanne Hledik[18] remembers her mum going to the Sydney Hungarian deli once a week to buy bread, because the bread at Scheyville was so unpalatable. The school provided food as well. The Scheyville diet included junket and sago and mutton. The mutton made Suzanne ill. It was also the first time in her life that she ate white bread, together with dripping and golden syrup. Vivi Kuru's[19] mother gave her lunch money because the lunches made at the Scheyville camp were done the day before, and would just be 'off'. Many people had a little gas burner in their room to cook food. These were a tremendous fire hazard. For many migrants, the main use of the telephone service was to communicate with local people of their own

---

[17] Eady, Deaconness Betty. Oral interview with Roger Donnelly 25 July 2009. Sydney.
[18] Hledik, Peter and Susanne. Email correspondence 5 January 2009 and oral interview Melbourne 17 January 2009.
[19] Kuru, Vivi. Oral interview Estonian House Sydney 2009.

nationality to buy food that wasn't available in the camp mess. Not everyone complained though – for Rita Blumanis,[20] the food was plentiful and she was in heaven getting jelly and custard. Her family thought they were in the height of luxury having the use of a kitchenette.

Some Australian-born children such as Norm Dale and his sister Marg were invited to festivals and celebrations at the camp such as Polish National Day, where such delicacies as porcupine cake and chocolate cake were on offer. For the Dales, if the food quality was the main complaint of the migrants, it was the thing that made it different. Being the children of the postmaster, they were invited to the 'national nights' and enjoyed dancing and 'miles of rich food. The meat dishes were heavier, having been made with lard and sauces.' Migrant women brought little treasures from their homeland such as coffee mills. These weren't seen as practical items in the Australia of the 1950s and 1960s.[21]

Enterprising teenage migrants published a 'Scheyville Club Newsletter' for the children. These newsletters show how plenty of social activities were organised for the fourteen- to eighteen-year olds. They show how they had become 'Australianised' yet maintained some of their own culture and were being part of the wider world. They were singing Elvis Presley songs, conducting their own anti-smoking campaign, going to the Royal Easter Show, spending Anzac Day on a picnic outing to Katoomba and finding Cracker Night a big deal.

Religion was also a part of everyday life at Scheyville. Val Dollin remembers the Baptist ladies coming with clothes. The nuns let her play the organ, and they learned national songs and put on a performance of the opera, The Student Prince. She remembers the nuns, particularly Sister Benedict and Sister Kieren, organising after school activities. Not everyone was keen on church though. Vivi Kuru remembers there being no Lutheran Minister, and her sister going to the Catholic Church, but her brother refused to go to church. Both Vivi and Elvi

---

[20] Blumanis, Rita. Oral Interview and email correspondence with Roger Donnelly 16 November 2008.
[21] Ginnings, Margaret and Dale, Norman. Op. cit.

Suviste were confirmed at Scheyville. You weren't allowed to get married unless you were confirmed.

Parents' work

Although life was idyllic for the youngsters, their parents faced significant hurdles adapting to life in Australia. Apart from having to learn a new language, which is always harder in adulthood, there was the pressure of finding suitable employment. The purpose of holding camps like Scheyville had always been to provide a stepping stone from which migrants could assimilate more readily into the Australian way of life and its workforce. The camps were not intended to be a place of long- term residency. Adults therefore faced the pressure of finding a job and moving out into urbanised Australia. However, for many people, finding suitable work was not easy. This was especially true for migrants who had specific skills, particularly those trained in professions such as medicine, science and engineering. Qualifications gained outside Australia were not generally recognised. It was not unusual for a migrant doctor or engineer to be obliged to accept a low-skill menial job.

The problem of recognising migrants' skills and professional qualifications was raised at Australian Citizenship Conventions. In 1955, Resolution 17 stated that the problem of 'the acceptance of the credentials of professional men among our migrants [should] be left in the hands of the immigration Planning Council'.[22] Resolution 18 drew attention to the plight of migrant doctors and members of other professions, with reference to those who came to Australia under the Displaced Persons Scheme. It also called for liberalisation of the age provisions for Commonwealth Scholarship, and that special scholarships be provided for migrant doctors and members of other professions. Passing a resolution at a government-sponsored convention was one thing: making it happen quite another.

---

[22] National Archives Australia. Reference: A462. Item 663/27.

Mr Dale, Scheyville postmaster, befriended a resident who was a doctor, but due to the quota system put in place to exclude foreigners, this doctor put himself through university again here. Ironically, one of the books he had to study was one that he had written himself in Europe!

Gerald Sinsig's[23] stepfather was an experienced tradesman who, on coming to Australia, had left a job in Germany that fully utilised his skills. In Australia he had to work as a labourer for almost fifteen years before he managed to get a job that put his skills to good use. His mother, who was trained as a secretary, became a jack-of-all-trades in Scheyville where she worked for a time on the cleaning staff, then moved on to assistant nurse in Scheyville's hospital, followed by a term as assistant kindergarten teacher and culminating with a typist's job in the camp's office. It is unfortunate that Australia did not at that time make a greater effort to recognise immigrant skills where they existed so that they could be utilised for the benefit of everyone. In my opinion this is the only blemish in an otherwise laudable postwar immigration policy.

'Dad was an indentured migrant. This meant that he had to work for the government for two years' explained Val Dollin. 'He worked at the Port Kembla steel works and came home monthly. When Mum became ill and was in Orange hospital, his indentureship ceased for a while for him to look after us and mum between working part-time with Edgell, picking vegetables. When mum was better, he returned to his job at Port Kembla, coming home monthly till his indentureship ceased in late 1953.'[24]

While they were at Scheyville, seasonal work picking vegetables on the neighbouring farms provided a break from the camp and some cash for the migrant women and children. The availability of this labour was considered important by the farmers. An exchange of letters between the Vegetable Growers Association of New South Wales and the Acting Secretary of the Department of Immigration in June 1960 prompted the Secretary to reaffirm that the government had no intention

---

[23] Sinsig, Gerald. op. cit.
[24] Dollin, Val. op. cit.

of closing the Centre and that arrangements would stay for local farmers employing centre residents on a casual basis. However, having migrants posted to Scheyville specifically to meet the wishes of farmers, was refused. The Department wrote 'it does not appear practicable to place temporary rural workers at Scheyville for the specific purpose of performing seasonal work as such a procedure would deny them the opportunity of settling into permanent employment as soon as possible.'

Females with children were disadvantaged due to lack of social interaction outside the camp. When they found employment, it was often in a workgroup with fellow female migrants.

Some migrants could be categorised as difficult in relation to job seeking: files in the National Archives provide examples of the difficulties of the migrants wishing to work in their chosen field and the attempts of the bureaucracy and industry to place them.[25]

A Mr Nolet had been a tea and plantation manager. In 1961, he applied to the CSIRO but had little chance of working in his chosen field. When referred to the railways he announced that he wanted to be employed as a manager. He was also sent to Bonds to be interviewed for a storeman position, but 'talked himself out of the job.' A Dutchman, Michielsen, was referred to the railways but declared medically unfit for a station assistant job. He only wanted maritime managerial positions with organisations such as the Department of Shipping and Transport, Lighthouses and Navigation. His qualifications were deemed insufficient for such positions but he wrote to the Minister to have the qualifications for these jobs varied in order to make himself eligible. The tone and context of the letters in the file can be summarised as individuals regarding 'themselves in the "higher" bracket of employment positions and not prepared to accept employment in the unskilled field.'

Correspondence from the then AIS (Australian Iron and Steel Company, which was part of BHP Ltd) in 1958, indicates the pressure from government for industry to absorb migrant workers and the company's capacity to do so. On

---

[25] National Archives North Melbourne. File: MP690/1. Barcode 526382.

7 January 1958, AIS Port Kembla selected 109 workers at Bonegilla and was unwilling to accept any more unskilled workers. 'Critical' pressures during 1958 concerning absorption into the workforce and community resulted in 517 people being moved from the Greta and Bonegilla Camps. Hungarian migrants Csonka and Halasc were initially not acceptable to AIS because of them not knowing English but AIS was persuaded to alter their decision. The two men then refused employment, embarrassing the Immigration Department as this action did nothing to enhance the placing of other more deserving cases. The migrants had been given warnings from the Scheyville Camp Director should they be unemployed through their own fault whilst at a Commonwealth Hostel for non-payment of the tariff, they would be removed from the Camp. It was understood that they had been getting casual work with the farmers in the Scheyville District but not revealing any income to the Scheyville Camp Director.

A telegram from the Department of Immigration in Canberra to the New South Wales Department of Labour and National Service (the organisation responsible for finding employment for migrants) reminded the Camp Director that, 'due to the lack of English and consequent difficulties migrants would experience in establishing themselves in the community, we are reluctant to take eviction action except as a last resort.'[26]

Getting into real estate in Australia

For a time, only British migrants were eligible to apply for Government 'Housing Commission' homes. At this time, banks were cautious in advancing housing loans and housing was in short supply.

However, a series of resolutions passed at the 1955 Australian Citizenship Convention addressed the fact that 'large numbers of migrants have been brought here directly to aid our building programme, and it is recommended to Commonwealth and State Governments that after the claims of ex-servicemen have been met, there should be no discrimination against European migrants in the

---

[26] National Archives File MP690/1 Ibid.

provision of homes.' It was noted that eligibility for State Housing Authority homes is now satisfactory in all states with respect to British migrants, but 'in NSW, foreign migrants are still not eligible until naturalized.'

Things weren't easy out in the real world. Anne Birdsey said that the fellow who sold land to her father charged them more than he charged Australians. 'He made a killing on selling land to the "New Australians" but we were prepared to pay to get our freedom and move to our own place.'[27] After her family left Scheyville there were only a couple of families that her family stayed in contact with.

The Dollin home in Doonside was completed in 1959–60. Val had mixed emotions about moving into the new home in 1960. She says 'my parents didn't want to move us out of school till the end of my exams. I remember it being lonely. It was amazing to have so much room yet something was amiss.' She was missing her Scheyville friends.

Betty Eady saw hundreds of families come and go from Scheyville in her time as a religious teacher. She observed over a decade that 'when the migrants bought land, they'd build a half-house, just a couple of bedrooms, the dining room and the bathroom, they didn't build the back. Or else they would build the back part of their house and make the lounge room their bedroom, and a dining room and the bathroom and build the front on later when they got more money. Particularly around Windsor you could buy a block of land cheaply. The migrants would get a small house or half a house built and then sell it and buy a bigger one.'

The Latka family was at Scheyville for about two years, leaving in November 1951. During this time Stefania's dad stayed at the Chullora railway settlement camp and visited the family when he could. In December 1952 they could finally live together as a family in Australia. The family shared a house at Canley Vale while their own was built on a block at Cabramatta that her dad managed to buy. Stefania went to school at Canley Vale Primary, and Cabramatta High, where she grew up with German boys who 'had been on the other side'. Her

---

[27] Birdsey, Anne. Oral interview by phone with Roger Donnelly 5 November 2008.

mum hated Scheyville: 'it was the hut,' says Stefania, 'it gave mum a certain feeling. It reminded her of an army camp.'[28] Seeing other women fight each other, resulting from the different nationalities living closely together, didn't please her mum either; after all these years some people still won't talk to each other.

Racism and fitting in

Anne Kurovsky's Estonian family arrived at Scheyville in the mid-1950s; and recalls that 'we so-called New Australians did not socialise with the locals as they were far from welcoming. ... As time went on Australians became friendlier but at school my sisters and I didn't have any Aussie friends. On the train we were stared at, due to our accent.'[29] By contrast Anne has found with her own children, that once they went to school there was more English at home and the youngest two 'struggled' with Estonian. Perhaps it is because of the language difficulties but Anne's husband is still suspicious of strangers. To obtain an interview, this author had to have Elvi Suviste, Anne's best childhood buddy, act as an intermediary to gain the trust of this family.

Assimilation is not a one-way process. There is an interplay of factors: the natives of the receiving country, the immigrants themselves and the advice given by the government of the receiving country. Education was needed for the Australians to receive the newcomers, to understand the people from completely different economic, social and religious backgrounds. Sometimes the Australians gave evidence of their prejudice against the 'New Australian'.

The Dutch were one of the majority groups who inhabited Scheyville in the late fifties. A website, Dutchies Down Under,[30] contains an explanation, and examples of the replies to a project conducted by the Dutch Australian Cultural Centre, entitled DIMEX (Dutch Immigration Experience). Proudly, the site claims: 'Dutch immigrants are known as the "invisible migrants". The desire to re-start

---

[28] McDonald, Stefania. op.it.
[29] Kurovsky, Anne. Oral interview by phone with Roger Donnelly 4 February 2009.
[30] http://ozloggies.web-log.nl; http://dimex.dacc.com.au/DIMEXDECDest.htm; http://dacc.com.au/research.html. Hard copy printed off website 20 June 2008.

their lives in a new country and to assimilate within the Australian society as fully and as quickly as possible has been responsible for this description. Often parents decided to speak only English within the home so the children of Dutch parents could not even speak the Dutch language. Whereas other migrant groups felt the need to live close to each other and have created specific cultural areas or suburbs, the Dutch have never had that desire. In fact, some real estate agents will tell you that it was difficult to sell a house to Dutch immigrants where the neighbours would also be Dutch immigrants.'

As one respondent to the DIMEX Project wrote: 'Originally I was very much aware of a certain stigma as being a "New Australian", but if there was a stigma it seemed to shift as more and more migrants arrived from non-English speaking countries, and in place of the stigma I became aware of a certain appreciation of the German and Dutch personality traits.'

Hungarians are equally proud of having assimilated into Australian society. The 'Hungarians in Australia' website[31] tells us that about 15,000 Hungarians arrived in Australia as displaced persons in the years following World War Two. The majority of them were middle-class and professional people. After the uprising of 1956 yet another 15,000 Hungarians came to Australia. The common reason both groups came was to flee tyranny of one kind or another. According to Peter Hledik, 'they appreciated their ethnic heritage through Hungarian weekend schools, Scout activities, dance groups and other associations of cultural nature. They never formed a cultural ghetto and always adopted Australian citizenship.'[32] Keeping traditions of the home country were hard to begin though – Peter recalls his mum and friends going shopping in hat and gloves. Australians would look and point because they looked different and spoke another language. His wife Suzanne went to the Scheyville primary school, then Richmond

---

[31] http://www.hotkey.net.au/-aussiemagyar/HungariansInAustralia.html; Urmenyhazi, Attila 'Hungarian Immigration in Australia' *Australian Dictionary of Biography* http://adb.anu.edu.au/essay/13 Hardcopy from websites on 15 August 2008 and 29 October 2015.
[32] Hledik, Peter and Susanne. Email correspondence 5 January 2009 and oral interview Melbourne 17 January 2009.

Rural School, where she completed her Intermediate Certificate and gained entry to Burwood Girls High School. At that time there was no high school close by to complete the Leaving Certificate. She remembers having a 'beaut' school principal by the name of Zilla Bocking. It was a long trek to get to school each day and she was provided with breakfast and English lessons at lunchtime. Suzanne still has friends she made at Richmond Rural School. Through dedication Suzanne gained a highly prized Teachers College scholarship although it was difficult because she was not Australian born.

For some it is a mixture of fitting in but within their own emotional comfort zone. Rita Blumanis reconnected with her friend John at a mutual Scheyville friend's twenty-first, fell in love and is still married to him more than fifty years later.

Rita says 'a shared background is a strong binding factor. Both of us know what it is like to go for weeks, even months with hardly any food, to have one set of clothes to wear, and to not know if you are going to wake up in the morning. And to know the language but feel like an outsider no matter how hard you try to fit in. We do though still feel blessed to live in Australia and happy to call ourselves Australian Latvians.'

In addition to considering the attitude of the locals it is useful to gauge the attitude of the migrants to each other. A selection of random memories that surfaced during interviews I conducted with Scheyvillians in 2008 and 2009 follows.

According to Betty Eady there was a policeman who used to come and do night duty just to keep order so that people didn't get drunk.

Scheyville postmaster Mr Dale reported that 'there were a lot of tensions in the camp depending on who sided with whom in the war. The feelings engendered during the war and in the camps in Europe festered. There was less problem with differences in religion.'

Lack of privacy was a concern for Suzanne Hledik: 'there were communal showers, no water closets. The place was institutionalised, and there was no privacy which was an issue when dad came to visit at weekends.'

Joe Wrona's mother was the 'Shaman' – the village witch. All the Dutch hated the cooks, because all the cooks were Poles. Joe had some arguments with other children. Overall though the family got along with people because they believed they had come to a place where they felt safe.

Val Dollin claims that a lot of children witnessed domestic violence, there being sometimes three children and two adults in a three-metre by three-metre cubicle in a hut. Quarrels were hidden from the children for the most part. Everybody knew everybody else's business. Her mum confided to her that it wasn't easy being a mum and seeing fights between the children. From time to time tension between national groups rose to the surface but deep down people knew they had to comply with the authorities.

Elvi Suviste[33] said that the majority of fights between the children occurred after the Dutch and Germans arrived. They were 'migrants' whereas the Balts were refugees or 'reffos'.

People were suspicious of each other, and weren't supposed to iron in their room. They would blow the fuse. Keeping a kero lamp in the room wasn't the safest practice given the size of the rooms but many did so.

Vivvi Kurru also had some work in the canteen at Scheyville, and was sent on errands; it turned out that that the husband of the lady who worked in the canteen was having an affair.

Anne Birdsey said the northern Europeans and Slavic people had fights. Frustrations came out after having a drink. It was mainly the German language spoken in the camp.

---

[33] Suviste, Elvi. Oral interview with Roger Donnelly and phone conversations and emails November 2008-February 2009.

According to Valda Seibelis,[34] each ethnic group seemed to keep to themselves and Stefania McDonald remembers seeing some women fight, which resulted from conflicts between the different nationalities. Even now some people won't talk to each other.

Reunions

Former migrants have held a number of reunions over the years. The first of any size was held in Australia's bicentennial year 1988, when funding was available. When Scheyville National Park opened in 1996, another reunion was organised by various migrant groups. Another get-together was held on Sunday 17 April 2005 as part of the New South Wales National Trust Heritage Festival. This was hosted by the National Parks and Wildlife Service (NPWS) with assistance from the Migration Heritage Centre New South Wales. The visitors' book held at the National Park Office for this reunion records 289 former migrants as attending. The media release advertising the event said to 'bring your own picnic lunch; a photo display and complimentary tea and coffee will be provided. We encourage visitors to participate in the recording of oral histories and bring non-fragile memorabilia for show and tell.' Val Dollin distinctly remembers people chasing their cultural history and background who hadn't attended earlier reunions.

On 15 May 1911, the name of the Pitt Town Co-operative Settlement Post Office had been changed to that of Scheyville. A hundred years later, a celebration was held on the actual Centenary, 15 May 2011 at the site. The New South Wales Governor, Marie Bashir, herself the child of Lebanese immigrants attended, as did a hundred OTU graduates, and a handful of Dreadnoughts. Of the 1500 who attended, the majority, approximately 1200, were former migrants and their families. The fact that 1200 migrants attended illustrates a number of things about the different ways that different groups and individuals 'spread the word'. The former military men used their Associations to contact members and supply a

---

[34] Seibelis, Valda and Ivars. Oral interview Beecroft NSW with Roger Donnelly 28 November 2008.

reliable list of attendees to the organiser. The migrants contacted each other on an informal, person-to-person basis. Although their ethnic organisations placed notices in the respective newsletters, no formal communication was used, and small groups of people contacted each other, agreeing to meet on the day and share memories. Some hadn't seen each other for forty years.

The attendance numbers at the centenary celebrations were thus inverse to the amount of direct communication to the National Park's office. My observations on this day suggest that a number of migrants still live within a twenty-kilometre radius of the site, whereas reliable OTU Association records prove that former national servicemen are scattered throughout the nation.

Barbara Albury commemorated her stay at Scheyville with a play which she performed at the Centenary Celebrations in 2011. The play Hungarian Sunday was first produced in 1998 as part of the Olympic Arts Festival in Sydney. Dealing with the experiences of Hungarian migrants coming to Australia, it was praised by the Sydney University academic Dr Ziita Weber, in her study of postwar migration, 'for the skilful way in which it encapsulates concepts of change, loss and grief'. Barbara was invited to perform the play in Hungary at an international conference – the World Conference of Hungarian Women – in 2007. It was also reported in the Hawkesbury Gazette (14/7/99 p.4) that Scheyville Migrant Hostel provided the inspiration for a new Australian play Time Present Time Past that opened on Friday 23 July 1999.[35] It explored the difficulties people faced in a new country and their hopes for the future. Described as 'touching and humorous, the play also gave an intimate view of enduring friendships which are being tested when old friends meet for a game of cards. Much of the action took place in the late fifties as the migrants found a new life at the hostel after World War Two.'

The hospital

Aspects of the operation of a hospital offer further insight into the fabric and functioning of the Centre as a community. As early as 1949, when the Centre

---

[35] *Hawkesbury Gazette* 14 July 1999 p. 4

first opened, concern was raised about the establishment of obstetric facilities at Scheyville. Thus, Scheyville had its own well-equipped hospital available for women and children. A special nursery for newborn babies was included. Other amenities included a crèche, where children from two to nine were cared for while their mothers were in hospital.[36]

When the Scheyville Centre first opened, the Camp Director had to obtain authority by phone from Canberra to book four cases in to the Richmond Private Hospital, as that was the only accommodation available.

Before a double-certificated Nursing Sister was found, the services of a European-trained medical attendant were utilised as a male orderly. A European-trained nurse had to assist Dr Carroll, who visited three hours per day Monday to Friday.

Dr Carroll expressed concern about the great deal of eating carried out in the rooms. 'Centre rules with regard to food in the rooms are utterly disregarded.' He had also observed that a great deal of trouble came from the fact that the meals for all inhabitants had to be served and completed within one hour. He was sure better results could be obtained if meals could be staggered.

The Sanitation and Hygiene Reports of 31 August 1951 and 9 October 1951 state that there is a known mosquito menace in the warmer months, that mice are being trapped and that the Camp Controller, Colonel Brown wasn't in agreement with the Health Inspector's feelings on the keeping of pigeons. 'The Health Inspector's Report suggests that pigeons kept in lofts in the camp area by residents should be discouraged. I am not in agreement with his feelings in this regard. The pigeons are doing no harm and as pets provide much enjoyment for families and their children.'[37]

A memo dated 19 December 1951 to the Superintendent of the Telephone Branch of the Sydney GPO from the Head of the Immigration Department reveals

---

[36] National Archives of Australia Series A1658/1, File 556/17/1. Quoted from Folios 1 to 112 for this section.
[37] National Archives of Australia Series A1658/1, File 556/17/1. op. cit.

that some fifteen months earlier an application had been made to provide a direct phone service between the Scheyville Centre Hospital and Windsor Exchange.[38] Seeing that couldn't be done, it had been requested an extension be made from the centre switchboard, enabling the hospital to be plugged in to the Windsor Exchange when the manned switchboard at the centre wasn't working. The situation had to be described as dangerous to get action.

A flat was made available for the Matron and single rooms for nursing sisters. When Senior Sister Coppo, who was domiciled in half a hut, said she was anxious to have one room as a lounge room, the Director informed her that he wasn't agreeable as other Australian staff in the centre may press for similar treatment.

Reports of earlier years indicate the sewerage system and laundry arrangements were not satisfactory. The hospital kitchen stove was insufficient- it was only a three-plate domestic stove catering for twenty-five persons. Maternity cases were taken to private hospitals. Return times for the new mothers and babies varied from immediate to twenty-four hours, depending on pressure at the hospitals. The building report of the maternity wing in 1953 revealed the building badly infested with borers.

In September 1952 a memo to the Deputy Director of Health Sydney stated 'this department is under constant pressure by the Treasury to institute charges for all services provided in migrant centres and Treasury suggested that the migrants should pay 24 shillings per day for inpatient services and five shillings for outpatient services.' The health department stuck to the view that such charges would be detrimental to the medical services and would prevent migrants attending early for diagnosis and treatment. The result would be that infectious cases would be hidden, antenatal treatment would cease and serious diseases would not receive adequate treatment. Under those circumstances it wasn't considered possible to charge for any services at the centres.[39]

---

[38] National Archives Series A1658/1, File 556/17/1 op. cit.
[39] National Archives Series A1658/1, File 556/17/1 op. cit.

Other interesting observations included the fact that in 1955 'it was known that the making of cheese and allied products was prevalent in this camp, and that of the 150 gallons of milk consumed daily by the camp population of 986 Germans, Poles, Dutch and Greeks, 10 gallons was raw milk.'

In 1956 a review of the Immigration Medical Service agreed 'that in view of the type of migrant now being received in Australia and in view of the smaller numbers held in Centres, there is no longer the need to provide the complete medical service at all Centres'. It was proposed that 'all chronic cases, cases likely to require hospitalisation for longer than three months, be transferred to Bonegilla Migrant Hospital, which will become the Centre for these cases. Few economies could be effected at Greta and in future only one medical officer is to be employed.'

Between September 1957 and February 1958, 653 people had arrived direct from overseas vessels. Dr Carroll had opposed closure because of the shortage of midwifery beds in the area, the fact that the camp was used as a Reception Centre as well as a Holding Centre increased demands on the hospital facilities. Windsor Hospital, six miles away, was reluctant to accept centre cases and both the small hospitals, Richmond and 'Lindenow' couldn't cope with Centre cases for a full hospitalisation period.

The centre population was maintained at approximately 1000 people and hospital inpatient statistics indicate that there were between 164 and 284 patient days per month.

A discussion paper on the hospital's future in 1958, pointed out that the Windsor midwifery hospital refused to take centre cases and that the nearest public hospital where full midwifery treatment could be obtained was Crown Street Women's Hospital, some forty-six miles distant.

The inpatient section had been closed in July 1959, and residents informed of the advantages derived from joining approved Hospital and Medical Benefit Organisations. Medicare, and universal health cover for all Australians didn't yet exist.

Perusing files on the hospital give an indicator of other aspects of the site. Details, such as there being 700 migrants; mainly Dutch, at the camp in June 1960, confirm the nationality of the majority, and we learn there was a quick turnover of people every two to three weeks, confirming the role of the site was changing from that of a Holding Centre to a Reception Centre. This trend supports the fact that the type of migrant coming to Australia was changing. The hospital was functioning as an outpatient department and most of the cases trivial. There were minor infections in children and the occasional broken bone to treat; mosquitoes were less of a menace. The ambulance wasn't used much but no alternative vehicle was available for midwifery cases. There was a prenatal clinic and Sister Jones travelled to and from Clovelly daily. Hospital positions at Greta Camp had also been made redundant.

Schooling! Pupils remember

For Val Dollin, 'beginning high school was like leaving a safe haven and beginning life in the outside world. There were three of us who started at Richmond High School that year. The majority of my friends went to Windsor Catholic High School. It was fun travelling on the bus to Richmond but it wasn't much fun being the only migrant in my class. I was called a "wog" etc. asked to say words I did not know or was unable to pronounce, but I got by and soon made firm friends throughout my high school education.'

Mr Robb, the initial school principal was of stern disposition. However, early pupils remember an easy-going teacher who made them feel at ease grappling with the new language. Says Gerald Sinsig, 'it was much easier to learn English there compared to the over-regimented and disciplinarian classroom in Germany.' Mastery of the English language also affected the roles that the younger people found. John Blumanis went to Richmond High but because of language difficulties left at age fifteen and went to work at the Riverstone Meat Works.

When Gerald Sinsig and his mates' grasp of English improved 'they were considered ready to attend Richmond High School. We had grown fond of our teacher and the prospect of being plunged into a new environment was not at all appealing. We also had to now contend with a ten-mile bus trip daily. We soon discovered though, that in true Aussie fashion, our school mates in Richmond were very friendly and readily accepted us into their circle of friends. These new travel arrangements came with a fringe benefit. Until the mitigating effect of the Warragamba Dam came into effect, there were frequent floods in the Hawkesbury area that cut Scheyville off from Windsor and Richmond for a week at times, which meant no school and being able to have a holiday of sorts roaming the bush.'

The teachers at Scheyville were great encouragers. Vivi Kuru says she was encouraged by her teachers to go nursing but this would have meant leaving her mum and boarding at the Prince Alfred Hospital. Instead, she got a job at Houseman's Department Store in Windsor. Vivi then went to secretarial college and got a job as receptionist with McDonald, Wagner and Priddel, who were the engineers for the Opera House project. She had completed her first year of high school at Parkes and was put into second year at Richmond High when she arrived at Scheyville at the age of fourteen. She says 'you just coped as best you could. I tried Parramatta High School after doing my Intermediate Certificate and then went to Burwood Girls High. This meant long school days, catching the bus to Windsor and then train to Burwood.'

Rita Blumanis is another who was encouraged by teachers to do well. Rita's first year in a 'proper Australian school' was sixth class at Fairfield Primary. By then she had basic language skills but knew nothing of the history, geography and mathematics learned in earlier classes. She sat the entrance test to graded High Schools and achieved entrance to Parramatta High School, a top school in the area, by sitting a department non-verbal intelligence test because her teacher had faith in her ability. Rita later became a primary school teacher.

For Francesa Moor (Samethini)[40] the first song she learned in English when she arrived in 1960 was the National Anthem, *God Save the Queen*; it was

---

[40] Moor, (Samethini), Francesca. Extract from Migrant Visitor Book dated 23 September 2007., Scheyville National Park Office.

sung at assembly before entering school for the day. For Elvi Suviste[41] the hardest things to grasp were the change from metric to imperial measurement and the concept of pounds, shillings and pence. Elvi completed her Intermediate Certificate at Richmond Rural School and did typing and secretarial studies. This was what she wanted to do, but her mum wanted her to do the sciences but Elvi wasn't interested in a nursing or medical career. The mothers of the migrants had the same aspirations for them as other Australian mothers. Education was seen as a key to success in life.

Betty Eady remembers different facets of life at Scheyville as she was an adult and a staff member providing religious instruction. The things she remembers are wide ranging; as can be seen from the following:

> A pre-school kindergarten for children between three and five years was available and about 80 children attended each day.

> A free library was popular with all ages. Many books were in English and some in other languages.

Those adults working in the kitchen and the preschool, and all the teachers had to learn English. As noted by Betty Eady, 'the ones that worked in the kitchen, they wouldn't employ them unless they went to night school to learn English. If they didn't try, they lost their job and they would get someone else who would go to English lessons.' The mantra was – no English, no job. Records indicate that night classes for adult migrants were held on Monday and Wednesday evenings for two hours in 1950. The teachers were members of the Scheyville Migrant School staff. This activity was taken seriously, judging by the petition letter to the Schools Inspector in December 1950: 'our attention has been drawn to the fact that instruction in English and Elementary Civics to New Australians should be discontinued after one year.'[42] The migrants were reminding authorities that

---

[41] Silveste, Elvi. Oral interview with Roger Donnelly January 2009.
[42] State Records Office NSW. Item number and title: Education, Scheyville Holding Centre, 14/7837.

opportunities to hear and speak English at Holding Centres were limited and that classes also provided them with the opportunity for different nationalities to come together and learn the Australian way of life. New South Wales Records indicate that English classes for adult migrants were conducted till 1957, when an Education Department memorandum notes that day classes for adult migrants had been discontinued.

Schooling! The official stuff

A precis of the School Inspectors Annual Reports on the school and staff is attached as an appendix.

It summarises the inspectors' findings on the school accommodation, the assimilation of the students into Australian society, school discipline, students' English ability and their ability to settle into other schools, cultural activities, elitism, staffing problems, school sporting achievements, and the Social Studies Course for the years 1950 to 1964 (except 1962 and 1963 that were not available in the Archives).[43]

A careful reading of these reports would bring back memories for former pupils. They also confirm that Scheyville Migrant Centre Primary School was a microcosm of each nationality that attended there, but also reflects Australia's national immigration policy and a picture of the overall child migrant experience at school during this period.

The problems in providing education at Scheyville were in part symptomatic of problems in general in education at the time. One of the main issues facing the Education Department was the need to repair the neglect of school buildings and restore the size of the teaching force, both of which had suffered in the period of intense mobilisation for the war effort.[44] Not only was there a growth of enrolments due to the immigration program but there was a rise in the birth rate in Australia from 1946 which increased school enrolments. This urgently needed

---

[43] State Records Office NSW. Item number 1/9542.
[44] Barcan, Alan. 'Three Pathways to Change in New South Wales Education, 1937-1958.' *Education Research and Perspectives*, Vol 36, No.2, 2009.

repair work on government schools had to compete with the massive postwar housing schemes which devoured most of the available labour and materials. The new housing schemes created new suburbs which exacerbated the demand for new schools. Heffron, the New South Wales Education Minister, told the State Parliament in 1945 that it was not only 'populate or perish' but 'educate or perish'.[45] Migrant children at Scheyville and their parents certainly saw education as a potent aid to getting on in their new country.

Not only did the school at Scheyville compete with the needs of the state as a whole, but with the needs of other migrant camps. Greta Migrant Centre in the Hunter Valley accommodated 7000 people by 1951. Scheyville catered for 1000 to 1500 at any one time. Greta had two government schools and, from January 1950 to December 1959, a Catholic school. At any one time, Catholics made up sixty to seventy-five percent of Scheyville's resident population, yet while the camp had resident priests and nuns after 1956 it lacked a Catholic school.

The new 1952 Curriculum for Primary Schools (New South Wales) was a massive book of 523 pages, providing extensive guidance on the eight courses – Health and Physical Education, English, Social Studies and Scripture, Mathematics, Natural Science, Art, Handicraft and Needlework, and Music. History and Geography were incorporated into a new subject called Social Studies.

As Professor Sherington has observed, the transformation of Sydney is in relation to changes in Regionalism and Education. His thoughts apply to Scheyville. 'Since World War II, regional diversity has emerged as one of the significant features of education in a city which has become a metropolis well beyond what was conceived in the nineteenth century. ... Population growth was stimulated by the postwar baby boom and then sustained by continuous patterns of immigration. Sydney became a city of changing demographics and age relations leading to a focus on young people as the "future" as well as a current problem requiring action. The social experience of Sydney in these years [1951–2001] was very much related to providing educational facilities. In such provision the "local"

---

[45] Barcan, Alan. op. cit. p 55.

became related to "regional", particularly as Sydney became more divided by the specific social and ethnic characteristics of its population.'[46]

Conclusions

Conditions which greet present-day immigrants differ dramatically from those that confronted the postwar arrivals in those experimental years.[47]

The memories retold in this chapter are of those of individuals who were children when they arrived in Australia. Their parents didn't have an easy introduction to Australia. Some facets of their upbringing ingrained a sense of duty to be financially prudent and willing to work hard. It has also heightened their opinion of the more recent migrants, particularly the 'boat people' of the early 2000s, as 'having it too easy'.

The postwar migrants joined their fates with that of Australia seven decades ago and Australia's development has been significantly shaped by those who came.

Because Australian authorities and professional organisations refused to accept many of the qualifications that migrants held, Australia lost the opportunity to benefit from their expertise. The male migrants had to learn English in a hurry to communicate in the workplace and their children had to master English to succeed at school. Females with children were disadvantaged due to lack of social interaction outside the camp. When they found employment, it was often in a workgroup with fellow female migrants. Tough rules may have been enforced but these migrants were better off than many of Australia's more recent arrivals. A 2011 report by the Australian Survey Research Group, 'Settlement outcomes of new arrivals' shows that more than sixty per cent of refugees had failed to get a job after five years and eighty-three per cent of refugee households now rely on

---

[46] Sherington, Geoffrey and Campbell, Craig. 'Education.' *Dictionary of Sydney,* http://www.dictionaryofsydney.org/entry/education 2008.
[47] Panich, Catherine. *Sanctuary- Remembering Postwar Immigration.* Allen and Unwin Australia. 1988. P xl1 of Introduction.

welfare payments for income. More than sixty per cent of those without jobs had a poor command of English.[48]

The adult migrants resident at the Scheyville camp experienced negatives as a result of being so far from the Sydney CBD; the same distance provided positives for the children. Recollections of the Scheyville Migrant Experience are split into the trials of the parents and the happy memories of the children. The majority of people who contributed to this book were children when they were at Scheyville. The memories are therefore layered in the respect that they spoke on behalf of their parents for a version of what life was like as an adult. The other layer of memory is that of themselves as a child.

In 2018 Australia processes refugees on Manus Island. In 1949 two SAAR or Quonset huts came from Manus Island to Scheyville. These huts were a real social hub of the Scheyville complex at the time because they housed the kitchen and dining rooms for the refugees and other migrants that followed. Thus, Scheyville still has links to our immigration processes.

These huts have also provided a significant contribution to the memory-scape of the site as well as their physical heritage value.

This is an important era in the Scheyville story because it adds to the layers of significance. In previous uses of the site, and the subsequent use of the site during the Vietnam War, the historical community of Scheyville was male. The period 1949 to 1964 is the only period when women and children made up the majority of the centre's population. Scheyville's other uses had been oriented towards men and boys.

Scheyville migrants reflect the multicultural diversity that occurred in Australia after World War Two. Regular reunions of migrants reflect the spiritual, cultural and social significance that the site holds for them. The layout of the site, peculiarities of some structures and other infrastructure introduced during the migrant era is also of significance.

---

[48] Australian Survey Research, *DIAC settlement outcomes April 2011*

Physical aspects of heritage are only part of the site's importance. The oral testimony of former migrants, tell the story of daily life. It is history at the 'Parish' level, but it is rich in meaning. It is a shame that the parents of those who contributed to this work are no longer with us.

Their stories relate to the physical landscape features such as the bush surrounds, the hut precinct, meal time and the school, hospital and post office. The tenor of this work is deliberately positive

This was a time of settled leadership at the top levels of the Public Services. This became apparent when reviewing government files. The head of the Commonwealth Immigration Department from 1947 to 1961 was T.H.E. Hayes, and from 1944 to 1960 the New South Wales Education Minister who oversaw the 1952 rewriting of the curriculum was Bob Heffron. Each of these men provided a line of continuity.

This chapter further explains what newcomers thought of Australia. It also asks what Australia, in providing these facilities, made of them. It prompts further thinking about the make-up of our population and how Australia took in, and still takes in, strangers.[49]

This chapter has examined what the State wanted from the migrants from the perspective of a child migrant at Scheyville and how that was achieved; there were many positive outcomes even though there were many challenges.

---

[49] Pennay, Bruce. *So Much Sky. Bonegilla Reception and Training Centre 1947-1971*. Migration Heritage Centre, NSW, 2008.

Father Gilroy with Father Doyle and Father Tierney

Bishop Lyons and Father Tierney at the opening of the Catholic Church, 1955

Children going to church

Father Doyle with Sister Benedict and Sister Anna Marie taking first Holy Communion with children

Father Tierney with Rozalia

Father Tierney with a first Communion recipient

Deaconess Betty Eady

The Roman Catholic Church, Scheyville

The Nun's Cottage, second migrant reunion, 1997

The role of the churches

Education and immigration policies were two major factors that influenced, assisted and shaped the assimilation of the post–World War Two migrants into Australian society. A third and equally important factor was religion. At Scheyville Migrant Centre the main 'players' in the religious stakes were the Roman Catholic Church and the Presbyterian Church of Australia.

The Catholic Church itself was on a new journey after the war with changes within its doctrine and having to cope with the phenomenon of so many of its faith moving from country to country. In 1952, the landmark *Exsul Familia* (Apostolate Constitution of Pope Pius XII on migrants) codified the Catholic Church's responses to migration. The document expressed the Church's interest in enabling the preservation of each immigrant's culture and language, whilst providing them with access to a sacramental life.

Although Roman Catholics constituted some sixty-five to seventy per cent of the migrants who went through Scheyville, there was another passionate voice on the ground. For ten years, Deaconess Betty Eady of the Presbyterian Church ministered to the spiritual needs of the members of the Protestant churches. Being able to interview Miss Eady gave a rare insight into the daily life of a church representative being involved at the parish or 'real' end of what matters between a church and its parishioners. Having verbal input from one side of the religious fence complemented the written records that detail the experience of the priests and nuns of the Catholic Church. In doing this, some insight into how the experience of church representatives with different ethnic groups varied. Religion and culture cannot be totally divorced.

The role of religion in the immigration and settlement process can be considered as having both a material and spiritual aspect. In the material realm, religious groups within various traditions see the provision of basic needs such as clothing, bedding and food as part of their mission. At Scheyville the Society of St Vincent de Paul did a great deal of practical work. The Catholic Church offered far more social services than other congregations.[1] Through formal and informal channels, social services were extended to migrants, especially in the earliest days of each migrant's settlement. The value of this hospitality provided an immediate connection between the new immigrant and a faith tradition.[2]

Belonging to a faith and having a community feeling fulfils both social and spiritual needs. Nation, Church and family would have been among the significant groups to which migrants belonged.[3] At Scheyville the migrants were definitely not excluded from the Church, while its presence at Scheyville ensured that rituals were preserved.

Betty Eady hits the ground running

Recollections from the 'Protestants' representative' on site.

Miss Eady was asked by the Presbyterian Minister at Ebenezer Church Windsor to help the children at Scheyville in 1952. She stayed at Scheyville for ten years.[4]

She trained at St Andrews's Theological Hall, where deaconesses trained with the student ministers and had to do the same subjects as the men. They also had to do some special subjects at Teachers College, work with community organisations, and learn about children's health.

Miss Eady gave a unique insight into aspects of the daily schedule at the camp:

> I was given no plans. It was just a case of show initiative to teach the migrant children and help the twenty-two different nationalities settle in to Australia. I started kids' clubs for after school and after dinner activities. Every Monday afternoon at 3.30 pm till 5 pm, a club was

---

[1] Ebaugh, H.R. & Chafetz, J.S. *Religion and the New Immigrants: Continuities and Adaptations in Immigrant Congregations*. AltaMira Press, California. 2000.
[2] Noseda, Mary. *Belonging: The case of Immigrants and the Australian Catholic Church*. Thesis submitted for the award of Doctor of Philosophy, Australian Catholic University. 2006. p 43
[3] Ibid. pp 14–16.
[4] Eady, Deaconess Betty. Oral interview with Roger Donnelly 25 July 2009.

held in the church for the children, with toys and games for the children to enjoy.

Monday night at seven there was a Fellowship meeting for teenage girls and boys. It commenced with hymns, chosen by the young people, prayers, Bible study and discussion, then closing hymn and prayer. Some refreshment was served, followed by games and music.

Four other clubs were held in the recreation room in the centre every week for junior and senior girls and boys.

A women's meeting was held every Tuesday night at which various handcrafts were taught.

I went to the school every day for half an hour. Religious instruction was given every day at the school in the Centre. About thirty children each day were taught hymns and prayers and told a Bible story or shown Biblical films. The public school had ten teachers and a headmaster with average attendances of three hundred and fifty children.

The children were so attentive because they knew that if they learnt English, they would get a good job. One of my methods for teaching the younger children to count was to give each child a ride on a rocking horse, and they would count up to ten.

To help teach the Christian story I used to get films sent out from the Presbyterian Headquarters every fortnight. I found that using pictures was one of the best ways to communicate, along with talking slowly. Speaking slowly was appreciated. I also taught basket work, sewing, and other handcrafts. My kids club operated till five pm, and more activities were conducted after six pm. The Church had a holiday home in Katoomba. Myself and some friends who helped cook, regularly took groups of twelve boys and twelve girls there for a break from the Scheyville camp.

Apart from the Catholic nuns and priests, the only other regular representatives of the protestant denominations to help at Scheyville was the Dutch Lutheran and Dutch Reform Minister who came once a month and conducted a service. Anyone who wasn't Catholic came to Betty. The ratio of Roman Catholics to Protestants was three to two.

Sunday School for the Protestant children was conducted on Sunday afternoons at three pm with about one hundred attendees and once a month a family service was conducted. There was a junior class and a senior class. There were flowers for the Sunday service and afterwards the flowers were given to the mothers. A half hour story was told and then the younger children did colouring-in activities while the older ones had a story. At Christmas time churches from Riverstone and even a bus load of young people from Hurstville would come to have afternoon tea and bring presents.

I remember the Postmaster, Mr Dale, and visits from the CWA who made cakes. I introduced the CWA to Scheyville. The main contact from locals was via the CWA, but not all the ladies had a car so this made it harder for them to get out to Scheyville. Colonel Brown, the Commandant lived in a big cottage that had been divided into two; the other camp supervisor lived in the other half. I was given the use of a big recreation room to conduct my classes, and I also had a smaller room where I used to keep donated clothes. I learnt handicrafts myself from the CWA.

As the migrants left the Centre for their new homes, hostels or other Centres, their names, addresses and other information was sent to the head church office in Sydney, from where they were distributed to the nearest Minister or Deaconess in that district, who would then visit the families.

I was the full-time church representative at the Centre whilst Reverend Prisk, the Presbyterian Minister of Pitt Town and Ebenezer churches was Chaplain of the Centre and attended to any baptisms, marriages, deaths or special situations. Special church services were held on Mother's Day, Sunday School anniversaries, Easter and Christmas.

The method of scheduling classes as explained by Deaconess Eady matches the evidence in the Catholic archives that both conducted activities. When the Catholics were conducting an activity for the boys, she would be conducting one for the girls. She also did hospital visiting at the camp hospital and at the Windsor Hospital.

In the booklet 'A Deaconess's Memories',[5] Deaconess Eady writes, of her relationship with the Catholics, 'We worked together, so when I had a girls' club they had a boys' club. This meant that the children had clubs nearly every day. The Sister [Catholic] also started a basketball team.'

Miss Eady was not paid a wage, supplied her own car and even had to contribute towards petrol. She was provided with a room in the staff quarters at Scheyville.

Miss Eady also taught handcraft at Stockton in Newcastle once per week.

Quoting from Madeline Dunstan's notes on the 200th anniversary of Ebenezer Church in 2009:[6]

Deaconess Betty Eady spent ten years in the Pitt Town and Ebenezer Charge, doing her wonderful job at Scheyville Migrant Centre. She showed the patience of Job, trying to understand all those children from

---

[5] Eady, Deaconess Betty. *A Deaconess's Memories*. 2002. Booklet held at The Ferguson Memorial Library, Headquarters of the Presbyterian Church Strawberry Hills Sydney.
[6] Dunstan, Madeline. 'Ebenezer Church – 200 years.' *Ferguson focus* (Newsletter of the Ferguson Library)

so many different countries. The Government set up a school but there was no church or Sunday School for quite a while, so we were the first Sunday school and play group. The school teacher's young son came along sometimes; he seemed to understand them better than we did, even though he was Australian.

In a 1997 interview with Jeannie Barker and Ross Wallace, staff of Scheyville National Park, Miss Eady was quoted as saying:

> In the beginning there was a priest but the two nuns came later for the Roman Catholics. In that Church Lutheran, Danish and Dutch reform services were held, it wasn't only Presbyterian. There were a number of Hungarian Presbyterians as well as Catholics. When the Lutheran man didn't come, then any kid or family that wasn't Catholic came to me.[7]

Scheyville immigrants and the Catholic Church

Writing about a decade-long involvement of an institution such as the Roman Catholic Church gives a 'warts and all' exposé of the time. Former residents can also relate to the years they were there. It shows solid progress was made in keeping the Catholic 'flock' and allows mention of the sometimes strained relationships that surface in a tight-knit community. How those situations were resolved and the frustrations of dealing with a bureaucracy with seemingly many masters can be highlighted. Whereas Miss Eady was available for interview, by the time I started my research, those priests and nuns who had been associated with Scheyville had passed on. The Roman Catholic Church Archives was a great source of information.

---

[7] Eady, Betty. Transcript of oral interview 10 July 1997 with Jeannie Barker and Ross Wallace, Scheyville National Park Rangers.

Father Tierney's report, 1953

In 1953, Father Tierney provided a report about the Scheyville Camp.[8] He believed that 'from the Catholic point of view, the camp life was not the best solution for migrants'. In writing such a report he put aside the many nationalities mixing together, and the coexistence of different denominations which he said often led to 'indifferentism'. He was critical of the lack of privacy, no proper family life in such communities: husbands away most of the time except weekends and the children exposed all the day long to bad influences. 'They are seeing and talking about things that even adults are ashamed to talk about.' He claimed that 'good parents and good people are taking great pains to keep their children under control and give them a good Catholic education, but the odds are sometimes heavy against them.' He continued:

> Many families actually lack a good Catholic education, and some are not even conversant with the basic principles of Catholic life. Many a family is formed by former soldiers who were enlisted in the Army as young boys and were consequently only summarily instructed about the religious principles.
>
> Other men were at forced labour camps in Germany where they were even denied the Catholic religious practices, not to speak of any kind of Catholic religious instruction.

In many cases, Tierney claimed, the same applied to the women. Only families derived from marriages contracted before the war or at the beginning of the war had sufficient knowledge about the religious life.

He saw the priest as being really necessary in a camp community: indispensable for the children in a camp and perhaps to a lesser extent for the adults. The children were seen as being still good at heart and receptive of good

---

[8] Roman Catholic Archives, St Marys Cathedral Sydney. Box D23. Correspondence relating to the Scheyville Migrant Camp.

advice and of Catholic instruction. When he first arrived at Scheyville only twenty children attended Chapel, but through 'organising them' the number of children attending Mass rose to as high as 130 to 150 for a Sunday. Two masses were held at Scheyville on a Sunday, the first at 9 am and the second at 11 am.

Father Tierney bought copies of the Children's Prayer Book with pictures, distributed 120 of them and, with help, read the prayers throughout the Mass, which helped to keep the children occupied. Ten teenage girls also formed a choir, and another teenager played the organ. He claimed, that by organising (read involving) the children, the number of adults attending mass increased from between thirty and fifty, up to one hundred.

The 'sore point' at Scheyville, according to Father Tierney, was the Scheyville Centre School. He regretted not being able to go into the classes more than once a week for more than one hour, and that this was on the day set aside for visits from the Ladies of the Legion of Mary. All the difficulties, as Tierney saw it, came from the Headmaster, who 'appears to be more of an anti-cleric than anti-Catholic. I discussed my position with the Headmaster many times but the Headmaster didn't give on a single point. I decided to leave the matter and avoid a quarrel.'

The Legionnaires of Mary went to Scheyville each Wednesday to assist with Catholic instruction.

The Windsor Branch of St Vincent de Paul made regular visits, but by September 1953 it was being expressed that a very special need was a Catholic Chapel, as the existing one was used by all religious groups.

Chaplains at work, 1954

A letter from Father John Bird to Cardinal Gilroy mentions the Father Tierney's report: 'There is no doubt that the presence of a Chaplain in these camps is essential. A comparison between the enclosed Report and those of twelve months ago reveals a most heartening growth of Catholic life in the Camp. I pass on to

Your Eminence a recent statement by Father Tierney that he is both happy and content with his work at Scheyville.'[9]

By March, the Chaplain's Report stated that the Polish Catholics were a great disappointment. Ninety per cent of the camp were Polish, yet 'not even their own priests are able to make much impression on them. Their laxity seems to date only since their arrival in Australia.'

In September 1954 special authority was granted by Gilroy to Father Tierney to perform marriages at Scheyville. Tierney was appointed as Curate at Windsor and Bishop Lyons, as Vicar-General, implemented the decision.

The Catholic Church also reinforced the message of the Australian Government when its hierarchy travelled to Rome. A Special Report on migration matters arising from Monsignor Crennan's overseas visit from June to October 1954, noted that Australia's contribution to the International Catholic Migration Commission (ICMC) finances was £1,000 ($2,000) in 1953. Crennan suggested that contribution should be £5,000 ($10,000) as 'few, if any countries anywhere are so dependent for continued survival, on immigration, as is Australia – Australia stands to benefit from a close link with the Catholic migration bodies.'[10]

Italian migration officials expressed warm appreciation to the Australian hierarchy of the Catholic Church for the help given to Italian migrants. All were in agreement that Australia offered a most suitable country for their people.

Such was the growth in the work of the Church with migrants, the Sydney Diocesan Office, of which Father Tierney was Director after his time at Scheyville, had two migrant Chaplains in 1949 and over seventy in 1987. Many priests paid to come out from Europe, while parishioners paid for a car and medical expenses. 'The programmes of these migrant Chaplains attest their zeal and contact with people.' Father Peter Diaczyozyn of the Ukrainian Rite travelled in turn each Saturday to Queanbeyan (320 km), Maitland (190 km), Cowra (480 km) and

---

[9] Roman Catholic Archives, St Marys Cathedral Sydney. Box D23. Correspondence relating to the Scheyville Migrant Camp.
[10] Roman Catholic Archives, St Marys Cathedral Sydney. Box D13. Correspondence relating to the Scheyville Migrant Camp. Special Report on Migration Matters.

Scheyville (50 km), and once a month he gathered Ukrainians for devotion at the Sydney suburb of Chullora.'

In addition to the New Settlers Committee, the Sydney Diocese had other organisations such as the Catholic Welfare Bureau to help find jobs, and acted as a social agency and family consultation bureau, and the Legion of Catholic Women provided Counsel and a case work service to those who needed help with personal, family, marital and child guidance problems.[11]

Interdenominational conflicts, 1955

There were organisations in each Diocese to assist migrants, and eighty-three Chaplains to New Australians listed in the 1955 Catholic Directory. The nationalities of these priests were Italian, Polish, Czech, German, Maltese, Lithuanian, Hungarian, Dutch, Ukrainian, Slovak, Latvian, Slovene, Croatian, Dalmatian and Australian.[12]

Migrant Centre correspondence[13] refers to help being provided in a number of ways, including assistance to a Lebanese woman who had three young children, aged five, four and two, whose husband had left her: she needed to make a living. There are numerous letters in the files concerning cases that went to the Churches Matrimonial Tribunal, as well as letters detailing help for couples wishing to obtain housing finance.

Correspondence dated August shows that Catholics at Scheyville wished to get their own school up and running.

The difficulties and frustrations of obtaining money to procure such items as projectors and screens are highlighted in various letters between priests J.F. Bird, Eris Tierney and the Reverend T. Leonard in 1955. One letter, written in 12 August 1955, complains, 'The Deaconess is a Protestant worker who has

---

[11] Memo to His Lordship, Bishop Lyons. 1954 and paraphrased from Mecham, Father Frank. *The Church and Migrants 1946-87* St Joan of Arc Press 1991.

[12] Roman Catholic records

[13] St Mary's Archives

obtained from the Director of the Camp amazing facilities which were withheld from the Catholic Chaplain.'

The tone of this letter and others indicates that the Catholics thought that the Deaconess was obviously receiving favouritism from the Camp Director.

In April 1955, Cardinal Gilroy had lunch at Scheyville after confirmation services concluded.[14]

Policies and procedures within the Church for activities at the holding centre seem to have been tightly controlled. On 2 June 1955, Reverend Bird wrote to Cardinal Gilroy, explaining that His Lordship Bishop Lyons had obtained permission for Father Tierney to celebrate an Evening Mass on the first Friday of each month in the Scheyville Holding Centre the previous November. This permission had been granted for a trial period of six months. Since the six months was up, Father Tierney would appreciate a renewal of permission for the Friday evening Mass. He assured the Cardinal that the attendance 'is very good', and that 'the Mass is necessary'.[15]

By August 1955 the Chaplains' report stated that there had been a remarkable change in the people. Eighty per cent of the Polish people were practising and loyal to the priest. There were seventy attending Friday evening Mass.

Thus, there had been a turnaround in interest and religious activity.

From earlier correspondence, the Catholic priests seemed concerned they would lose some of 'their turf'. Tierney wrote: 'the ladies [visiting nuns] are doing a good job here. If they were not here the children would be at present without any Catholic instruction, and the same applies to the adults. The increased Catholic activity particularly among the children has been taken notice of by the other denominations. The Church of England and Presbyterian ministers are visiting every Wednesday giving instruction to children of other denominations. This is one of the reasons why a Catholic priest must be here, if for nothing else than to

---

[14] St Marys Roman Catholic Archives.
[15] Roman Catholic Archives

keep an eye on what is going on from these quarters.' Before the Catholic Church was built at Scheyville, Tierney had written, 'it's a pity the chapel is not only for the Catholics, but also for all other denominations. I tried to organise the chapel to serve for all purposes, and was happy to preserve the Blessed Sacraments there, also during weekdays.'

The churches were seen as co-operating to help the Government's assimilation agenda and were referred to in the Resolutions at the 1955 Australian Citizenship Convention held in Canberra from 25 to 28 January 1955.[16] In the 'thank yous' at the Convention; there was 'a special thankyou to the children's choir of The Scheyville Immigration Centre'.[17]

Stretching Church finances, 1956

In December 1956 the Sydney Catholic Committee for New Settlers wrote to Gilroy advising that it was: 'hard on money for the Migration Chaplains'. There were twenty-six chaplains to whom they had to pay a monthly travel allowance and the salaries of five of the twenty-six. After receiving £540 [$1080] from Monsignor Crennan's Office, they had to pay out £1652 [$3104] per annum. The Office was also expected to give a portion of the annual collection to the upkeep of the Federal Catholic Immigration Office. The Sydney Committee complained that it was rare for the Chaplains to get 'stole fees'[18] or part thereof. They had to fight for a National Chaplain to get a stipend of three pounds three shillings when he said a 'National Mass' in a parish. They fought for the Chaplains to keep 'stole' fees.[19]

Senior members of the Catholic clergy also did their part in welcoming migrants to Australia. When the first group of eighty-three Hungarian refugees arrived at Mascot Airport on 3 December 1956, Reverend Monsignor Crennan,

---

[16] Australian Archives ref. A 462 Item 663/27
[17] Ibid.
[18] Stole Fees are fees paid by a member of the laity to a Priest for administration of a sacrament or performance of a rite in the Roman Catholic Church.
[19] Roman Catholic Archives, St Marys Cathedral Sydney. Box D18. Correspondence relating to the Scheyville Migrant Camp.

Director of the Federal Immigration Committee was there to meet them. Crennan reported 'that of the eighty-three, some twenty-seven were Jewish people who were given immediate private accommodation by their Jewish friends, and that the remaining fifty-five, comprising thirty families, were transported to Scheyville. Seventy per cent of this number were Catholics.'[20]

A second contingent of sixty-seven arrived the following day. Apart from twenty Jews the remaining forty-seven, again comprising thirty families were sent to Scheyville. Fifty-five per cent of these were Catholics. Crennan reported on 21 December 1956 that no other Hungarian refugees had arrived, and that, for the future, no more would be coming to Sydney. The Immigration Department had made arrangements to accommodate the remainder of the 5000 Hungarians at Bonegilla in Victoria. Crennan reported that 'all of the Hungarians in these two groups who went to Scheyville were almost destitute. In many cases their only possessions were the clothes they were wearing.'[21]

When Father Doyle, Camp Chaplain, saw the sorry state of these people, he immediately contacted the Sydney headquarters of St Vincent de Paul. Within a matter of hours material help was at hand. The Society gave Father Doyle £150 ($300) in cash to provide the refugees with necessary toilet requisites. Five lorry-loads of clothing were also dispatched. Father Doyle distributed this clothing and 'all refugees were provided with a complete wardrobe of very good quality wearing apparel'.[22]

In addition to this help, Gilroy had a special appeal to Catholics at all masses in Sydney on 9 December 1956; £3100 ($6200) was received on this one Sunday and handed to St Vincent de Paul to assist it in its charitable work for the Hungarian refugees arriving in Australia.

By the time of Crennan's report on 21 December, 'a number of the first refugees had already obtained work and private accommodation'. The Immigration

---

[20] Roman Catholic Archives. Box D18.
[21] Roman Catholic Archives, Box D18.
[22] Roman Catholic Archives. Box D18. Report on Hungarian Refugees in the Archdiocese of Sydney dated 21 December 1956.

Department had special English classes for them at Scheyville and there was one hundred per cent attendance at the classes.

> Already the camp Chaplain, (Father Doyle) reports that he is able to have simple conversations with them. Almost daily, Australian families and Hungarian families visit the Centre and take the newcomers away and spend the day with them.
>
> All Hungarians in Scheyville will spend Christmas as guests in private homes. Countless gifts of food and clothing have been sent to Scheyville by private individuals. They were brought in contact with Hungarian Associations.
>
> Every effort will be made by Catholic Organisations, Government Departments such as the Department of Labour and National Service to assist and 'assimilate' the refugees as they arrive. Father Doyle reported that he had a satisfactory attendance at Mass, and that St Vincent de Paul would do for others what they had done for the first arrivals. Already a considerable sum of money and clothing had been sent to Albury for the next group.[23]

The Church was also subsidising a number of migrant children attending Catholic schools in the Sydney Archdiocese. Of the 133,319 children attending Catholic schools, 3427 paid no fees, 2846 were on reduced fees, and 7046 were full fee-paying students.[24]

In another letter to Mr Maher, (Executive Secretary of St Vincent de Paul), Father Tierney asked that the St Vincent de Paul organisation care for the two Kolomiejts boys at Westmead. They were at Scheyville and their mother died there. Father Diaczyen hoped that the boys could continue at Westmead until they completed their Leaving Certificate.

---

[23] Ibid.
[24] Roman Catholic Archives. Box D17.

The St Vincent de Paul Society also had a Court Probation Committee that helped migrants who had been in trouble with the law. Help was provided by reminding authorities of the conditions at Scheyville, such as the lack of family life with husbands away, cramped living conditions, and trouble with the new language. The Society provided migrants with assistance in learning trades, and attempted to stir interest in parish or other outside activities to keep migrants busy so they were less likely to have time to get into trouble.

Supporting Hungarian Catholics, 1957

Father Bird believed that the St Vincent de Paul Society was the only Society to make any effort to do something for the migrants. No work of the Society could be more important to assist in keeping them in the Catholic faith, for without it a terrible loss could occur, the families and children being lost to the Church. Father Bird exhorted all members of the St Vincent de Paul Society to carry Christ's message to all migrants irrespective of rebuffs and insults.[25]

Pressures were also coming from within its ranks. There was concern over a letter from a Mr P. in April 1957 who was writing to Hungarians in Australia trying to get them to boycott Mass. He accused the Hungarian Bishop of being a Communist, and accused the Church of spiritually neglecting the Hungarians.[26]

In a letter from Father Tierney to J.B. Maher of St Vincent de Paul, he explains that the Church would not help anyone return to a communist country such as Hungary. 'Catholics in Australia are ever willing to assist dissatisfied migrants get out of a "capitalistic" country and return to real freedom'.

During 1957 the New South Wales Catholic Immigration Office continued its work on behalf of the Hungarians. Permanent employment was found for 197 persons, and casual work for 214 persons. St Vincents provided £1752 ($3504) for casual work, sent medicines to relatives in Hungary and given £650 ($1300) in what was termed quick relief.

---

[25] Roman Catholic Archives, St Marys Cathedral Sydney. Box D17 Correspondence concerning the Scheyville Migrant Centre.
[26] Roman Catholic Archives. Box D17.

The placing in employment and accommodation was the work of one individual, a Mr Belaorszaczky.

The Catholic nuns at Scheyville also prepared the girls at the camp for a custom that was part of Australian society in the 1950s, that of the Debutante Ball.

In June 1957, cases of bigotry were reported at the camp, and the Camp Commandant, Colonel Brown wrote to the Immigration Department's Head Office in Canberra. A complaint had been made at the Scheyville Camp Amenities Committee claiming that that leatherwork classes held in the Catholic Chapel were only for Catholics.

There was one recreation hall available to hold classes, and Miss Eady, the Presbyterian Deaconess, had use of that for her craft classes. Nevertheless, the Committee wrote, 'the Committee feel that whilst the leatherwork classes are open to all denominations, it is not entirely politic to hold these classes, to which the Amenities Organisation contributes ten pound a month, in the Catholic Chapel. It is requested that full use be made of the Recreation Hut when available.'

Father Doyle was forced to reply to this indirect threat of losing a monthly £10 ($20) contribution. He stressed the point that no mention was made of religion, nor were classes in any way connected with a religious service. There was a full program of activities for children at the camp. Due to a clash of programs, Miss Eady had use of the only hall available and the Catholics held activities in the rear of the Roman Catholic church. Statistics kept by the Church indicated that some twenty-two per cent of attendees at the activities provided by the Catholics were non-Catholics.[27]

Practical and spiritual progress, 1958

The 1958 New South Wales Statistical Report indicates that a total of 4,395 interviews had been held with migrants. Some 150 migrant ships had arrived in Sydney during the year. All these ships were met and the migrants aboard

---

[27] Roman Catholic Archives, St Marys Cathedral Sydney. Box D23 1956-1959. report dated 26 June 1957.

welcomed on behalf of the Catholic Church. Interviews included 3408 instances of individual counselling, 253 interviews relating to travel loan applications and 403 sponsorships involving 1128 people. The New South Wales Migrant Office had placed 176 people in employment and arranged accommodation for 146.[28]

In July Crennan wrote to Doyle that he had the 'very happy feeling that the spiritual life of the people at Scheyville is maintained at a high standard.'

In this year, some twenty-five public school boys attended the classes held by the Catholics on Friday nights from 6.30 pm to 7.30 pm.

Father Bird was the Catholic priest at Scheyville prior to Father Tierney, in 1953. In a 1958 speech to the St Vincent de Paul Society New Settlers Committee, at Blakehurst in Sydney, he stated that he knew the pitfalls and disadvantages that the migrant camp priest came up against. He said that he had been the Chaplain at the Scheyville Camp of 1500 persons in 1953, and that he was not given much assistance by the Camp authorities which made the work heartbreaking. There was no church building at the commencement of his service, but eventually the inmates got one built by their own efforts, and one Mass was held each Sunday, and now (1958) there were four Masses each Sunday and each was packed.[29]

Moving migrants on, 1959

On 7 April 1959, Father Tierney wrote to Cardinal Gilroy, quoting from the Migrant Office's statistical report, that 'the large sum of £32,000 [$64,000] collected in travel loan money is a pointer as to why migrants are not as generous to the Church here as might be expected'. Tierney reminded the Cardinal 'that the majority of migrants now have to pay their own fares, except for British and Dutch migrants. Catholic migrants who cannot pay their own way get an interest-free Travel Loan from the International Catholic Migration Commission (ICMC) through its offices in Europe, and Giunta Cattolica in the case of Italians. The

---

[28] Roman Catholic Archives, St Marys Cathedral Sydney. Box D18 Correspondence relating to the Scheyville Migrant Camp.
[29] Ibid.

Sydney Office acts as a collecting agency for both the ICMC and Guinta Cattolica Organisations.'[30]

It appears that in 1959 the Immigration Department believed that some residents at Migrant Holding Centres were not making an effort to leave the camps and live in an 'Australian community'. In a letter from Monsignor Crennan to Father Doyle he notes that 'Doyle expects an increase of Dutch migrants, following departures of the older residents. I was just speaking to the Chaplain at Greta camp. He told me that numbers of the old residents had been instructed to find private accommodation. Evidently there is a drive to move those people who give the appearance of wishing live indefinitely in the Centres.'

The Church kept statistics on its flock, and these were included in the bimonthly reports submitted by the priests.

Father Doyle reported in May 1959 that of the 833 people in camp at Scheyville, some 519, or sixty-two per cent of the total centre population were Roman Catholics. One hundred of the 108 families took the Latin Rite and eight, the Greek Rite. Offerings from the families to the Church were two to three pounds ($4-$6) per week. Twenty to thirty people attended daily Mass, and catechisms and sacraments being taken totalled 450 for the month.[31]

The impact of migrants on the Australian church, 1960

In a letter and report to Cardinal Gilroy on 4 May 1960, Father Tierney wrote of the effect the migrants had on the Church and what contribution they had made. 'More than half of all migrants who have come to Australia in the post-war era are Catholics.'

The Dutch are the best Catholics from the Australian viewpoint as to how a Catholic should practise his faith.

---

[30] Ibid.
[31] Roman Catholic Archives. St Marys Cathedral Sydney. Box D23. Correspondence concerning the Scheyville Migrant Camp.

> Seventy-five per cent of them [the Dutch] are practising and approximately one third of Germans. About eighty-five per cent of the Maltese are attending, but the Italians, Yugoslavs and Austrians have not good records. It is estimated that a little over one quarter of all migrants are going to Mass.
>
> Generally speaking, migrants are not a 'force' in parochial life. For example, few belong to the Sodalities or the St Vincent de Paul or other Catholic lay organisations. From the experts, integration into parochial life is a slow, natural development and integration cannot be expected until the second or third generations. In short, everything depends on the children of migrants.[32]

Note that this is 1960, and the clergy are now using the term integration, whereas in the early 1950s they were using the term 'assimilation' just as government departments were.

> "Admittedly, migration has placed a heavy financial burden on the Church, and the school system has felt the strain.
>
> To aid the assimilation of migrants into parish life, twenty-five European priests are actively engaged, under Australian Bishops' direction, as migrant Chaplains. Note that the Australian system differs from the American, whereas America adopted the system of National Parishes, the aim in Australia has been to assimilate migrants into existing parishes and not to form National Parishes".[33]

---

[32] Roman Catholic Archives. St Marys Cathedral Sydney. Box D18. Correspondence concerning the Scheyville Migrant Camp paraphrased.
[33] Ibid.

1962 and the priests are still busy

A letter from Father Victor Doyle to Cardinal Gilroy dated 2 January 1962 advises that at St Vincents Church Scheyville for the past five years he had conducted Devotions every evening, and Benediction of the Most Blessed Sacrament on Tuesdays, Wednesdays, Thursday, Saturday and Sunday evenings and evening Mass on the first Friday of the month.

The Catholic convent at Scheyville

Father Victor Doyle made repeated urgent appeals to the General Council for two sisters to visit the camp and prepare the children for the sacraments.

In a letter dated 6 May 1954, the acting secretary of the Immigration Department, A.L. Nutt wrote to Father Tierney stating, 'There is no objection to the erection of a Chapel on a suitable site in the terms of your letter.'

Two years later, in a letter from the Head of the Immigration Department, T.H.E. Hayes to Monsignor Crennan, dated 19 September 1956,

> Further to my letter of 29 August last, it is understood that Father Tierney proposes to erect a small cottage of approximately seven squares for accommodation of two Sisters, who will be engaged on religious instruction and visitation. Approval is granted for the erection of the building for the purposes mentioned at the expense of your Church.
>
> The Sisters will be able to partake of their meals in the staff mess without charge, or if for any reason this arrangement is unsuitable, they can draw rations on the same basis as staff occupying other residences in the Centre.[34]

---

[34] Roman Catholic Archives. St Marys Cathedral Sydney. Box D23. Correspondence concerning the Scheyville Migrant Camp.

Scheyville Speaks

Cardinal Gilroy blessed and opened the convent on 30 December 1956. This housed the two Sisters of the Order of St Joseph, obviating the need for the Sisters to travel from North Sydney to and from the Centre each Sunday to give religious instruction to Catholic children. Speaking at the opening Cardinal Gilroy said that 'It will also enable them to teach the children handicrafts to occupy part of their leisure time at the Centre. Scheyville's reputation is growing day by day in the economy and social life of Australia. People have come here in their thousands – they have been received by Australians in a way that makes them realise that they are most welcome, not as mere guests but as fellow citizens.'[35]

Gilroy made special mention of the work of members of the Legion of Mary from Sydney who had assisted during the last six years in the religious instruction of the children, and of the Poor Clare Sisters from Richmond who had given signal assistance also, until the responsibility had been taken over by the Sisters of St Joseph at North Sydney.

Cardinal Gilroy exhorted all Catholic parents at the Centre to do their part in educating their children 'so that they will be a credit to the land of their birth and origin, and an asset to the land of their adoption.'

The history of the Josephites at North Sydney reveals that Sisters Mary Horan and Margaret Smith took up residence in January 1957. They and Sister Anna Maria Trinca were the longest serving Sisters of Joseph nuns at Scheyville.

> Their first duty was to give catechetical instruction to two groups of children in the camp per day; about 300 children attended the instructions. Classes to prepare children for First Communion and Confirmation were conducted every evening at 6.30pm.
>
> The physical layout of the camp imposed problems on the everyday routines of child care, which made child-rearing one of the camp's most frustrating aspects. With typical ingenuity the sisters arranged, after

---

[35] 'Cardinal Gilroy Opens Convent at Migrant Centre' *Windsor and Richmond Gazette (NSW: 1888–1961)* 23 January 1957: 7.

school each afternoon, outdoor sport for the older children and indoor games for the smaller ones. Evening classes were held to interest children in handicrafts such as basketry, leather work, embroidery, pottery, felt toy-making and textile painting. On Saturday afternoons some sixty to seventy children attended sewing lessons and enjoyed their first attempts at cooking.

Folk dancing was the main feature for recreational hours on Sunday afternoons. The two sisters who were serving migrant children when the camp eventually closed in 1964 were Sisters Margaret McLeod and Sylvia Markulin.

The camp had a floating population of over 3000 per year and approximately 900 children passed through the sisters' hands each year, until eventually by 1964, as other housing became available for migrants, the Scheyville camp was no longer needed.[36]

Like the church which it adjoins, the convent was erected by the Society of St Vincent de Paul within the Blacktown Council of the Society.

An appeal was launched for £200 needed to furnish the convent, the Society having undertaken to meet the fullst of the building – a matter of some £3,000 ($6000), as well as the full £10,000 ($20,000) cost of the church. The collection totalled £300 ($600) by the end of the day.[37]

In 1968 the Commonwealth Government paid $4000 to buy the church building at Scheyville from the Archbishop of Sydney. The Church paid the money to the St Vincent de Paul at Blacktown as they were the organisation that bore the cost of constructing the building.[38]

---

[36] Burford, Kathleen E. *Unfurrowed fields: a Josephite story, NSW, 1872-1972*, St Joseph's Convent North Sydney, 1991.
[37] 'Cardinal Gilroy Opens Convent at Migrant Centre' *Windsor and Richmond Gazette (NSW: 1888–1961)* 23 January 1957: 7.
[38] Purchase Order N540902 dated 23 January 1968 to purchase from the Trustees of the Roman Catholic Church for the Archdiocese of Sydney, the Chaplains quarters on behalf of the Department of Army

A letter from St Vincent de Paul to Cardinal Gilroy dated 2 April 1963 records:

> The Church and Chaplains' Quarters were blessed by His Lordship, Bishop Lyons on Sunday 3 April 1955. The Convent was blessed by Your Eminence on Sunday 31 December 1956. The total cost of the work including interest was £11,783 [$23,500]. The whole of the work was paid for by the Blacktown Council of the St Vincent de Paul organisation.[39]

Father Tierney

The following short biography of Father Tierney is included as he was instrumental in the provision of services to Roman Catholic migrants settling in NSW after World War Two.

Father Eris Tierney was Director of the Catholic Immigration Office in Sydney from 1952 to 1972. Born 19 September 1921 and ordained a priest on 21 July 1945, he died in 2009 at his home in Bateau Bay (Diocese of Broken Bay) where he lived in retirement.

Much of Father Tierney's work at the Catholic Immigration Office is recorded in Father Frank Mecham's book The Church and Migrants. Father Tierney generously and zealously assisted refugees and migrants in many ways, from providing interest-free loans for travel to Australia to finding employment and accommodation. Many Catholic immigrants arrived in Sydney each month (in one year, 1000 per month); with the migrant chaplains, he met them all on arrival.[40]

---

[39] Roman Catholic Archives, St Marys Cathedral Sydney. Box D18 Catholic Immigration papers, Scheyville Migrant Centre correspondence.

[40] Australian Catholic Migrant & Refugee Office Newsletter. 1st edition 1999. Article on Father Tierney located on website www.acmro.catholic.org.au; Mecham, Father Frank. *The Church and Migrants 1946-87* St Joan of Arc Press 1991.

Training officers for Vietnam

An overview

It was an experience they would not forget. An experience shared by some 2700 young Australian men between 1965 and 1973. The experience they underwent was an officer training course.

Scheyville became the home of the OTU on 1 April 1965 when the national flag was raised for the first time. The OTU was established to meet an Army requirement to train selected National Servicemen as officers. After attending a selection board where about 120 men were chosen from each national service intake of between 2200 and 2500, the OTU cadets underwent twenty-two weeks of rigorous training. Those awarded the opportunity to attempt an officer training course were selected on the basis of educational qualifications, intelligence quotient and personality.

Upon graduating as probationary Second Lieutenants the men were posted to Army units around Australia, and many served in South Vietnam, Papua New Guinea, Malaysia and Singapore. Many Scheyville graduates were in action within twelve months of graduation, and some were in action within twelve months of being enlisted. The initial aim formulated for OTU was to train platoon commanders for the infantry. Later, the aims were modified to train men for equivalent roles in other arms and services. Those allotted to the Infantry Corps would go straight to their battalion, but those allotted to other arms and services underwent specialist Corps training as gunnery officers, engineers or as Service Corps Officers.

Some 1871 of those young men would undergo the total Scheyville experience. For some of the remainder, being dispatched to another Army unit to complete their national service would be a relief. Yet, for many, the disappointment of leaving Scheyville early was to remain a bitter memory indefinitely.

Scheyville's corps of Officer Cadets consisted of young men who had been dragged away from banks, universities and farms – drawn from all walks of life and thrown into national service. The government had stolen two years of their lives, so from time to time, cadets would think to themselves, 'why am I doing this – the Army isn't my career'. They were under real pressure: the fear of failure was enormous, and yet the determination to succeed was extremely strong. The determination to succeed has been so strong among those who experienced Scheyville that this group of Australian males, collectively, must rate in terms of career success in post national service life as one of the most successful groups of people in Australian society from their generation. Other schools and institutions have notable graduates but those institutions have existed for 50 to 100 years. O.T.U. is different because it only operated for seven years. This is a point that deserves more research.

Many Scheyville graduates achieved success in a wide range of civilian endeavours. Scheyvillians have made their mark in business, aviation, educational institutions and, in lesser numbers, the public service. Many remained in the Army to lead very successful military careers. Fourteen graduates attained the rank of Brigadier, and approximately 130 attained the rank of Lieutenant Colonel or above. Not all achieved this rank in the Regular Army; some combined a successful civilian career with leadership positions in the Army Reserve.

Prominent positions in Australian society occupied by Scheyvillians have included those of Deputy Prime Minister (Tim Fischer) and Premier of Victoria (Jeff Kennett). Two other individuals – John Bradford initially a Liberal, and later an independent member for McPherson on the Gold Coast, and Terry Gygar, who was a Liberal member of the Queensland Parliament for fifteen years – have also served in Parliament.

According to David Sabben, who commanded one of the three platoons involved in the battle of Long Tan in 1966:

> If there was one word I would use to describe OTU, it would be "competition". The Army didn't just want the best – it wanted the best of the best, and then some. We were always competing. Against each other all the time, because assessments were continuous; against the

clock, which insisted on only providing 24 hours in each day; against the curriculum, which was deliberately set to not allow us time to do everything, thereby forcing us to prioritise our time and tasks; against ourselves, to ensure our best performance, even when cold, wet, hungry, or weary beyond words, and often under pressure to get results from equally cold, wet, hungry and weary peers.[1]

Another graduate and Vietnam veteran, Gary McKay, sums up the training process as being a case of "being broken, remoulded, trained, challenged and tested". He believes he was being manipulated, coerced and prepared for a lifestyle that was to be the catalyst in his development as an adult, and stay with him for the remainder of his military service. Cadets were pushed, prodded, screamed at and cajoled in a way that was similar to tearing the insides out of an old factory and completely renovating the insides. 'On the surface nothing had changed, but once you looked past the facade you could see that there had been a reworking of the place where business is done.' The instructors at Scheyville 'were not just trainers, they were conditioners and hard taskmasters'.[2]

Instructors instilled the importance of gaining information from all sources, analysing a problem and making a balanced judgement. Two other things remain constant in the memory of each cadet. Firstly, the fact that they didn't really get a chance to prepare for an exam, and secondly, the extent of motivation engendered within each individual.

Don Keyes recalls that the pace was so frenetic that 'there were no preparation periods for exams. If you didn't get it right when you sat in the classroom, you could forget about it when you hit the exam'. The examination on a particular topic may not have been for weeks after being taught, and they came dotted all over the place. The fact that lectures went till 9.30 pm, five nights a week, and until lunch on Saturdays meant that there was no going back to their room and

---

[1] Donnelly, Roger. *The Scheyville Experience* University of Queensland Press, 2001, p xi; email from David Sabben 18 October 1999.
[2] McKay, Gary, 'On Being a Scheyvillian'. *Scheyvillian* No.2 1992.

honing up on what was missed in the classroom. That produced a pressure all of its own. Cadets had to concentrate one hundred per cent of the time, and stay focused, as they were worked hard physically during the day. Keyes continues: 'you may have been at a particular lecture for one subject, and the next item on the timetable may have been a very hard physical training session, or even a physical training test; next item would be a forty minute exam ... next a fieldcraft lesson. That sort of pace didn't exist all day every day at the other training institutions. At Duntroon, for instance, there was homework, but the normal instructing day ended at 4.50 pm each day, Monday to Friday.'

To last the distance at this pace required a degree of motivation not needed to excel at other courses or institutions. Each cadet had a different reason for wanting to succeed, but one thing common to all was the determination to succeed. The OTU cadets' motto of *'nil bastardum carborundum'* (pig Latin for 'don't let the bastards get you down') may have been used at various times by different groups of individuals, but for Scheyvillians, according to Keyes, 'it was really only the negative expression of what the motivation really was'.

Some aspiring young officers had their spirit broken. However, it was an inescapable fact that OTU cadets were being trained for war, and within a matter of months of graduating would be responsible for the lives of thirty-three other soldiers. In the larger scheme of things, according to McKay, 'a few individuals not being able to make the grade was small change compared to the total responsibility an officer on operations would have to deal with. Scheyville made individuals aware of their capabilities both physically and mentally. It challenged them, and once those challenges were met, confidence was gained. The OTU course instilled the process of gaining information from all sources, analysing a problem and making decisions with confidence and trust.'

Some 365 Scheyvillians served in Vietnam, and for them, although OTU had an impact on their lives, the Scheyville experience was just one phase of their career. Experiences endured in Vietnam not surprisingly take precedence over their training at Scheyville, tough though that training may have been. For many of those who didn't serve in Vietnam, and particularly those graduates from about mid-1969 who had little opportunity to serve in combat, the Scheyville experience was perhaps the most significant work-related endeavour of their lives. This showed in their responses for my 2001 book The *Scheyville Experience*, in their approach, and in their enthusiasm to tell their story. It was an anticlimax for many. All that training, anticipation, fear mingled with excitement – and then to realise that their contribution wasn't needed.

No matter whether they were required to discharge the enormous responsibility of commanding a platoon in Vietnam, or to serve in the Education Corps within Australia, there is no doubt that life would have been different for those who went through Scheyville, had they not had the experience. As many former Scheyville Directing Staff have stressed, the pressure and frenetic pace of OTU was intentional so that possibly nothing else faced by the cadet in his life would be as hard.

The Australian scene

When OTU Scheyville began in 1965 Australia was still in the Menzies era of conservative values, but by the time it closed in 1973 a transformation in accepted social behaviour had occurred. The Whitlam Government came to power on 2 December 1972 using the slogan, 'It's Time'. Indeed, it had been a time of monumental change in attitudes. Conformity was no longer expected, nor taken for granted by many.

The role of women in society was being questioned and the term 'Women's Liberation' was coined. Germaine Greer expressed these attitudes when she published *The Female Eunuch* in 1970. The establishment of the Women's Electoral Lobby was a clear indication that such views reached a receptive audience. As indeed was the debate, particularly in Roman Catholic circles, concerning Vatican II and the encyclical Humanae Vitae, which reaffirmed opposition to birth control at a time when the contraceptive pill had freed many women from unwanted pregnancies.

In the late sixties Australians enjoyed a low level of unemployment, and relatively low inflation level. Society expected young men to be able to get a job, and those who didn't make a concerted effort to do so were branded as 'lazy, long haired layabouts' by many members of the older generation. It was possible to work hard for seven or eight months and then spend a couple of months 'beach hopping' in a Holden panel van, complete with surfboards on top and a mattress in the back, then find employment again within a relatively short time.

Television became a major influence on popular opinion, and this meant for the first time that images of a war were brought to Australians each night in their suburban lounge rooms. Yet responses from some hundred or so Scheyvillians interviewed, concerning their political preferences at the time of their being conscripted, indicates that they had little or no interest in politics. It appears that young Australians, particularly in the early days of the country's involvement in the Vietnam War, felt insulated from the fighting, dying and rioting of the world at that time.

Musically, the world progressed from the clean-cut image of the Beatles singing *'All You Need Is Love'* in 1967 to the authority-defying style of the Rolling Stones. The Stones were openly telling fathers of the time that they really were after their daughters by singing *'I Can't Get No Satisfaction'*, and *'Let's Spend the Night Together'*. By 1972, the heavier rock sound of Led Zeppelin blasted out songs such as 'School's Out', and the hippies were firmly entrenched at Nimbin. It appeared as if the youth of the 1960s and early 1970s reacted to the Vietnam War by growing their hair long, talking of 'free love', and refusing to accept everything their parents did or said as gospel. Society was becoming more permissive.

The Age of Aquarius escaped those who experienced Scheyville. Youths of a similar age marched against the war in Vietnam, rebelling against authority and enthusiastically displaying their nonconformity. OTU was an institution that provided the very antithesis of such a lifestyle. Both its graduates and those who instructed there appear to have been attracted to traditional ideas.

Significantly, all four graduates subsequently elected to Parliament represented conservative parties. Research for both this book and The Scheyville Experience brought me into contact with more than 150 individuals from different parts of Australia, spanning all facets of OTU's eight years of operation. Although it is highly probable that many Scheyvillians have voted for the Australian Labor Party at some time in their life, no respondent was able to clearly identify, or remember any Scheyvillian who has been seriously involved, especially for a lengthy period, with the Left in Australian political life. The response to the questionnaire for this project by Captain Brian McCarthy, formerly the controversial head of the Airline Pilots Federation, indicates that even he is no avid fan of the Labor Party or former Prime Minister (the late) Bob Hawke.

Perhaps the feeling about political preferences at Scheyville was best summed up by former Deputy Prime Minister Tim Fischer in his comment that 'My political views were not influenced by OTU Scheyville, although I gathered that left-wing views were not all that well regarded.' This opinion was supported by comments by Lieutenant Colonel A.G. Clark (retired) when recollecting the voting return registered at OTU in the 1966 federal election. Clark was visited by the successful local candidate on the Monday after that election and advised that a total of 256 votes were cast at the Scheyville polling station, 250 of which were for the conservative candidates and only six for Labor. Although the polling booth was available for use by any voter, it is likely that only a handful of people not connected with the OTU would have voted there. Although voting patterns may have changed at the Scheyville polling booth by 1972 when the Labor government was elected, the voting return in 1966 clearly indicated support for the Coalition.

The strategic basis of Australia's defence policies in the 1960s

The shift in social values during the time of OTU's existence was matched by military and political shifts across the region. In the early 1960s the Australian Government and her major allies, Britain and the United States, judged the general instability in South-East Asia to be a matter of grave concern. Communism was seen to be a major threat and communist China was considered to have southward expansionist policies. The 'domino theory', which posited that one South-East Asian state after another would topple and collapse under communist pressure from the north, was widely accepted.

France had been forced to vacate Indochina, which left Vietnam partitioned into two states, one being communist North Vietnam. Neighbouring Laos and Cambodia were weak, unstable and considered ripe and ready for communist picking. There was also uncertainty regarding the ability of the newly independent states of Malaysia and Singapore to withstand communist pressures. Indonesia's continued policy of confrontation towards Malaysia, a nation created by democratic process and a member of the Commonwealth, was viewed as an element of instability in the region.

According to the Commonwealth Government Defence Report of 1965, 'Australian defence had been characterised since World War II by a progressive increase in international defence responsibilities and commitments. These had been assumed to meet our own security requirements and as a contribution to the security of the peoples of South-East Asia. They required the stationing abroad of substantial elements of the Australian Services in Malaysia, Thailand and South Vietnam and involved the deployment of more regular fighting units than at any time since the Korean War.'[3]

Australia had accepted certain obligations through alliances and three regional security agreements. The first of these were its Commonwealth responsibilities. Britain was anxious to withdraw militarily from South-East Asia once independence had been granted to Malaysia. Australia had maintained its contribution to the Commonwealth Strategic Reserve since 1955, and in 1964 acceded to a request from Malaysia to counter threats from Indonesia. Secondly, Australia had entered into an alliance with New Zealand and the United States to provide mutual defence co-operation in the Pacific area. The third of the regional

---

[3] Donnelly, Roger. *The Scheyville Experience*. UQP 2001. p 68; Commonwealth Government Defence Report 1965, p 5.

security arrangements to which Australia was a party was the South East Asia Treaty Organisation, which was intended to provide protection against various forms of military aggression from communist countries.

Since 1962, a training team of thirty Army instructors had been engaged in training South Vietnamese forces in jungle warfare, village defence and related activities, in support of their resistance to the Vietcong insurgents directed from North Vietnam. There has been a debate over the sequence of events that led to Australia increasing its contribution to the Vietnam War. The debate has centred around the existence of a 'request' from South Vietnam, or pressure applied by the United States to accept a bigger strategic military responsibility, or whether it was a decision taken unilaterally by our own government. Whether or not such a 'request' was ever made, Australia did increase its involvement in the Vietnam War after 1964.

The re-introduction of selective National Service

Various forms of military conscription have been imposed throughout Australia's history. To understand how the approach to introducing conscription in 1964 developed, it is worthwhile to recall briefly the course of the conscription debate in Australia during the twentieth century.

The first form of conscription in Australia was introduced in 1911. This limited scheme took the form of military training for twelve- to sixteen-year-old youths. During World War One, a referendum on the matter of conscription for overseas service was defeated. A form of conscription was introduced during World War Two; conscripts were initially not required to serve outside Australia's territories, although these areas were subsequently extended. The next compulsory service scheme began in 1951 when eighteen-year-old males were called up for between three and six months. After several reductions in scope this scheme was abandoned some years later.

Recognising the need for a more rapid expansion of the Regular Army than could be achieved by voluntary enlistment, the government decided in November

1964 to introduce selective National Service training. Intakes of twenty-year-old national servicemen were based on the number needed to build the Army to a strength of 37,500 by the end of 1966. The actual strength of the Regular Army at 30 June 1964 was 23,493 personnel. During Australia's involvement in the Vietnam War the target strength was raised to, and reached, 45,000 men.

New Defence legislation enacted in 1965 made provision for the inclusion in the Permanent Military Forces of national servicemen who were obliged under the National Service Act (as amended in 1964 and 1965) to render two years continuous full-time service in the Regular Army Supplement and three years part-time service in the Regular Army Reserve. The amendment also provided for the extension of the liability to render continuous full-time service in time of defence emergency and in time of war, and further required that national servicemen, in common with all members of the Defence Forces, could be required to serve either within or beyond the territorial limits of Australia.

The National Service Scheme introduced in 1965 therefore differed markedly from previous schemes. The age of the national serviceman had been raised to twenty years and he was to serve for a period of two years. The scheme was not universal, and national servicemen were selected by ballot. There were to be four intakes per year, each of about 2000 men. The numbers balloted in had a direct relationship to the needs of the Army and its ability to absorb the recruits. The ballot system, though on the face of it fair and impartial, proved later to be a controversial decision. The most significant aspect of the scheme was the clear implication of overseas service in operational areas.

The Army recognised from the outset that the National Service scheme must be as self-sufficient as possible and the relevant technical and non-technical skills of those called up should be quickly identified and put to the best possible use. Defence planners estimated that approximately 125 national servicemen in each intake could be identified and trained as officers. Planners also estimated that the officer course should last about twenty-two weeks. This meant that with four intakes per annum there could be a maximum of 250 National Service Officer Cadets undergoing training at any one time.

A national serviceman had to volunteer for officer training. Volunteering for officer training was one of the few choices that a conscript would have during his period of national service.

The two-year duration of the national serviceman's commitment and the twenty-two weeks available for officer training were significant and interrelated. The requirement was for the national service officer to complete all administrative procedures, leave, movement needs, plus subunit training and unit training within a period that would leave him with twelve months uninterrupted service in an operational area, should that be required. Such thinking was revolutionary at the time, as far as officer training in Australia was concerned.

It is worthwhile pausing to reflect on the effect that this method of national service had on the size of the Army generally and the make-up of the officer corps. Before the Vietnam War, Australia had three battalions of Regular Army personnel. By 1969 the Army had nine regular battalions and a strength of 45,000.[4] (In 1959 the officer corps of the Regular Army numbered 2402 and included 631 graduates of RMC Duntroon. By 1970, the officer corps strength was 4380, but only 909 of these were Duntroon graduates. In the years between 1963 and 1972, 1287 officers graduated from Portsea and 465 from Duntroon.[5] Scheyville produced 1871 officers in the period from 1965 to 1973. This figure includes 68 cadets who had formed the OCS (Officer Cadet School) wing at Scheyville in 1972–73 but were compelled to graduate from Portsea.)

Early days

The decision to raise the OTU, whose primary role was to train selected national servicemen as officers, was made by Army Headquarters (AHQ), in

---

[4] Commonwealth Government Defence Report 1969, P 35.
[5] Coulthard Clark, Chris D. *Duntroon: The Royal Military College of Australia 1911-1986*, Allen & Unwin, Sydney 1986.

November 1964. The time frame from concept at AHQ level until the first intake of officer cadets arrived in July 1965 was approximately eight months.

The job of establishing the OTU was given to Brigadier Ian Geddes. Geddes was to be the first of four Commandants of OTU and remained there for some two and a half years.

While AHQ directed the unit be raised, responsibility for the detailed development of the size, shape and modus operandi of the unit was delegated to Geddes as Commandant.

The site

It became clear to Geddes, upon reporting in at Headquarters, Eastern Command, Sydney, that there was no suitable Defence site available to adequately house the unit with all its special needs such as messes, staff and cadet accommodation, parade grounds, close training areas, sporting fields and classrooms. For that reason, Eastern Command had consulted other government departments and discovered that the migrant hostel at Scheyville was the best site they could find. With the first intake only six months ahead the amount of renovation and building that could be carried out was strictly limited.

On his initial visit to Scheyville late in 1964 with engineers, architects and builders, Geddes found the site still occupied by a large number of migrants. Generally, he liked the area as it was semi-isolated, had large training areas, was near the Richmond airbase, and potentially provided all the accommodation needed.

Provision of sporting facilities to cover all the team sports such as Rugby and Australian Rules, considered so important in the training of Army personnel was found to be a problem. There were no playing fields when the Army moved onto the site early in 1965, and it took a long time to build all that were needed.

In addition to playing fields, a tennis court and squash court were to be built. A ground and area beautification plan was embarked upon with thousands of trees being planted, while cannons and other memorabilia were borrowed from the Australian War Museum. A major construction cost was the erection of a 30-metre small arms range. This was to save hundreds of man-hours which would otherwise have been spent travelling to and from the firing ranges at Holsworthy.

To further ensure the young potential officers would fit into their units, as pleasant a mess as possible was created at OTU. The cost of silverware and mess fittings as well as a large cooking and waiting staff was high, but favourable and widespread publicity was gained from making a point of inviting distinguished guests to dining-in nights.

The Defence Report of 1965 notes a Federal Budget allocation of $300,000 for the provision of all facilities at Scheyville.[6] It was a tough assignment for the Department of Works to carry out all renovations in five months. Work was still going on when the first intake arrived.

The very high failure rate of thirty per cent was seen as a matter for serious concern after the unit had its first graduation parade. Great pressure was brought to bear by AHQ to reduce the failure rate. However, after examining and researching the unit's procedures thoroughly, Geddes asked AHQ to obtain the equivalent figures from similar courses in the United States and Great Britain. To his relief it was found that the pass rates at OTU were slightly better or much the same as other institutions. Although far from happy with a thirty per cent failure rate, at least OTU staff knew the problems weren't peculiar to their institution.

Frank Miller and his rose-coloured glasses

It is marvellous what the mind remembers after time; latent observations that stick in the mind and then surface like a light bulb moment. Frank Miller has never forgotten the perceptive observations and advice from one senior classmate. This guy served in Vietnam. He made the point to Frank that there were some people who had been born in Europe but acquired Australian accents, some had English or Scottish accents. But none with European accents passed the course.

Another point made to Miller was to the effect that 'you think it's tough and full on here – but stop and reflect on what it would be like to be out there as a

---

[6] Commonwealth Government Defence Report, 1965, p 33.

private soldier. Here we're treated well in the sense that each day goes quickly, you are constantly learning skills that would better prepare you for later life and, despite what you may think with the discipline and pressure, you are treated regally. Your own room, and the wonderful mess with steward service to boot well illustrate this point.'

This same cadet also advised of other 'tricks of the trade' to pass the course. One that still comes to mind for Miller concerned the cross-country runs. The cadet had observed that, after the first 300 yards or so, most people just kept their place – neither falling behind nor passing others. To end up acceptably near the front at the finish all you had to do was sprint to a reasonable position at the start and you would stay there!

He put a new perspective on things.

> Much was done in the army to promote the impression that the OTU course was excruciatingly difficult. I recall my 2RTB CSM [Company Sergeant Major] telling me on my departure to Scheyville that "this place (2RTB) is like a picnic compared with what it's like there!" Yet, coming from a time-demanding four-year university degree, and, apart from the higher physical imposts, OTU wasn't that bad. (Perhaps I now see things through the 'rose-coloured glasses' of time.)[7]

In reality, everyone involved had a vested interest in portraying the course as being exceedingly tough – graduates included!

Graduates from several intakes expressed their perception that things were being progressively slackened over the years – a view encouraged by the seniors. In addressing OTU Association gatherings Miller often singles out those from Class 1 of 1965 – the first ever. Through extrapolation he claims they had it by far the hardest of all – and therefore they must all be superhuman to have graduated.

One of Miller's warmest memories of Scheyville was of the summer sunsets there. He reminisces, 'For my final term I had a room geographically

---

[7] Email from Frank Miller to Roger Donnelly 12 February 2019.

nearest the road and furthest from the Parade Ground. Once the day's toil was behind us, we had a time for "personal administration". This involved having a haircut (almost a weekly obligation), picking up and dropping off laundry, and cleaning boots, webbing etc. The latter task I came to find relaxing – almost therapeutic. What with a Marlboro Red cigarette aglow, and transistor furnishing a contemporary musical background, I thrilled as the warm sun set below the still bushland. So peaceful, so serene! It was really something to behold.'

Greg Rogers and the disappeared ones.

Greg is one of the thirty per cent who failed the OTU course, yet he returned to his job at Victoria Police with increased confidence and self-respect. One Superintendent noted on his file that Army training had had a positive effect on his ability. Promotion followed. In 1977 he aided the Inspector in charge of Special Branch to plan, organise and carry out the security arrangements for the visit of the Queen. He had been selected for that role because of his police service, status as a detective and because he had a Commonwealth security clearance and had undertaken his officer training at Scheyville. 'The Commandant, Studdert, said to me I was to leave (and confirmed in writing to my family sent by mail) that while I was capable, there was not enough time to develop my skills and ability to graduate.' However, Rogers believes that Scheyville had been good for, and to him.[8]

Computers – first used by the Army at OTU

Scheyville was somewhat of an experiment for the Army. The far-sighted Geddes believed a more suitable assessment system should be used than was employed at RMC or Portsea. A fast and reliable method of gauging leadership potential, ability and progress was required. The workload required by such a system was to be kept to a minimum so that staff would not be prevented from

---

[8] Email from Greg Rogers to Roger Donnelly dated 14 July 2019; Donnelly, Roger. *The Scheyville Experience* p 128. Comments by Lt. Colonel David Ford, questionnaire response, 1996 relating to time to train officers.

carrying out their prime function of instruction at the level required. Electronic data processing of both objective and subjective examinations complemented the measurement of personal qualities.

The use of computers to measure leadership qualities in potential young officers was regarded with suspicion in the Army, outside of OTU. Many of Geddes' colleagues and superiors regarded computers as impersonal things that the Army shouldn't be involved with. They didn't understand that they had their place as effective management tools to quickly process volumes of data.

Geddes' request for computer assistance was coldly received; after arguing long and loud, he found an ally in Bruce White, the Secretary of the Department of the Army. Based on the savings of the clerical staff, approval was granted to contract IBM to process material from the assessment system.

Guidance officers, the Father-Son regime, extra duty parades and debussing exercises

Geddes believed that there was a greater role for Guidance Officers at OTU than at RMC or Portsea. He reasoned that 'theoretically, every cadet who went to Portsea or the Royal Military College had discussed the matter with his parents, recruiting personnel, read brochures and wanted to become a soldier'. Individuals coming to Scheyville had not volunteered for service in the Army and would need to be persuaded about the satisfaction of leading a platoon and doing it well. Hence, it was decided that the degree of guidance and personal attention given to Scheyville cadets should be greater than that at RMC and OCS.

To this end, each course was divided into small groups of four to eight cadets and an instructor allocated to each group.

To complement the role of Guidance Officers, a Father-Son regime was instituted. The philosophy behind this was simple. It was believed that from a training point of view it was good to have a senior cadet coach a junior cadet. This helped the Directing Staff, as it gave bewildered newcomers some assistance to settle in to the school's routine, and was particularly valuable for housekeeping items such as bed making, equipment layout and assembly and care of equipment.

Inherent in the philosophy was the belief that to have a senior cadet take an interest in another person's welfare was good training for these future leaders.

Naturally, intake number one didn't have senior cadets to play the role of Father so NCOs were used. Part of the Father-Son relationship was the mutual trust developed by using it for disciplinary purposes. In a cadet's first week at OTU, any punishment in the form of EDs (extra duties) awarded to the newcomer had to be borne by the senior cadet or 'Father'. In the second week, both Father and Son did the punishment together; after that the cadet was responsible for his own misdemeanours.

Immediately after reveille at 6 am each morning, cadets were required to stand outside their room with all their bedding over their shoulder. To a civilian this may seem absurd. However, one must bear in mind that these cadets were training from 8 am until 9.30 pm every day. Although they were under enormous pressure, it was important that they get a good night's sleep. If a cadet knew he had to remove all his bedding every morning then he would be more likely to avoid the temptation to try and save time by sleeping in a sleeping bag on top of his bed to save time in the morning to make his bed.

Extra Duty Parades were also instituted from the beginning of OTU These took place immediately after reveille each morning. The Directing Staff knew that cadets needed every minute of every day to do their own work. If a cadet had to appear at an ED Parade for having dirty boots yesterday then he had been robbed of time for today. After attending the ED Parade he had to run back to his hut, have a shave, shower and scrub his boots again because they probably got dusty, shine his brass, make his bed and be on parade. If the cadet had time, he could eat breakfast. If not, go without! As Regimental Sergeant Major Moon said, 'we supplied breakfast but we didn't give them much time to eat it, and the whole day consisted of this sort of pace.'

Sport, sport, sport!

Sport played an important part in life at OTU as it helped to mould character, build up physique and encourage team spirit. Consequently, cadets were expected to take an active part. The sports program introduced cadets to a variety of sports so that after graduation, they could organise and supervise most games. To achieve this end, Company Sergeant Majors maintained rolls showing the games played by individual cadets on sports days.

Sport was played on at least one afternoon during the working week and on Saturday afternoon.

The major sports played were Rugby and Australian Rules. Soccer and hockey were also played during summer months. Minor sports included basketball, hockey, soccer, softball, volley ball, cricket, athletics, swimming, triathlon, military pentathlon, cross-country running, road relay, tennis and squash.

The accent was on team sports, which wherever possible were conducted on an inter-platoon basis. Sport was an important part of the assessment process as it gave staff an ideal chance to observe how cadets behaved, how they responded to intimidation, what their endurance was like, and their will to win.

Dining-in nights and etiquette

The pace at Scheyville was leavened by a few social functions. Apart from the Graduation Dinner and Graduation Ball, usually two or three dining-in nights were held each intake. Directing staff tried to impress upon the cadets that they were not being assessed on dining-in nights, but few cadets ever believed that was the case. After all, as junior officers they were required to mix with everyone from private soldiers to generals, and attend cocktail parties attended by politicians and other dignitaries.

Instruction periods were held on basic manners, table layout and basic etiquette for social functions. The format of dinner in the Officers Mess, rules about how to pass the port, permission to smoke, not talking 'shop' or politics and proposing the Loyal Toast were taught to all intakes. In some intakes a limited number of specially selected cadets went to the Women's Royal Australian Army Corps (WRAAC) School at North Head for a dining-in night. Intakes from 1969 onwards had visits by representatives of wine and tobacco companies. Senior executives of some of Australia's largest corporations, including BHP and Boral, also attended. Advice on how to roll and smoke cigars was taught, along with wine appreciation. The big companies were interested in 'head hunting' OTU graduates because they were leaders and potential managers.

Weekend leave

There was no leave granted to the junior intake before the midterm Church Parade or the end of the fourth week of training, whichever was the sooner. It was then only granted if the cadet had qualified in the cross-country run. Leave commenced after Saturday sport at 6 pm for those who weren't confined to barracks or had extra training parades. Failure to return by midnight Sunday meant a charge of absent without leave and subsequently being confined to barracks for a couple of weeks.

It was on a cadet's first taste of leave that he noticed how regimented he had become, even though it had been only four weeks since marching in to OTU. As recalled by Peter Morgan:

> The first day we had leave we were taken by bus to the train station. It was our first time out in civilian clothes. If our short hair wasn't enough of a giveaway, our uniform civilian clothes surely drew attention to us. Everybody had to wear grey trousers, polished black shoes, white shirt, skinny OTU tie and blue blazer. Anyway, when the bus pulled up at the rail station, we began falling in behind the first person to get off. It was probably not all that long, but it was certainly noticeable that we were waiting for someone to give the order to march … somewhere. One of our group who must have been less indoctrinated than the rest of us, suddenly broke ranks and took off to a shop that sold ice-creams. After some hesitancy, everyone did the same. But the effect of our recent regimentation didn't stop there, because even though we could see there

were several shop assistants behind the counter, all ready to assist, we again started to form a queue behind the first person.[9]

Cadets proceeding on leave were not permitted to proceed beyond Gosford in the north-east; Wisemans Ferry to the north, Wollongong to the south and Mt Victoria to the west. Paragraph 95 of the Standing Orders stipulated that all hotels within a thirty-mile radius of OTU were out of bounds on Sundays except during Graduation Week, when the Commandant granted approval.

Graduation and Gough

Graduation in December 1972 for Dick Adams and his class was extra special as theirs was the last group of national servicemen to graduate. This group was told that graduation was only tentative, as Gough Whitlam and the Australian Labor Party had been elected to government, and the National Service scheme would be abolished. People were leaving the Army in droves, and this group wasn't sure if they would be allowed to graduate. For Adams and his mates, it felt as if 'they had been trained to Olympic standard, and all of a sudden the rules had been changed.' Some of this group graduated, went to their first postings, and then resigned their commissions. This illustrates how important these individuals felt about accomplishing goals, as they weren't prepared to leave the Army while they had a hope of graduating from OTU.

That special feeling lives every Anzac Day in Sydney for Dick Adams. As a Superintendent of Police he still gets a lump in his throat, because the New South Wales Police band always strikes up the Scheyville theme tune of 'The Road to Gundagai' as the contingent marches down George Street past the Sydney Town Hall.

The syllabus and daily routine

A normal training week at OTU consisted of twelve periods each weekday, from 7.45 am to 9.30 pm, with five periods on Saturday morning and compulsory

---

[9] Donnelly, Roger, *The Scheyville Experience*. University of Queensland Press 2001, p 103.

sport in the afternoon. There was an additional requirement for cadets to work at least five full weekends during the twenty-two-week course. Training was carried out in three wings: Individual Field Training, Advanced Field Training, and Military Arts. Field training also included two periods living in the bush. In the junior term, this was five or six days as a member of a rifle section, and in senior term, ten days training in the duties of a Section Commander and a Platoon Commander. The junior cadets were used as riflemen during five days of the ten-day exercise.

To rework the cadets' minds in the space of twenty-two weeks meant that the instructors not only had to be dedicated and efficient, but they had to have a syllabus that was honed to the task.

Returning members of the Australian Army Training Team Vietnam and battalions that served in the early stages of Australia's involvement in Vietnam provided ample evidence that changes to training techniques were essential to achieve efficient military operations against the Vietcong. With such a background, Chief Instructor Maizey brought a philosophy of making field exercises as real as possible at Scheyville. Certain elements of the war being fought in Vietnam were introduced.

Firstly, helicopters were used as often as possible as this was the means of getting about in Vietnam, particularly to conduct cordon and search operations or inspections of villages.

Secondly, a mock Vietnamese village complete with hides, false walls, dogs and chooks was set up in the Colo-Putty area on the property of a person who gave permission to OTU. This was used for the cadets' final exercise, making the training realistic. For the first three intakes Maizey was at Scheyville, the Red Beret Parachute Platoon from Williamtown was used as enemy. However, to introduce more realism, females were introduced to the exercise. The first females introduced were wives and children of Scheyville staff, but later the whole of the WRAAC OCS played the part of the enemy. All participants, including children, were dressed in black pyjamas. On one exercise 'it was so fair dinkum that a very pregnant officer's wife who was in a wire enclosure needed to go to the toilet and the unsuspecting cadet who found her had quite a shock.'

A major syllabus revision was undertaken shortly after the arrival of Commandant Studdert. This was prompted by Army Headquarters request to review the OTU Charter. The Charter was changed from that of producing primarily infantry officers to training a national service cadet who could undertake the duties and responsibilities of a junior officer in the Regular Army. It wasn't so much a change in the wording of the Charter, as the addition of the idea that the cadet was being trained as a national service officer, and that he would only be there for two years. The notion that cadets were to be officers in the Australian Army was a much more general concept and that he had to be effective during the period of his obligation, introduced a range of effects on what was being taught.

Portsea 'overflow classes' join the Officer Cadets

One change important to the life of Scheyville as an institution occurred in 1972. A proportion of two intakes in 1972, and the final intake in 1973 were from the OCS Portsea. These cadets became known as the Portsea 'overflow classes'. The output of Portsea was stepped up in 1972 to support the expanded infrastructure of a 45,000-strong Regular Army and 35,000 Citizen Military Forces. This remained until reductions in Defence occurred in 1973 due to the abolition of the National Service scheme. To meet this temporary peak of demand, which the facilities at Portsea could neither accommodate, nor be expanded in time to meet, an OCS Wing was opened at Scheyville on 1 February 1972. In total, 68 OCS cadets completed the OTU Scheyville course.

In theory, the courses conducted in the OCS Wing, Scheyville were the same as those at the Portsea campus. In reality there was a difference, even though the block syllabus was similar. Everything at Scheyville was done at a faster pace than Portsea, while their colleagues at Portsea retained the steadier pace which had replaced the frenetic activity of the early OCS courses. One beneficial effect of the six-month OTU cycle for members of the 'overflow classes' was that their junior apprenticeship lasted only three months, with the remainder as senior class with its rank, privileges and exemptions. The downside for an OCS 'overflow' cadet was that he saw two contemporary classes of OTU graduate before him.

The limited privileges at Scheyville – such as leave restricted to Saturday nights and Sunday – reflected the old OCS course, although no married OCS cadets were sent to OTU. The 'overflow' classes were exposed to the rigours of Scheyville's computer-processed assessment process, not yet in place at Portsea.

The initial feeling for most Portsea cadets thrust into OTU life was 'why me?' For several weeks there was the feeling of having been dumped at Scheyville while the more privileged on the other side of the fence enjoyed the imagined greener pastures of Portsea.

The cadets in the last class of 1973 remember OTU with fondness. Chris Grigsby and Ray Dousset for example, claim they identify more with OTU than Portsea, although they have a tinge of bitterness because they were not allowed to graduate as Scheyvillians. When they did go to Portsea they took great delight in showing off some of the small bonuses of life at Scheyville such as wearing GP boots and a Herbert Johnston peaked cap. Their Portsea contemporaries were still wearing the old AB boots and gaiters worn by school cadets.[10]

OCS Portsea – Graduating Class June 1973 and Scheyville

Scheyville offered commissioned service rather than service in the ranks for national servicemen. Duntroon offered a university degree and a guaranteed career. Portsea drew from a wider social, racial and employment base than the other two. Around two-thirds of the cadets in the 1973 class at Portsea had prior military service, including operational service in Vietnam, Malaysia, Cambodia, the Philippines and on the border between Papua New Guinea and West Irian. Arguably Portsea served as a promotion school for serving soldiers and non-commissioned officers in several allied armies, allowing some Australian civilians the privilege of participation. Portsea was often referred to as a finishing school for the Army Apprentice School at Balcombe. Those who entered Portsea as civilians

---

[10] Donnelly, Roger, *The Scheyville Experience,* University of Queensland Press, p 112.

did so for many reasons: in search of secure jobs or upward social mobility, to escape a boring existence or to avoid national service.[11]

The intellectual capital of Scheyville

To illustrate the intellectual capital that existed in those selected for officer training at Scheyville an analysis has been made of the first intake of 1970. After perusing statistics and reading widely on the make-up of the intakes, this 1/70 intake is seen as representative of those selected. A booklet with details on the one hundred graduates was consulted. Of the 100 graduates named in the booklet, biographies had been supplied for eighty-three graduates. Of these one was killed in action in Vietnam and the booklet didn't mention his life prior to national service. Of the remaining eighty-two biographies, forty-six had a university degree before entering the Army and a further sixteen had institute of technology qualifications, qualified as Chartered Accountants or were non-degree qualified primary teachers. Only nineteen of those who graduated from Scheyville in that intake hadn't entered with a tertiary qualification. Some twelve had a science degree, fifteen were engineers, three were lawyers, six were already pilots and thirteen were teachers. Such was the breadth of academic achievement prior to commencing national service.

The cohort

The cadets came from different strata of the community but had qualities of leadership and a higher education than their fellow national servicemen. The graduates included some from the OCS Portsea cohorts of 1972 and 1973 and those who were going to be trained as Army aviators. The majority of the national servicemen who attended Scheyville went to government high schools. Interestingly, the same applies to graduates of RMC Duntroon in the same period – roughly sixty to sixty-five per cent of each cohort attended public schools, while Catholic and independent school graduates each made up eighteen to twenty per

---

[11] Officer Cadet School Portsea, Class of June 1973 www.ocsportsea.org/class-lists/class-jun-73

cent. The make-up of the Portsea graduates may have been different but the cohort of OTU Scheyville and RMC graduates was similar. So much for the view that Army officers came from elitist private schools!

A day in the life

This book is about people, and how they reacted to an alien situation. But how does an author present the 'soul' of the place called OTU Scheyville? Drawing on a technique used by D.J. Dennis who wrote a book on the experiences of 161 Reconnaissance Unit in Vietnam, called *One Day at a Time*[12], Geoff Houghton has written a poem that is an anecdotal compilation of events and encapsulated them into a single day. No matter at what time the cadets were at Scheyville during its eight-year existence, the events happened at the same time of the day. His poem is like a diary of one day in the life of a group of young conscripts. It illustrates the pressure of the place, the time and space problem that all individuals had to endure to successfully complete the course. (Both Dennis and Houghton are Scheyville graduates.)

OTU an ode to you

It's freezing cold and dark; the bugle's blare is stark,
It's not yet six, we're standing in a row like bricks,
Half naked half frozen, and to think we are the "chosen",
Draped in our bedding, this sure as hell ain't no wedding,
Rushing madly here and there, not one minute can we spare,
A mad dash ahead, to shower shave and make the bed,
Us lucky ones are off to eat, the others have EDs to warm their feet.
With food barely down the hole, we rush to salute the flag on pole,
Then it's lessons, strategy and drill, or a run or two up the hill,
Never a moment to spare, the bastards run our arses bare,
A hasty morning tea is all we get, a short reprieve again we're set,

---

[12] Dennis, D. J. *One day at a time: a Vietnam diary,* University of Queensland Press St Lucia, Qld 1992

Scheyville Speaks

Rush and change its time for sport, many battles bravely fought,

With little or no room for error, we live in harsh and constant terror,

Here today gone tomorrow, don't know who deserves our sorrow.

The violent roars from our instructor, sounding like a mad conductor,

Faces stern with lots to learn, a moments peace is what we yearn,

But sure as hell there is no respite; the NCOs have us in their sight,

Thank God at least it's time to eat, lunch allows us to rest our feet,

But alas too soon the meal is done, and our boots weigh a tonne,

Again we start this endless grind; it really starts to play on your mind,

Sweating striving off we go, the damned instructors never letting go.

Then at last it's dinner time, we change again to look our prime,

A well-earned beer in the mess, before we sit to eat in formal dress,

There is no room in this timetable, for any of those who are less than able,

Back to class, we knuckle down again, never ever showing the pain,

Then at last comes half past ten, once more we breathe and sigh amen,

Boots and gear ironed and polished, now sleep our exhaustion to abolish,

It seems like only seconds passed, not long have our dreams to last.

Oh God, not again, the bugle is such a pain! [13]

Not all stories of the training are of a serious nature. It is easy to forget that some other national servicemen were at Scheyville in various supporting roles. John Henry remembers working in the Sergeants Mess as a member of the Catering Corps during 1969–1970. He was good at his catering job and earned his corporal's stripes whilst at Scheyville. As a left hander John had difficulty with weapon handling. Unashamedly, he admits he wasn't the best person at drill and sometimes

---

[13] Houghton, Geoff. Intake 3 of 1971 at O.T.U. Poem emailed to Roger Donnelly Wednesday 17 August 2011.

saluted with his left hand. Unknowingly, this foible led him to have cult status with the cadets. However, to complete his corporal's training he had to give a lesson in "saluting on the march" to the officer cadets. Despite certain mistakes the Company Sergeant Major assessing him said that he couldn't possibly fail him.

Women of Scheyville

In many ways the instructors, especially married personnel, had a tougher deal than did the cadets. Facilities were not available to cater for families. Only ten families were in quarters near the base, with most occupying Housing Commission dwellings or rented cottages at Riverstone. A few families rented at Windsor or further afield.

It was difficult for officers and NCOs with young families because it was virtually a seven-day-a-week job. The children were in bed when they got home, and hadn't risen in the morning when Dad left for work.

Some staff chose not to bring their families to the area for what was normally a two-year posting. For Dick Flint, his posting would have meant shifting his family from Canberra to Penrith. One child was at high school, one was about to enter high school and the youngest was about to go from preparatory school to primary school. Both he and his wife believed that transferring them from one school to another would have been a disaster. The family was left in Canberra and Flint commuted to Scheyville on Monday mornings between 2 am and 6 am so he was there for reveille. They were two difficult years for the family, but Flint believed that the family wouldn't have seen much of him had they been just down the road from the married quarters. Flint's day began at 5.45 am and he rarely got to bed before 11 pm.

Neil Weekes also attests to his time at Scheyville being so hectic that his wife regards it as 'a black hole in their married life'. Weekes was one of seven Scheyville graduates who returned as instructors.

When the Weekes' first moved to Scheyville, they had to find their own house. Married quarters were neither as good nor as available as they now are, and the family moved to a house near Blacktown, which is some distance from the camp. They were a one-car family, and Lyn Weekes didn't have her driver's licence at the time. Even if she had, Neil would have had to drive to work, as the bus service was infrequent.

Even shopping in Windsor on a Saturday or Sunday was a problem as there were lectures on Saturday mornings, sport on Saturday afternoons and church on Sundays.

The owner of the Blacktown house put it up for sale and the family moved to another private rental property. At that time married quarters were allocated on a points system, based on length of service and time on the Married Quarters Waiting List. As Weekes was a very junior, temporary captain with just five years service, he was too far down this list to be allocated a married quarter. Consequently, he was also not entitled to a removal at public expense. He had to find alternative accommodation and arrange his own removal, at his expense. As he was absent in the field, all this organisation fell on Lyn's shoulders. Near the end of his posting the Weekes' were able to occupy one of the ten married quarters at Scheyville.

Life was also harder for married cadets such as Geoff Daly. His physiotherapist wife came to Sydney and worked in a hospital while Geoff was at OTU. On weekends he would stay in the nurses' quarters at the hospital. He was afraid of being caught because it would mean being marched out of Scheyville.

The first night he went to the nurses' quarters he counted the doors down the passage to his wife's room. On his second visit he had to try and find the room on his own. With the Matron's door at one end of the passage, he counted the doors until he thought he was at the correct one. When the door opened, he saw a lovely person in a diaphanous negligee in front of him. In that split second, he could see this girl screaming for help and the Matron's door opening at the end of the passage. It was a relief when she asked if he was Geoff Daly, and directed him next door. Going to the toilet was also a humorous affair.

According to Brendan Killen (1/69):

There was an unintended party and beneficiary of my Scheyville attendance – my wife Vicki. We had only been married six months when I commenced National Service. My first two weeks at Scheyville were a huge personal challenge when the reality of separation from Vicki for maybe six months overtook the self-satisfaction of selection for OTU. In response to my tearful call to her from the Cadet's Mess one night she told me to stay strong and that she would come to Sydney from Adelaide to be closer and support me. Vicki gave up her nursing job, moved to Windsor, took work at Turramurra, and began her support campaign to help me get successfully through Scheyville. She worked afternoon shift at a nursing home in Turramurra – imagine what that meant in travel time (and risk) with the less-than-reliable cars we drove in those times!

My point is this – Scheyville gave both of us the opportunity to shape our lives like nothing else ever could. It (National Service) forced other people outside the process to make sacrifices just like Vicki did. Whilst she was supporting me, no one was supporting her (she was only twenty at the time). When I was selected to attend Scheyville, Vicki was also selected; when I graduated as a Second Lieutenant and Vicki pinned my pips on my epaulette she shared the success we both had. Many good people like my wife grew from the Scheyville experience to contribute significantly in the community, professions and most importantly in providing the foundation for solid family units. People like Vicki magnify the contribution Scheyville graduates have made to Australia.

1966 Seniors March-off Parade
These and the other photographs of the Office Training Unit by courtesy of
Neil Leckie and the Committee of the OTU Association

1966 Slow March on Parade

1968 Fiancée Helen Wallace (later Mrs Ramsay) pinning on Don Ramsay's pips

1967 Charlie Koch, a Lex Neville photo

1967 I. Dobie, J. Churchill, K. Hopkins and others

1968 Helicopter Drills

1969 Dress Presentation

1970 HQ, Officer Training Unit, Scheyville

Colour Party Graduation, 1970
L to R: Aostris Zalaiskalns, Tony Sonneveld, Jon Bates

Cadets' Mess Ante-room looking north

OTU Education Wing

Through the pipes with a whizz bang

Courtyard of the Administration Centre at Scheyville

1967 Sports

Most intakes had a 40% failure rate. Once marched out, your photo was blacked out.

The Traverse exercise

The Monkey Bars training exercise

Balance Beam practice with SLR

Vietnam and its aftermath
Vietnam: A picture

At home–

The waiting youths, the chosen names,

The greedy licking of draft-card flames,

From Labor benches a political cry –

"Murderers, sending our boys to die!"

Prime Minister Holt's catch-cry today,

"All the way with LBJ."

The crowds of banners in demonstrations,

The "Save Our Sons" organizations,

A split within the nation.

And in Vietnam–

The sweating green,

The treacherous ground,

The sniper's bullets' unnatural sound.

A gaping wound,

A corpse's sneer,

The bloody stretchers at the rear,

Village children

With terror-driven eyes,

Skeleton bodies and pitiful cries,

Asians the same;

No way to know,

Peasant or Communist, a friend or a foe.

A split within a nation.

Sue Baldwin, 5E1, Lismore High School. 1966 *The Lens Magazine*

A poem or a song encapsulates facts, opinions and feelings more succinctly than thousands of words in an essay. The above poem was written within fifteen months of Australia committing a battalion of troops to Vietnam and the commencement of the National Service scheme. Yet, this seventeen-year-old schoolgirl captured the situation that was to persist for another seven years very efficiently.

The Miracle of Marie

War is more than bullets, blood being spilled and the dead body count. From the chaos, the churn of emotions and disappointments come some heart-warming stories that remind us that love still abounds. The following story weaves together the connections of an Army pilot who trained at Scheyville, who won a bravery award for his courage and flying skill in Vietnam, and an exciting story of adoption under war conditions. The reader is reminded that one of the fellow Australians he rescued with his helicopter on operations was a fellow Scheyville graduate. Here is the story of Marie:

> Marie's actual birthday is unknown but guessed to be about 30 December 1970. A Roman Catholic nun found her in the streets of Vung Tau, South Vietnam in about mid-January 1971. At the time, I was serving as an army helicopter pilot with 161 Recce Flight based at Nui Dat. My loving wife, Liz, and I already had three sons. Unfortunately, our only daughter, Wendy Marie had died in May 1969, aged only four and a half months. Wendy was a catalyst for an idea of trying to adopt a Vietnamese orphan. We had no idea how we might adopt in Vietnam.
>
> On one of my rare days off, I hitched a ride on a Caribou aircraft from Nui Dat to Bien Hoa where I met up with a couple of American military policemen. They drove me to an orphanage where I saw a large room full of babies in cots. Several of them were of mixed race such as half Negro Vietnamese, half Mexican Vietnamese, and half white American Vietnamese; the rest were Asian. Some had boils, some had skin rashes. The stench of wet nappies was overwhelming. There was one attendant.

This was just a sample of the many unwanted, out of mind and out of sight war orphans. The toughest of soldiers would have had tears in his eyes at the sight of these babies. I returned to Nui Dat with a mind full of vague determination to proceed with an adoption.

On another day off I visited the Baria Catholic School where I met Reverend Mother, Sister Augustine. Many Australian soldiers visited this school. It was a place of peace where we felt relatively safe amidst innocent children. I discovered that as well as teaching the normal students, Sister Augustine and her companion Sisters, and helpers, cared for about fifteen orphans.

I asked if I could adopt one of her orphans. Eventually we agreed upon a little girl. Marie was not as yet at Baria. She was still at Vung Tau with other nuns of the same Order of Saint Paul of Chatres. Soon the nuns brought Marie to Baria where I saw her for the first time, but neither Sister Augustine nor I knew how to adopt. So far, I have been calling the girl Marie but at that point in time she had no name, no documentation, just a babe.

Sister Melanie gave the baby a Vietnamese name, Nugyen Thi Thu Huong, plus Marie Jeanne when she attended the Baria Court House to achieve a birth certificate. No legal process could commence without a birth certificate.

At about this time, Liz saw an article in the Melbourne *Sun* newspaper. It concerned Rosemary Taylor, a remarkable lady working towards adoptions of war orphans out of South Vietnam, mostly to France. The paper mentioned the Saigon lawyer she used for adoptions. On the next available opportunity, I hitched a ride to Saigon.

I visited Rosemary and the lawyer who wanted $2000US to process the adoption. I also discovered that I needed a Presidential Dispensation to adopt because, by Vietnamese law, to be eligible to adopt, one had to have been married for ten years and have no other children. Rosemary told me that she could finalise the adoptions of six orphans into America or France in the time she could get one child to Australia. With the lawyer's help, the process of our Vietnamese adoption began. Until my tour of duty ended, I regularly visited Marie, known as Jeanne to the nuns because Vietnamese people use the last name, whereas we use the first.

At the end of October 1971 my tour of duty ended but the adoption process did not. I was still in the Army, based in Holsworthy. Liz and I also had to commence a formal Australian process of adoption for Marie. In about late April 1972, Marie's Vietnamese passport arrived in the mail. It contained an exit permit from Vietnam. From April into May I heard that an area where Marie was kept for some time, on a small farm run by the nuns a few kilometres east of Baria, was being rocketed.

I became very worried. I told the New South Wales child welfare people of my fear for Marie. To their credit they fast tracked Marie's entry permit to Australia. After telling my Commanding Officer that I was going to Vietnam, "with or without leave Sir", I headed to Melbourne, firstly to attend my mate's wedding as best man and then onto Saigon. I should add that the Army was not happy and I had already been refused an Indulgence Passage which could have meant a free RAAF flight to Malaysia to save a dollar. I wore civilian clothes but my hair style alone made me look like a soldier. I had posted a letter to Sister Augustine about ten days before I left for Vietnam but she never received it. I had desperate hopes that someone might meet me at Saigon Airport but that did not happen.

When I left Vietnam at the end of my tour, the airport was extremely busy. When I returned it was dead quiet. The only Australian soldiers left in Vietnam had the task of guarding our Embassy. There were no Australian soldiers at Nui Dat or Vung Tau. I had but two addresses in Saigon. I took a taxi to Phu My where I hoped to find Rosemary Taylor. I got caught in a heavy rain shower wetting down my growing sense of terror.

When I arrived at Phu My, Rosemary was not there and I was told that Marie was not there. Now I was really starting to sweat, thinking I might have to catch a civilian bus to Baria. As I departed the Phu My complex, I went through a large gate. I was about to be swallowed up by a throng of pedestrians and a myriad of smelly two-stroke motorcycles when a Vietnamese person ran after me and told me that Marie was in another building in Saigon.

She gave me an address which I found with the help of a taxi driver. Had I been one or two seconds earlier in my departure from Phu My, I would have merged with the crowd. Sure enough, Marie was there in the care of Margaret Moses, an ex-Australia Mercy nun who spoke fluent French and had volunteered to assist Rosemary Taylor. Marie looked skinny but otherwise okay.

Suddenly I realised I needed a current International Health Certificate for Marie to depart Saigon. Margaret made a phone call and gave me an address for a volunteer Australian doctor running a clinic in Saigon. Her instructions were to go straight to the head of the queue; this got me a few dirty looks from the locals. Marie was jabbed three times and I returned to Margaret.

Then I realised that everyone had to wait two weeks after the smallpox vaccination to discover if it had worked. When I told Margaret about the "wait" she took the Certificate and made a neat change to the date. Now I hoped I could get Marie "out of there" I booked a flight for the following day.

I had few hours to spare and went for a walk. To my utter amazement I bumped into one of the nuns who lived and worked at Baria. She had not gone to Saigon with any hint of meeting me. Just have a think about the statistical likelihood of such a meeting in a city of about five million people. Coincidence – not likely! This Nun could then return to Sister Augustine and confidently advise her that I really had come to collect Marie.

Margaret Moses gave me a bed for the night. I didn't sleep much because I could hear artillery exploding on the outskirts of Saigon throughout the night. I left Saigon the next day, 1 June 1972, but not before I told Margaret not to stay too long because it was dangerous. She stayed to the very end, 1975, and got killed along with many orphans in cardboard boxes, in a large American Star-Lifter aircraft which suffered a decompression failure when the large rear door blew out in flight. Margaret is listed as one of our war dead. What a heroine she was! Rosemary Taylor also stayed to the bitter end and has continued similar work in Thailand with disadvantaged children even as I write this story.

After a brief stopover at Kuala Lumpur and a night at Singapore, I arrived very early at Perth Airport where I had to go through Customs and Immigration before catching a local airline flight to Melbourne. I got plenty of scrutiny at Perth but I didn't think much about it. I eventually arrived at Melbourne where I was met by Liz.

Within a day we drove back to New South Wales. We now had four children, including Marie, because Robert was born six weeks before I left to serve in Vietnam in 1970. He is three months older than Marie. He has been an amazing son who has been very tolerant and caring of Marie from the day she arrived in Australia.

I learnt why I was given thorough scrutiny by the authorities. The Victorian child welfare authority at the time, in contrast to NSW, had refused entry to five Vietnamese orphans whose exit permits from Vietnam were soon to expire. These five were smuggled as far as Perth where a throng of pre-warned media personnel were waiting. The media made it so embarrassing for the Victorian adoption authority that the orphans were allowed to stay.

By returning to NSW as soon as we did, we avoided all media contact and Marie grew up as one of our family having nothing to do with the news media. When I left the Army in late 1973, we moved back to Melbourne until I accepted a job based at Tyabb. The jobs have changed but Liz and I still live at Tyabb. Our family grew to five sons and two daughters, all of whom have grown up. Marie is happily married; has two sons and a daughter and lives in Tasmania. Liz and I have fourteen grandsons and six granddaughters.

In 2012 I convinced Marie that it would be a good idea for her, Liz and me to return to Vietnam to show her the places that I had told her about over the years. So, in July 2012, over forty years since Marie left Vietnam as a baby, we headed for Vietnam, an eight-day round trip. Marie met Sister Augustine and Sister Melanie. Sister Augustine is now 95 years old. Marie visited Vung Tau and Baria. She saw the room where she had slept at Baria as a baby. I revisited Nui Dat and found what is left of Luscombe runway. I reckon I got within forty metres of where my tent had been in the rubber plantation. We visited Sister Augustine twice. She was overjoyed to see us. According to Sister Augustine, I was the only Australian soldier to adopt a child from the Baria orphanage. It was a very emotional trip for all of us. Marie plans to return to Vietnam with her husband and three children within two years. Note well that Liz did the hard yards. While I was away working, sometimes for months, she was the one changing nappies and feeding our tribe. She is a wonderful mother.[1]

Sister Augustine

---

[1] Email from John Sonneveld to Roger Donnelly 16 April 2019 containing the story of Marie.

Scheyville-trained helicopter pilots in Vietnam

As the jeep became the symbol of World War Two and Korea, the helicopter became synonymous with Vietnam. They allowed Battalion Commanders to recce and plan before operations. They could also study the terrain in a way never before known.

Scheyville not only trained 'nashos' to be platoon commanders, it provided officer training for Direct Entry Aviation Cadets who were ultimately offered Short Service Commissions of five years. Hence the majority of helicopter pilots who took the troops into battle and evacuated the wounded in Vietnam were Scheyville graduates. It is worth mentioning some of their work; one Battalion Commander who made maximum use of them was Brigadier Colin Khan. Khan commanded the 5RAR on its second tour of duty to Vietnam in 1969–70.

According to Brigadier Khan,[2]

> Because my aggressive use of recce helicopters it was always beneficial to me to have the same pilot when possible. I did have Peter Bysouth but especially a young man called Jellie (he was killed after I left). Jellie and I suffered a number of near misses from machine gun (MG) fire, and once an RPG explosion near our tail.
>
> On another occasion, we were almost captured by NVA [North Vietnamese Army] in an action in Long Binh Province. I wanted to land to talk to my Company Commander in action. – I asked the Company to "throw smoke" for identification – when the pilot and I identified the colour and started to land, firing broke out and my Company Commander called out on the radio that we were not landing in his position. The NVA had come up on my radio net and were luring us in to land in their location – knowing our routine of throwing identifying smoke.

---

[2] Khan, Brig. Colin. Letter to Roger Donnelly dated 27 January 2010.

And of course, the main benefit of a helicopter to me was for ground recce and planning before an operation or movement.

I was an avid user of the Sioux. EVERY morning soon after dawn, I had my Sioux at my Fire Support Base and I would spend between four to eight hours every day, airborne over my Area of Operations (AO), following the actions of my troops and supporting them. No Commander spent more time in a helicopter and I was completely wedded to their use.

Certain pilots who knew my aggressive use of Sioux were better than others – but all were good – I never found one of our young pilots wanting in courage or professionalism.

I always said to the pilot what I wanted to do, where to go and how close and low to enemy positions I wanted to go. It was not a matter of being "boss" – if the pilot expressed a particular concern and it was a technical or a flying matter – I always acknowledged and supported his judgement. I never recall any disagreement – even when I would at times use the Sioux as my mini gunship to allow me to "strafe" an enemy position with my weapon.

In conclusion, you should observe I was a constant, major user of our young helicopter pilots, who were outstanding in their professionalism and courage.

Without them, I could not have commanded a very successful Infantry Battalion that killed more enemy than any other battalion. These aircraft were, to me, a battle winning factor and I could not have succeeded without them.

The Directing Staff realise the training is for real

Directing Staff who served at Scheyville in its early days possibly didn't realise how much pressure they and the cadets were under until the first of the graduates was killed in Vietnam. Gordon Sharp graduated with the first intake but was killed during the Battle of Long Tan in 1966. As Regimental Sergeant Major Moon reflects, 'when the message came through that Sharp had been killed and the CO read it out, I was shocked because up until then it was just another training camp. I had realised before but this brought it home that this was for real.' The pressure didn't become any more intense as there was already so much pressure on staff as well as cadets, and no more could be fitted into the syllabus, but from that moment on, every person knew what a serious job they were doing.

The death of Gordon Sharp impacted on the thinking of Geddes and his instructors in relation to the allocation of graduates to their Corps. It made them more discriminating, whether that was consciously or subconsciously, in deciding which young officers would go to the Arms, that is, Artillery, Armour, Infantry and the Engineers. To quote Geddes, 'Gordon Sharp's death heightened our determination and responsibility to make certain that particularly those fellows going to Infantry were ready and right for the job.'[3]

Another day in the office – the hot and steamy rice paddies or jungle

The narrative which follows is based on the experiences of Brian Vickery, Gordon Hurford, and others, as recounted in *The Scheyville Experience* and in other interviews to the author:[4]

Dawn is breaking. Having 'harboured up' for the night, the platoon is ready for 'stand to', a serious time of the day. Will the presence of the pyjama-clad ones be announced early today? That would mean no breakfast, no early morning

---

[3] Donnelly, Roger. *The Scheyville Experience*. QUP 2001 p 82.
[4] Donnelly, Roger. *The Scheyville Experience*. QUP 2001. Paraphrasing Brian Vickery p 44.

cigarette before the patrolling starts. Death-delivering gunfire would break the peace. All men rub their sleep-deprived eyes, quietly move to their posts and look out into the jungle. The silence is deafening. Better than the alternative!

Up above, the thump, thump, thump of the rotors on the Sioux chopper announce the arrival of the battalion Operations Officer or CO to do an early morning recce. A fleeting thought goes through the infantryman's mind that the two blokes above were on the beer last night. Lucky them. At about 5 am, a rat the size of a household cat had tried to drag his backpack away. While he was beating it to death with his entrenching tool a burst of automatic fire came from within a nearby village. Had he enraged the gods? The bloody rat escaped. We have been on operations now for two weeks. The tropical heat has provided ever-increasing discomfort through sweat blisters and prickly heat. Ants tumble out of trees down the back of necks and eat us while at rest. Rest is the operative word. We never get a good night's sleep out here. But the fifty-pound pack still has to be carried. How many times will it or my giggle hat get snagged on the vines or the bamboo?

Having contact with the enemy is one thing; the ever-present threat of mines and booby traps reminds us that we are indeed vulnerable. No two contacts are ever the same, although in most instances the action lasts no longer than thirty minutes.

Vietnam is an infantry platoon commander's war. (A few occasions like the battles of Coral, Balmoral and Long Tan punctuated this.) This will be another day of enacting the policy of search and destroy, or search and clear which are our techniques for uncovering the enemy camps, caches and strong points in the jungle. This is our 'bread and butter' just like Gary McKay said. This tried and true method of saturating an area with patrols was learned in the counter-guerrilla operations against the communist terrorists in Malaya. The foolproof way to ensure that an area was clear of enemy was to physically pass over it on the ground.

A good wash, a shave and a can of beer behind the barbed wire at Nui Dat would go well, but at least some of the time out here in the dankness we get to smell the enemy but not see him. Thank God for the thickness of the jungle!

First contact with the enemy isn't always 'the walking down the track and suddenly it's a contact with one or two people and it's over with quickly' situation. Today, Brian Vickery's platoon will conduct a cordon and search operation at An Nhut Village. The villagers will not understand him when he tries to speak with them. A lone VC will be discovered hiding behind some matting in the house.

David Webster's platoon is operating near Thua Tich. It will discover a small enemy camp based around the caves in the riverbank and find the horseshoe shaped bedding rolls of the type used by the VC. A member of his platoon will tread on a booby trap that malfunctions – thankfully!

However, the lead section had followed a track down into a creek and had shots fired at them. The forward section returned the fire and a sweep was performed down the creek. During the sweep four people were encountered – two children and two adults. Unfortunately, the two children and the elderly male died. The woman lost a leg. This is an edited version of the contact as explained by Webster. The story doesn't end today. The mental anguish will never subside and a digger will commit suicide some thirty years afterwards. Notes from his diary will reveal he felt persecuted by reports and comments made when he returned from Vietnam that he and his mates were child killers.

Ten or so hours later the platoon will harbour up again. The diggers will gouge out another shell-scrape for the night. The sky will be quieter once the planes and helicopters have left the stage and their crews retired to the wet bar for the evening. The dull routine will continue. A kind of gloom will descend as darkness takes control. The canopy closes over again for another night.

Perhaps there will be time for something to eat and a hot brew before manning the perimeter?

Dusk has fallen. Another long day in the Vietnam jungle that will be followed by another long night.

Welcome to the sometimes explosive, sometimes boring dull routine reality of the Vietnam War.

Anzac Day remembering

Like a significant portion of the Australian population, Scheyville graduates attend Anzac Day ceremonies and reflect on the human tragedy of war. For Gary McKay, each Anzac Day is different because 'I travel to various locations a lot as a guest speaker. But the most memorable was when I was in Gallipoli training to be a tour guide with the AWM [Australian War Memorial] and was asked to read the Second Lesson at the Dawn Service. Hard to beat that (except it was freezing). I sat next to a Turkish Captain who had to read Ataturk's *"Ode"* and he was so nervous he could hardly walk.'

Most find the playing of the 'Last Post' as the most moving part of Anzac Day as it is a signal of farewell and acknowledgment that they are departed. One sharp observation of the day is that of DP who finds the most moving part seeing older women who are war widows. It is poignant and sad to see media coverage of the widows and children of casualties of later theatres of war such as Afghanistan 'the tumult and the shouting dies/ The Captains and the Kings depart' ... and these women are left to do it alone.

The observation of a minute's silence is perhaps more significant for someone like Gary McKay who served in Vietnam as a platoon commander. He says that he always runs through the names of the men in his platoon who he lost in battle (four) and those who have died since 1972 (five, as at 2014).

As for a summation of a Scheyvillian's own Anzac Day or personal pilgrimage, it is all summed up by McKay: 'When I was drafted and was told I was going to war I was a bit excited by that idea. The reality is a lot different. You can't wait to get into action and then can't wait to get out and back home. The novelty of being shot at wears off very quickly. I can see how many males would respond to the testosterone effect. Until they see their first corpse blasted apart or then see one of their mates shredded by bullets or shrapnel. You very quickly grow up and the shiny bravado soon wears off to a dull lustre that might reappear years later.'

Role of the buildings and site in memory

The first Commandant, Geddes, remembered converting the former Migrant Camp, and how the Parade Ground was a place at the core of the Scheyville Experience. On his first visit to the site in late 1964 he found it still occupied by a large number of migrants. Generally, he liked the area, as it was semi-isolated, had large training areas, was near the Richmond airbase, and potentially provided all the accommodation needed.[5]

The case of Turk Ellis on the parade ground is an excellent example of how memory alters over time. As I was researching my previous book, *The Scheyville Experience,* I was told the story of their graduation day. A final practice parade was conducted in the morning. At the end of the practice, and just before 'falling out' to make their final preparations, Cadet Turk Ellis was called to the front of the parade where he was addressed by the RSM and the Commandant. Cadet Ellis fell to his knees in front those assembled. They were later informed that Cadet Ellis collapsed because he had just been told that his father wouldn't be attending the parade because he had been killed in a motor accident on the way to Scheyville. For forty years the fellow graduates of intake 1/70 recalled the above. In 2010 I attended the 1/70 class reunion in Sydney and at Scheyville, where I finally met Cadet Ellis. Explaining how many of his fellow graduates had each, independently recited the circumstances of that graduation day incident to me over a period of years I sought clarification as to the authenticity of the story. Turk Ellis explained that he had indeed been called to the front of the parade. He had collapsed. His dad had died on that morning. However, he said, that his friend's recollections were not exact. The Unit was still formed up, but had left the parade ground, and was waiting for the order 'to fall out'. His dad hadn't died in a car accident. His parents had stayed in a motel the previous night, had sex, and his dad died of a heart attack! Memory changes over time.

---

[5] Donnelly, Roger, *The Scheyville Experience*. p 73.

Physical and other memorials to the OTU

There is a stone memorial to their fallen at the RMC Parade Ground, as well as a number of plaques on the obelisk at the headquarters of Scheyville National Park, at North Head, the Seymour Vietnam Veterans' Walk and with the National Servicemen's Association Memorial in Adelaide.[6]

Scheyville also lives on at Duntroon. RMC Duntroon is the repository for the history of all the officer training establishments in Australia. Not only does the newly revamped Australian Army Museum Duntroon hold memorabilia from Scheyville, Portsea and Georges Heights, but the Sergeants Mess also holds many pieces of OTU memorabilia. Duntroon has three ovals – Duntroon, Portsea and Scheyville – and regular exercises are named Exercise Duntroon, Exercise Portsea and Exercise Scheyville (completed at the Scheyville Oval). There are also plans for Exercise Georges Heights (the location of the former WRAAC Officer Training School).

In November 2018 a new activity, named 'Plan Scheyville', commenced. It entailed a 22-week lead-up (the same time as many Scheyville classes) for a Military Skills team to prepare to participate in a Military Skills Competition at West Point in the USA, competing against around fifty of the world's best teams. The OTU Association has supported Plan Scheyville by presenting each of the participants with an OTU Scheyville tie to wear with their civilian clothing during the competition, which took place between 12 and 19 April 2019.

The bond is formed: the OTU Association

In 1976 Gary McKay MC and Les Boag decided to arrange an OTU reunion in the 6RAR Officers Mess at Enoggera. About fifty attended, of whom some forty-four signed the attendance list. Thus, the OTU Association was established. Such was the bonding that had obviously occurred during the training of these 'nashos', that every class has had a number of reunions, and a number of

---

[6] *Scheyvillian* Journal No 1. of 2019

national reunions have been held. Another one is scheduled for October 2022! At the 2013 reunion, some 600 graduates and partners attended a formal dinner, 410 marched in the Sydney Anzac Day march and 444 attended a church service at Windsor.

One of the Association's long-standing commitments has been to the Lord and Lady Somers Camps. Held in January each year at Somers on Westernport Bay, Victoria, they have been the focal point of the Association's involvement with youth development. They provide an inspiration similar to that received by the young soldiers at Scheyville. The sixteen- and seventeen-year-olds go through a week's intensive activities that promote teamwork, leadership and self-understanding.

The Queensland Chapter of the association also supports youth leadership; its 'at risk' youth charity is Vitae Limited. In November 2017 they donated $2500 and a further $2000 in late 2018.

Not many organisations or institutions have this level of comradeship that has existed for fifty years!

Scheyville graduates – the unintended benefit of the Vietnam War.

Journalist Alan Ramsay lamented in the Sydney Morning Herald[7] that the Australian commitment of combat troops to Vietnam was a 'foul corpse nobody will claim'. Stephen Barton reflected on what he called the 'little known unintended benefit from the foul corpse'. He swiped at those who wrote that Scheyville was a sinecure for privileged sons, and supports my argument that Scheyville graduates are one of the most successful, in material terms at least, cohort Australia has ever produced. Most schools can't claim as many successful sons as Scheyville. If they can, they haven't done it in the space of seven years! And what was it that made Scheyville graduates so special? To quote Barton,

---

[7] Barton, Stephen. *Sydney Morning Herald,* 29 April 2005

'National Service, while burdening the Army with the demand of training thousands of young men dragged from the streets by the misfortune of a ballot, also gave it access to a pool of talent otherwise denied it.'

The last word on the 'experiment' that was OTU Scheyville is from Brigadier Peter Pursey who became a Commandant of RMC Duntroon:

> On the relevance of officer training, we have entered a new century and; in my opinion, the training that we undertook at Scheyville, well prepared us for the tasks which we had to undertake. The training was right for the time and the quality outcomes of all Nashos is testimony to that in my view. The question of whether it could be repeated today is another question. I doubt it. In 1960 and 1970 the training was focused on Vietnam and jungle warfare. OTU had a program to match that need. Society was relatively understanding of the requirement. Until a government makes a major commitment of Australian soldiers to a conflict; I am uncertain whether the Nasho/OTU concept could be repeated. I think it most unlikely. Attitudes and society have changed markedly since 1970 and the general public would be much more democratic and vocal about committing young people to a war outside our shores. Even if they did allow it, the complexity of war in the modern era would make the OTU syllabus unsuited for the needs of today.[8]

The above comments do not represent an official view of the Australian Army.

---

[8] Questionnaire response and fax from Brigadier Peter Pursey, 18 May 2000. Also appears in Donnelly, Roger, *The Scheyville Experience* QUP 2001 p 188.

Four battles and a National Park emerges!

A journey from dilapidation and 'Far-outs-ville' to New South Wales Heritage Listing.

Introduction

In October 1996, Pam Allan, Minister for the Environment in the Carr Government officially declared the site a National Park; in 2010, Frank Sartor, Minister for Climate Change and the Environment, signed off on the inclusion of Scheyville National Park on the State Heritage Register.[1]

A reliable estimate of 1500 people attended the Scheyville Centenary Celebrations on 15 May 2011.[2] Staff and event organisers were pleasantly surprised by the attendance, and even more so, by the event winning a prize in the Greater Western Sydney 2011 Tourism Awards and being a state finalist in the Events Category. In my opinion it is fantastic that Scheyville became a National Park. It was also gratifying to attend the Centenary Celebrations. Following the discovery of correspondence leading to the change of name from Pitt Town to Scheyville during my doctorate research, the then National Park Manager, Jonathan Sanders had acted on my flippant suggestion that such a celebration be held.

Such accolades mask the fight to preserve the natural, cultural and built fabric over the preceding thirty years. Apart from a five-year period between 1978 and 1983 when the Hawkesbury Agricultural College used the premises for overflow student and staff residential accommodation, the site had been neglected. This chapter describes the threats to the site which were averted between 1983 and 1996. There was a thirteen-year gap between the old Agricultural College closing its Scheyville Campus and Gazettal of the Scheyville National Park on

---

[1] State Heritage Register NSW. Gazette date 9 April 2010. Gazette No. 51. Page No. 1853.
[2] Email dated 24 May 2011 from Jonathan Sanders Scheyville National Park Manager to Roger Donnelly detailing attendance figures.

3 April 1996. The central part of the former Pitt Town Common was threatened by four major development proposals during this period: the second Sydney International airport in the early 1980s; a maximum security prison in 1987; a super-sized waste dump in 1990; and an extensive residential development in 1992.

Certain places have specific groups attach a particular type of meaning to them, while other places are passed over as insignificant. Scheyville has been both It was sought after by governments for various uses then left to rot in the 1980s and early 1990s. Then all of a sudden it was rediscovered. When the Hawkesbury Valley community recognised they might lose it to a second airport, prison or waste dump, they realised how significant the site is.[3]

Scheyville becoming a National Park was a deliverable political objective of the Carr Government in New South Wales. Jonathan Sanders was the National Parks Department representative on the committee to provide input to the Sydney Metro 2000 Strategy. This committee was concerned with the urban sprawl nature of Sydney development and that the then Liberal Government was allowing developments to proceed without due consideration to the provision of water, sewerage and public transport, particularly in Western Sydney. Jonathan claims that if they had all proceeded as planned, 'every family would have needed four cars to access all amenities. In the last days of the then Liberal Government, that government was taking notice of the need to plan more carefully. Unfortunately, the Metro 2000 Strategy was still a draft document when the Liberals lost government. In the dying days of the Liberals, the then Housing Minister issued a decision that Scheyville would become a 20,000 people town.'[4]

When Bob Carr took over, his government scrapped the Metro 2000 Strategy work. He believed that 'it would just be another Lib pro-development-at-any-cost document'. Then in 2001 the Carr Government scrapped the Hawkesbury-

---

[3] Harrison, Rodney. *Understanding the Politics of Heritage*. Manchester University Press 2009.
[4] Email and phone call between Roger Donnelly and Jonathan Sanders 27 June 2013 and NSW *Parliamentary Debates*, Legislative Council, 20 February 1991.

Nepean Catchment Management Trust. According to Jonathan Sanders, this led to a policy vacuum.[5]

This section analyses the debates that surrounded the varied proposed uses of the site from 1973. The story of Scheyville's journey to becoming a National Park was a perfect example of the lengths that government instrumentalities often go to and repeatedly use the same logic to appease developers and concerned residents when population and housing pressures are exerted in our major cities. Councils and government departments sometimes lose sight of all the challenging issues that have to be balanced before a development decision is reached. They are not able to please all parties.

Kevin Rozzoli, the state Member of Parliament for Hawkesbury from 17 February 1973 to 27 March 1999, claims that 'after the College [Hawkesbury Agricultural College] vacated the site in 1983 it became dilapidated.' It was used by the Army and he visited the site to find 'wanton destruction'. The government tried to be 'risk averse'. He claims that even as the local member he wasn't privy to everything that concerned the site. 'Gradually adjacent wetlands that were part of the old Pitt Town Common such as Cattai, Mitchell Park and Longneck Lagoon were annexed by the National Parks as the government abolished the Boards of Trustees, of which I was a member. I suspect that the Major Airports Needs Study [MANS – study for the Sydney Second Airport], and the attempt to build a prison awakened a prompting of the public conscience.' This, with the fact that New South Wales land held by the Crown for no specific purpose could be the subject of a land claim by the indigenous community added to a feeling of 'let's give something to Western Sydney'.[6]

---

[5] Email and phone call between Roger Donnelly and Jonathan Sanders
[6] Phone interview 13 June 2013, Donnelly with Kevin Rozzoli.

The development of the New South Wales National Park Register

To put the remaining sections of this chapter into context it is necessary to visit the history of New South Wales National Parks.

The National Parks and Wildlife Act 1967 established national parks, state parks, nature reserves and the National Parks and Wildlife Service. In 1974 a new Act was introduced which tidied up existing legislation. In 1998, the National Parks and Wildlife Act 1974 still governed the operations of the National Parks and Wildlife Service.[7] In the late 1990s, under the Carr Government, there were several significant amendments to the 1974 Act. These included: The National Parks and Wildlife Amendment Act (Aboriginal Ownership) Act 1996; the National Parks and Wildlife Amendment Act (Regional Parks) Act 1996 and the Marine Parks Act 1997. A further number of new national parks were created with the passing of the Forestry and National Park Estate Act 1998.

In 1995 the New South Wales Government signed the National Strategy for the Conservation of Australia's Biological Diversity, which committed the Government to the establishment of a comprehensive, adequate and representative network of terrestrial and marine protected areas. The New South Wales Draft Biodiversity Strategy identified performance targets for establishing a Comprehensive, Adequate and Representative reserve system, based on comprehensive regional assessments, for forests by the year 2000 and for all other terrestrial and marine ecosystems by 2010.

By 30 May 1998, 4,551,372 hectares were reserved under the National Parks and Wildlife Act which was just under six percent of the total land area of New South Wales. As of the same date, there were 103 national parks with a total area of 3,764,654 hectares.

---

[7] Parliament of NSW Briefing paper No. 22/1998 by Stewart Smith titled *National Parks in NSW*.

Sydney's development can be seen as a tug-of-war. On one end is the team pushing for as much land as possible to be set aside from development. On the opposing team are those who realise that Sydney's population is expanding westwards and that infrastructure has to be provided for that increased population. Meanwhile, the Hawkesbury area is needed as a place for agriculture near Sydney.

Hence a number of considerations within Sydney Urban Development Strategies had an impact on the Scheyville National Park decision.

By 1988 the 'Sydney into its Third Century' document emphasised the road and rail networks as backbones, but was long on vision and short on practicalities. In 1995 'Cities for the Twenty-First Century' proposed a set of competitive hubs formed by clustering economic and residential areas and this underwent a modest update in the 1998 'Shaping Our Cities Plan' following political changes.

During the 1980s there was a significant increase in the number of Resident Action Groups (RAGs) in Sydney. Resident activism influenced local planning processes, the location of noxious facilities and subsequent urban form. This initiated important reactions by government at both the local and State levels. Urban collective activisms have been stereotyped as single-issue, self-serving NIMBY (Not In My Back Yard) groups. But as argued by Lauren Costello and Kevin Dunn, RAGs '… are also empowering forces, in which women and men are introduced to the political structures and become engaged in protest and resistance that can challenge the social and spatial order. RAGs can, either singularly or cumulatively, force a realigning of existing power relations and they can necessitate changed modes of governance.'[8]

One theme of this chapter is that the people of the Hawkesbury had to be vigilant. They had to become involved, as successive State Governments sought to foist certain developments upon them at the Scheyville site.

---

[8] Costello, Lauren N. & Dunn, Kevin M. 'Resident action groups in Sydney: people power or rat-bags?' *Australian Geographer*, 25:1, 1994, 61-76

'Far-outs-ville': the Scheyville campus of Hawkesbury Agricultural College

The Hawkesbury River region was the third area settled after European occupation. One of the main reasons for the settlement was the fertile land. Founded in 1891, the Hawkesbury Agricultural College (HAC) was the earliest training college of its type in New South Wales, and its first principal, John Thompson, played a significant role in selecting the Pitt Town Common – the future Scheyville – as the site of the co-operative settlement in 1893.

On 19 March 1976, HAC became a College of Advanced Education (CAE). An opportunity to rent Scheyville from the Commonwealth was seized by the College, and a five-year lease executed in 1978. The College had submitted a proposal to the Higher Education Board for specific funds to update Halls of Residence in 1976, prior to becoming a CAE.[9]

Leasing the Scheyville site fitted in with HAC transitioning to a CAE. It also coincided with a change in choices made by students in relation to accommodation.

It was resolved in December 1977 'that, subject to satisfactory results being obtained with regard to costs and management for the Scheyville complex after the meeting of January 4 [1978] Council delegate to the Executive the authority to lease or rent the property for use as accommodation from the Department of Administrative Services.' Interestingly, the future costs were to be apportioned between the College and the Army.[10] By February 1978 this was set at fifty percent each.

The College had noted 'the problems which existed for new students locating suitable off-campus accommodation or commuting to Richmond from home each day by public transport. Dr Swain said that it was not possible to give any indication whether the rejection of offers of places to prospective students

---

[9] Resolution No 76/3 20/2/1976
[10] Hawkesbury Agricultural College (HAC) Buildings and Equipment Committee Meeting December 15, 1977

could be linked to poor accommodation and transport.'[11] The student population grew from 583 in 1977 to 802 in 1978. The percentage of resident students for the two years, respectively forty-six and forty-five was only maintained by virtue of Scheyville.[12]

The Three Farms Committee of the HAC recommended that sixty to one hundred weaner beef cattle equivalents be purchased to graze an area of approximately 125 hectares, for finishing. This was in addition to recommendations to improve the buildings for student accommodation, buy a tractor and plough, and do a range of other improvements such as fencing.[13]

The Hawkesbury College history[14] notes that in 1977, 'difficult economic conditions facing the nation at this time were the major reason for the shortage of capital funds. The College, nevertheless, had its own major problem – an urgent need for more residential accommodation because of the rapid growth in student numbers. Thus, was born the Scheyville Campus.' There was 'a lot of money spent setting up Scheyville, which had deteriorated quickly after the Army's departure. It provided community-style living for students, was substantially self-governing, with supervision provided by a warden and residential tutors.'

There is little recorded of anyone's experience at the site during this period. However, an article by Ian Lees, a resident of Scheyville in 1981 gives a student's view.[15]

Lees writes that:

… the campus was known affectionately as "Far-outs-ville" due to it being a twenty-minute drive from the main campus. Catering and cooking were up to the individual, which led to the formation of "food

---

[11] HAC Equipment and Buildings Committee Meeting 11 March 1977 p 2.
[12] Braithwaite, B. M. and Hawkesbury Agricultural College. Old Boys' Union. *Challenge & change: the history of Hawkesbury Agricultural College 1966-1991* Hawkesbury Agricultural College Old Boys' Union, Richmond, 1991. p 74.
[13] HAC File 148/1/1 (ii) b, Report on the Utilisation of land at Scheyville 17 April 1978.
[14] Braithwaite, B. M. and Hawkesbury Agricultural College. Old Boys' Union. Op. cit.
[15] Ibid pp 94-95.

groups". The majority of buildings were single storey which resulted in the affectionate term "sweat boxes". It didn't really matter what the accommodation was like because the whole place worked! Other facilities on offer included squash courts, tennis courts, above-ground pool and grass ovals. Within the campus agriculture, horticulture, home economics, valuation and food students blended together in the multicultural melting pot. Communal living was the style of living. The food group proved to be the vital link as the masses congregated in the communal kitchens. The kitchen was the place where recipes were created, gossip caught up on and a mess generated. Thus, just as with the other eras of occupation – migrants, soldiers, FOOD was the important ingredient that held them together!

The bar opened after *Dr Who* and *Monkey* [television programs of the time] were over and was run on a roster system. It was in the bar and TV room areas that dances were held. Up and coming bands and theme nights were the order. These nights proved popular with all students only concerned how far to crawl before a bed could be found.

In many ways this recollection of Ian Lees illustrates that nothing had changed. Meal time was important, pranks were played (as in the Dreadnoughts era) sport was important, the droughts left the lawns to crackle under foot, and you could collect insects from outside the toilet block. Scheyville had its own community feel.

By 1979 the number of accommodation units at Scheyville had been increased from 100 to 150 and other facilities, such as a games and reading room, provided, yet the Master of Halls had been asked to make enquiries about the drop off in the student occupancy rate.[16]

In the Financial Statements for the period ending 30 June 1981, the Halls of Residence Report indicated 'a satisfactory situation up till June but below

---

[16] B & E Committee meeting 17, 5 June 1979

budget level of occupancy on both Richmond and Scheyville campuses'.[17] Nevertheless, it was agreed that the Scheyville Campus continue to operate in 1982. A working party to examine College long-term accommodation needs was set up and one aspect of this study was that a final report to the Principal be furnished by May 1982. (Council Meeting No 36)

That Report submitted to the Council meeting on 18 June 1982 noted 'a study of room occupancy in relation to student enrolment in recent years shows an increasing tendency for students to live off campus. In 1982 we have a record 1020 students enrolled with only 300 living on Richmond Campus and 63 at Scheyville on 19/4/82.'[18]

> Increasing numbers of students are coming from homes within commuting distance of College and the increasing proportion of mature age students are important factors in relation to the choice made by students of where to live. In 1976 off-campus accommodation was very difficult to obtain and expensive because of reluctance of owners to rent to HAC students and subsidised rentals for the RAAF Richmond personnel.[19]

By 1981 off-campus accommodation was much easier to obtain and rents became very competitive with campus residential fees resulting in a number of vacant rooms on Richmond campus. Taking these factors and a slump in the building industry, high interest rates and no demand by short course students for Scheyville-type accommodation it was resolved that the Scheyville campus be closed at the end of 1982.[20] The lease terminated on 7 January 1983. It was estimated that the Scheyville campus, if maintained in 1983, would have operated at a loss of close to $30,000.

---

[17] HAC Council meeting No. 35 14 August 1981.
[18] HAC Council meeting No. 40 18 June 1982. Item 10.1 Assistant Principal's Report.
[19] HAC Council Meeting 18 June 1982.
[20] HAC Council Meeting 18 June 1982

In 1985 a committee of inquiry into higher education in Sydney's west was instituted, and released a Report on 2 February 1986 recommending the establishment of a university that would absorb both the Nepean CAE and the Hawkesbury Agricultural CAE. The University of Western Sydney (UWS) was Gazetted from 1 January 1989.[21]

Police training activity 1980s

Dick Adams, a retired Assistant New South Wales Police Commissioner says that 'whilst it is common wisdom that NSW Police Special Weapons Operations Sections (SWOS) were the primary users of the facility and, by inference, caused much of the damage to buildings, they did, in fact only use the facility on one single day – as part of a joint exercise with the NSW Police Tactical Response Group (TRG). The TRG used the facility on numerous occasions – mainly to practice urban combat and building entry techniques. On some occasions, senior members of the SWOS attended in an observer role. In fact, the facility was also used by 2 Commando Regiment, Corrective Services and other organisations.'[22] This raises a question of who or what organisation was 'in charge' of the site at this time, to allow destruction of certain buildings, or is it a case of our values changing to the tune of wishing that at least some of those buildings had been spared?

The Scheyville National Park Conservation Management Plan notes:

> Much of the unexploded ordnance which was still hazardous in 1996 when the National Park was dedicated probably dated from this period of Tactical Response and Special Weapons Operations. The army took

---

[21] State Records Office of NSW Agency 2941. Files from 1 Jan 1972 to 31 December 1988
[22] Email from Dick Adams to Roger Donnelly dated Monday 5 November 2007.

responsibility in 1996 for detonating and clearing the ordnance. Some of it probably also originated from the military activities of the 1940s.[23]

It is also possible that some of this ordnance was left after the site was used as the OTU during the Vietnam War.

Paraphrasing from the Conservation Management Plan as detailed in The Scheyville Experience, the police enthusiasm for firing advanced weapons of localised destruction had brutal effects on some of the surviving buildings outside the Quadrangle area.[24]

Battle one: Sydney's second international airport

It is necessary to give a brief chronology of the airport saga. In 1969-70 the Holt Federal Government received a report on major airport requirements for Sydney. During the 1971-74 Whitlam Labor Government's term, a major cost-benefit study of alternative airport proposals was undertaken. The Fraser Liberal Government had the Major Airport Needs for Sydney (MANS) study completed. It sat on the decision for seven years. Malcolm Fraser and his Treasurer, John Howard, received ten proposals for a second airport site which were narrowed down to two: Badgery's Creek and Scheyville.[25]

Using four basic criteria, the 1985 site selection program identified nine potential sites within 80 kilometres of the Sydney CBD. A site at Goulburn was also included as representative of potential outlying sites. The sites were grouped into 'Closer Sites' and 'Mid-distance Sites'. Scheyville, along with Badgery's Creek, Bringelly, Holsworthy and Londonderry were the Closer Sites.

The Minister for Transport and Regional Development, Mr Sharp, played a strategic political game by nominating Holsworthy as needing an Environmental Impact Statement, along with Badgery's Creek, knowing it would be excluded as

---

[23] *Scheyville National Park Conservation Management Plan,* Department of Environment and Climate Change, 2009.
[24] Donnelly, Roger. *The Scheyville Experience* University of Queensland Press, St Lucia, 2001 p 199.
[25] Commonwealth, *Parliamentary Debates,* House of Representatives 29 May 1996.

being the second most expensive to develop. This was because of unexploded ordnance and relocation of Defence facilities. (Scheyville had been found to be the most expensive to develop.) This further delayed a decision. In 1986, the Government announced that Badgery's Creek had been selected. In 2000 the federal government advised that a further Review of Sydney's airport needs would be undertaken in 2005.

However, the Labor Party in 1984 had the list of ten sites that included Scheyville. The Minister for Aviation, Mr Beazley announced that the sites were narrowed down to Wilton and Badgery's Creek.[26] In response to a question in the House, the Minister for Aviation, the Hon Peter Morris said, 'I should be able to tell the Honourable Member by September which of the two sites has been selected.'[27]

Mr Cohen, Federal Minister for Home Affairs and the Environment, visited on Friday 10 February 1984. It was reported that 'the visit was in order to inspect heritage items which would be affected by the siting of Sydney's Second Airport at Scheyville. ... The Minister's portfolio includes the National Heritage, but he was unable to comment on the possible siting of an airport, as this is the responsibility of the Minister for Aviation, Mr Beazley. However, Mr Cohen will have some input into discussions in Cabinet.'[28]

The suggestion that Scheyville be the chosen site for the airport inspired the creation of the Hawkesbury-Hills Protest Committee and in February 1984 its Heritage Subcommittee published an extensive discussion of the historical and heritage values of the Pitt Town (Scheyville) area. They concluded that:

> The Pitt Town/Scheyville/Oakville/Maraylya/Box Hill area is relatively unique. It is rare to find a site which contains a continuum of evidence of human occupation ranging from early Aboriginal culture through to

---

[26] Parliamentary News Release, 18 September 1984, 84/79
[27] Commonwealth, *Parliamentary Debates,* House of Representatives, 25 March 1985, p 806.
[28] *Hills and Riverstone Press* 22 February 1984. 5.

contemporary civilisation. It is not uncommon to find piecemeal evidence of such occupation, but it is indeed rare to find an area with evidence of ALL stages of that occupation.

As the Hawkesbury area is one of the first European settled regions on this continent, the Pitt Town region is even more important.

The siting of an international airport there would be a crime against the national heritage, and on heritage grounds alone, this proposal must be dropped immediately. Once this threat is removed, Government at a national, state and local level must be on constant guard to ensure that this most unusual region is maintained as part of the Nation's Heritage.[29]

A petition signed by thousands of concerned residents was delivered to the House of Representatives on Wednesday 29 February 1984. (House of Reps, P148).

The committee's main report cited noise pollution, adverse effects on students studying, house values, access problems, quality of life, the pollution of Longneck Lagoon, floods in the area, and the fact that locating an airport at Scheyville would be 'incompatible with many of the objectives of the Sydney Region Outline Plan Review, prepared by the NSW Planning and Environment Commission.'[30]

Although the protest committee played a part in having the Scheyville site rejected, a more compelling case came from the Hyde Johnson Report, quoted below. This report may not have been finalised until 1990, but it considered the

---

[29] Hawkesbury-Hills Airport Protest Committee Heritage Report on Sydney's Second International Airport February 1984, p 21.
[30] Hawkesbury-Hills Protest Committee Health and Environment Review. Report prepared by the Health and Environment Sub-committee of the Hawkesbury Hills Airport Protest Committee. 1984.

results of 'an extensive program of research and investigations carried out over the period 1976 to 1982.'[31]

'The temperature and sunlight intensities in the Hawkesbury Basin are greater than in the eastern parts of the Sydney Air-shed. This causes a given concentration of emissions to produce photochemical smog at a faster rate in the Hawkesbury Basin than elsewhere in the air-shed. Also, the Hawkesbury Basin can act as a trap for emissions from within the Basin and for polluted air transported in from the east.' The trends in ozone concentrations between 1976 and 1990 predicted by the IER [Integrated Exposure-Response] model calculations corresponds closely with those measured at the SPCC [State Pollution Control Commission] monitoring sites. In the main findings of their report, Hyde and Johnson state 'in the absence of further pollution controls, urban growth during the next twenty years is set to give rises of up to 50% in western Sydney ozone concentrations.'

Thus, the anticipated increase in urban growth was known to increase levels of smog and 'on current projections it is likely that haze levels in western Sydney will increase, degrading the visual amenity of the region.'

Thus it can be seen that, as well as the usual reasons trotted out to prevent a massive intervention such as the building of an international airport, the cost and the likely air pollution problems inherent in the Scheyville area were going to determine that the airport shouldn't be built there. Although it isn't part of a scientific paper, if the committee had asked the former Officer Cadets and their instructors of the Vietnam era they would have known that the area was subject to fog in winter months.

---

[31] Hyde, Robert & Johnson, Graham, Pilot Study: Evaluation of air quality issues for the development of Macarthur South and South Creek Valley regions of Sydney, Final Report. Prepared for the NSW Department of Planning, NSW State Pollution Control Commission and the Commonwealth Department of Transport and Communications, December 1990

Battle two: A maximum security prison

In July 1987 the state Minister for Corrective Services announced that the Scheyville site would become a maximum security prison, holding 400 prisoners. This would have created a complex larger than Parramatta Gaol. The only other maximum security prison built in twentieth-century New South Wales had been at Parklea in 1982. Parklea prison is in the suburb of Blacktown, approximately ten kilometres from Scheyville as the crow flies.

The concept of such a prison close to Sydney and convenient for family visits, while being located on a very large site which would act as a buffer zone between the local inhabitants and the prison was strongly maintained by the Department of Corrective Services and even more strenuously condemned by the Hawkesbury community.

The proposal was dropped.

Not before much politicking was played though, with both the Labor and Liberal parliamentarians accusing each other of hypocrisy and cynicism.

The reasoning behind the decision dated back to major riots at Bathurst Gaol in 1970 and 1974 that signalled the existence of serious deficiencies in the prison system. As a result of those riots and their aftermath the New South Wales Government established a Royal Commission with Mr Justice Nagle appointed as sole Commissioner. His report was tabled on 4 April 1978 with 252 recommendations for sweeping changes.[32] In March 1988 there were 4015 prisoners within the New South Wales prison system, which rose to 6063 in September 1991, an increase of fifty-one percent in just three years.[33]

Thus, there was a dramatic increase in crime and incarceration at the time Scheyville was considered as a prime site for a maximum-security prison. By 1991 the Dillwynia Women's Correctional Centre (200 places) and the John Morony

---

[32] NSW Corrective Services Website and The Australian Prisons Project UNSW 2010 Section 2 Major Themes by Decade – 1990s www.app.unsw.edu.au. Copyright 2010. Hardcopy printout made 2012.
[33] Ibid.

Correctional Centre, Windsor, with 300 inmates had opened, in addition to Parklea (893 inmates). All these facilities were within ten to fifteen kilometres of Scheyville. The Labor government of 1987 had also 'acquired a training college at Windsor. All staff now go through an extensive period of training.'[34]

At the time of the 1987 announcement the government claimed fifty-seven sites had been evaluated before selection, but Scheyville had only become available in recent days, suggesting a hasty decision on the part of the government. No wonder the residents who lived near the prison site protested strongly. Some Pitt Town residents, such as Mrs Purtell, were more in favour of the prison proposal than when the airport proposal was brought forward over a decade ago. 'but the western suburbs just seems to be a dumping ground. There was the airport proposal, we have the waste dump at Londonderry, and the worst railway system. Then there is the matter of sewerage, where is all the extra sewerage going, Long Neck Lagoon [now part of the National Park] is already polluted.'[35]

In October 1987, the Opposition Leader, Nick Greiner, in response to a question of whether he would proceed with a gaol at Scheyville, commented on talkback radio station 2BL: 'No, we would not. Presuming it hasn't gone too far. The government said it looked at a number of sites. Typically, it hasn't released those sites. There are many towns in New South Wales, not far from Sydney, which would welcome a gaol as a means of reviving the local economy. We do not see a need to concentrate all the gaols in western Sydney. No, we would not proceed with the Scheyville Gaol.'

In March 1988 the Liberals regained power in New South Wales under Greiner. Twelve months after Greiner made the aforementioned comments, Mr Gibson, the Labor Member for Londonderry, (the electorate next to Hawkesbury) was attacking the government over its decision to build a gaol at Daruk. As Gibson pointed out, 'Daruk is in the electorate of Londonderry. That is a little news for the Minister. The gaol site was changed from Scheyville to Daruk. As the crow flies,

---

[34] NSW *Parliamentary Debates,* Legislative Assembly, 23 November 1987, p 16953.
[35] *Windsor and Richmond Gazette* 29 July 1987 Mrs Purtell p 3.

that is a distance of about ten kilometres.' So, Gibson was reporting 'on one promise that the Government didn't break, and that was the promise not to build a prison at Scheyville.'[36] A change of government had brought about a change of prison location from a Liberal seat to a Labor seat, yet it was still in the Hawkesbury Valley.

Battle three: A second-generation Macquarie town

Only this time it would have been more like a modern-day shanty town!

In December 1989 Hawkesbury City Council resolved to prepare a Draft Environmental Plan to rezone land at Scheyville for conservation and urban purposes. Detailed discussions were held between the council, the Department of Planning, the Department of Housing and the water Board to review the allocation of Crown and state-owned land for housing and conservation uses; examine various environmental and conservation issues and consider the inclusion of Scheyville in the Urban Development Plan. Council prepared a preliminary draft Local Environmental Plan which then became the focus of a number of studies aimed at investigating various environmental, planning and infrastructure issues. These studies were carried out over a period of more than two years to confirm the suitability of the site for urban development.[37]

In February 1991, the government announced that it was 'responding to the ongoing problems with housing affordability and availability in the Sydney region,' and that it was continuing to implement strategies specifically designed to help home-seekers. 'This work is largely being pursued through making more land available and special programs to increase home ownership and public and private rental opportunities. In the medium term, the Government plans the release of nearly 150,000 residential land lots located in the Rouse Hill and South Creek

---

[36] NSW *Parliamentary Debates,* Legislative Assembly, 13 October 1988, pp. 2294 - 1997
[37] Hawkesbury City Council. *Scheyville Draft Local Environmental Plan: A New Generation Macquarie Town.* 1992. Foreword to the document.

sectors, West Menai, South Penrith, Scheyville and other areas already identified for urban development.'[38]

In a memorandum to all aldermen on the Hawkesbury Council, the council's General Manager wrote: 'Such land releases will be subject to extensive planning and environmental assessment procedures to ensure that residential development does not proceed at the expense of the environment.' The foregoing appears to have been deliberately inserted as a statement to appease the likely knockers of development of that scale in the west and north-west corners of Sydney.

Draft plans were unveiled at the Hawkesbury Library in early March 1992 of plans for a model village development. This new community of about 20,000 residents 'will feature innovations in town planning and water cycle management – but its residents will depend on Hawkesbury Hospital for major medical services and improved public transport to link them with other suburbs,' said the Council General Manager.[39]

Billed as the new-generation Macquarie town, Scheyville would have a high concentration of medium-density housing. It was planned to have 4800 dwellings occupying a residential area of 385 hectares, about 70 hectares of open space within the proposed urban area and approximately 360 hectares of land proposed to be zoned Environment Protection (Forest Conservation).[40]

In a memorandum dated 28 April 1992[41] to all Aldermen on the Hawkesbury Council, the Council's General Manager wrote: 'With Bligh Park approaching completion the Council in 1989 resolved to initiate the necessary procedures to have the investigations undertaken to ascertain the suitability of the [Scheyville] land for urban purposes. At the same time the State Government announced its plans for the area's urban development. The decisions were based

---

[38] NSW *Parliamentary Debates*, Legislative Council, 20 February 1991.
[39] *Penrith Press* 18 March 1992. p 10.
[40] Hawkesbury City Council, *Scheyville Draft Local Environmental Plan* 1992.
[41] Hawkesbury City Council. File: GT130/2PT7/GM738:clh. Memorandum to all Aldermen from Town Clerk/General Manager on the subject of Scheyville Urban Development Proposal-Summary. 28 April 1992.

on recognition of a need to accommodate Sydney's population growth which is expected to add another million people to the existing city by early next century. As with Bligh Park the area was proposed largely to provide for the first-home buyer. It should be noted such areas are limited in northern and north-western Sydney.'[42]

It should also be noted that in 2001 the Hawkesbury Gazette (1/8/2001) was to report:

There was controversy surrounding the expenditure of profits from the Bligh Park Development. According to Council's Corporate and Community Services Director, a profit of almost $20m was made on the development since the project began in 1984, with the majority of money spent after 1993. These profits repaid the loan, allowed $5m on the Hawkesbury Sports Stadium and Oasis Swimming centre and $4.6m towards redevelopment of the of the Hawkesbury Hospital site as a library and art gallery and extensions to the museum.

With a change in government (from Liberal) there was a change of priorities and no follow through for the Three Towns Sewerage Treatment Plant Scheme. This was meant to be a dollar-for-dollar funding arrangement with the State Government.

The State Government has indicated its commitment to urban consolidation and has introduced a number of far-reaching measures to pursue this policy. The Department of Housing has indicated that urban consolidation will at best provide only a partial answer to the problem of the city's expansion, and that a substantial part of the foreseeable population growth will need to be accommodated in new urban areas, located on the fringe of the metropolis. ... Scheyville is envisaged as one of those areas. It will be carefully pre-planned and systematically developed to form a self-contained residential community, with its own shopping, community and recreational facilities, as well as primary schools and a high school, to meet the needs of the local community.

---

[42] *Penrith Press.* op. cit.

He also claimed that 'as the land is largely held in one ownership, it can be developed more economically and will therefore provide more affordable home sites than other release areas proposed within the North West Sector and elsewhere.' He later explained that 'the cost of a water reuse solution would cost approximately double that of simply irrigating open spaces and parks with reclaimed water' and 'would add to the cost of housing'.

In commenting on The Natural Habitat Study the General Manager said, 'the inclusion of wetlands and landscaping as part of the development will supplement and increase the diversity of habitat for birds.' The area available would not be increased so there was little likelihood of increasing the diversity of habitat.

The Council General Manager wanted to place 20,000 extra human beings in the area, many of whom would have wanted to have cats and dogs, yet he listed as one of the main conservation actions to be 'measures should be taken to protect native fauna from domestic animals'. In the preceding paragraph he mentioned that 'native mammal fauna is severely degraded throughout the surrounding forested and cleared areas, due to the existence of many exotic species including grazing animals, rabbits, foxes, cats and dogs'.

In the social plan it is recognised that a primary school, childcare services and a community worker would be needed but apart from some jobs within the 6000 square metres of retail floor space there was no mention of other employment opportunities.

He listed the studies that had been undertaken by the Department of Housing, Sydney Water Board, the Environmental Protection Authority and a number of consultants. Interestingly he stated that, 'as the studies have been received, they have been placed in the Library for public access and representatives of the action group, Concerned Residents Against Development of Longneck Lagoon Environs (CRADLE) advised. Later in the year, when the Local Environmental Plan went on display and only one copy was available for view and use in the Library, members of CRADLE and other members of the public complained of only having access to the documents for a period of four weeks (from 17 August to 18 September 1992)!

One of the comprehensive rebuttals of the proposal came from Dr David Hughes, President of CHANGE (Coalition of Hawkesbury and Nepean Groups for the Environment). Some salient points he made in his submission are paraphrased below, and include:

> This site has a greater degree of isolation than any yet developed within the Sydney region'. While recognising that 'the site is one of the few remaining large parcels of State-owned land in the Hawkesbury Basin that might be suitable for public housing, yet its almost total isolation from any major public transport or employment infrastructure sets the scene for the creation of another Mt Druitt or Green Valley. Unlike Mt Druitt, there is no rail nearby and unlike Green Valley, employment opportunities are at a great remove from its intended inhabitants. Similar problems existed, and have been commented upon in interviews for this project by post–World War Two migrants who were housed at Scheyville from 1949–1964.[43]

Employment opportunities were constrained by the fact that nearest major centres were Blacktown, 25 kilometres away, and Parramatta, 30 kilometres away, yet to reach these centres would entail a minimum twelve-kilometre bus trip and then travel via a single-track railway from Riverstone. It was speculated that the towns of Windsor and Richmond couldn't be expected to provide any more than a minor source of work. To cope, families would be obliged to own at least two motor vehicles or depend on tenuous public transport links. There was no guarantee that the bus company which had indicated its willingness to the Council General Manager to provide services to the area would do so.

---

[43] Hughes, Dr David. His research paper on the proposed Scheyville Housing Estate to the Coalition of Hawkesbury and Nepean Groups for the Environment. (CHANGE)

Roads in the area are narrow and often subject to flooding. Flooding in some years happened a few times and cut access to Windsor and Richmond for five days at a time. That meant that access to the nearest hospital at Windsor and urban centres would be cut for 20,000 people. The next nearest hospital is Blacktown which was experiencing public outcry over its lack of resources and Westmead Hospital is further away than the suburb of Mona Vale is from Cremorne. Lack of accessible adequate hospital facilities placed a question mark over the project.

New residents would experience inconvenience – it was proposed that demountable classrooms would be placed in the grounds of the nearest primary school, Glossodia, until numbers could justify the building of a primary school. The nearest high school was at Windsor and direct access during flooding would be impossible. The nearest tertiary facility is the University of Western Sydney at Richmond. Again, it would be inaccessible during flooding and the nearest TAFE facilities were at Parramatta and Blacktown which means a few hours travel a day for the youth of Scheyville."

Air pollution studies by the CSIRO and the Hyde-Johnson report into air pollution for the Western Sydney Basin (cited above) indicated that the final resting point of nearly all of Sydney's air pollution is in this very part of the Basin. As a result, heavy fogs are a regular feature adding to transport problems. Add the cars of the 20,000 inhabitants and those of the soon-to-be-developed North-West Sector near Rouse Hill and the region's atmospheric and transport loads would further increase. Remember, this site made the short list with Badgery's Creek as the site for Sydney's next major airport.

The site is one of the few remaining large areas of regenerating native forest in the Hawkesbury basin still in public hands. One species of plant (*Acacia pubescens*), classified as endangered and two others (*Dillwynia tenuifolia and Pultenaea parviflora*) classed as vulnerable were found in the natural habitat study to be in areas to be protected.

There were also economic and political issues. The Hawkesbury Council and the Department of Housing were the two entities wanting to develop the site and in the short term would make money. However, road, social service, hospital and educational infrastructure costs would have to be subsidised by other taxpayers. Studies at the UNSW[44] (according to Dr Hughes) indicated that the hidden public subsidisation of developments in isolated areas with the consequent extra costs, amounted to between $50,000 and $70,000 per home site. That equated to at least $240 million. Seventeen years later, the Planning Minister Kristina Keneally said that 'infrastructure costs of more than $100,000 per lot for 62,000 lots in the Macarthur South subdivision in Sydney's south-west were prohibitive, and that the distance from Sydney and lack of public transport went against the project.'[45]

At approximately the same time as the Scheyville proposal was being opened up for comment, the 'Sydney into its Third Century Metropolitan Strategy', and the 'Regional Environmental Plan No.20' were announced as being under review. The Hyde-Johnson Report commissioned by the Department of Planning, the State Pollution Commission and Commonwealth Department of Transport cast serious doubts upon further development in the Hawkesbury until comprehensive air pollution monitoring data could be made available to assist with development and housing decisions.

In his conclusion, Hughes suggested that the government of the day wanted to provide cheap homes for first-home buyers and was willing to develop one of the last remnant forest areas in public hands on the Cumberland Plain. Thousands of poor families were to be housed in an isolated area with limited access to employment, inadequate hospital and educational facilities and worsening air pollution. The region's existing unemployed youth and the teenagers

---

[44] Hughes, Dr David. Referring to Murphy PA. of the School of Town Planning UNSW 'Immigration and the Management of Australian Cities: The Case of Sydney'. *Urban Studies*. 1993;30(9):1501-1519. doi:10.1080/00420989320081471
[45] SMH article on 23/7/2009 Comment from Kristina Keneally, NSW Planning Minister 2009 to Matthew Moore.

who would come to the area would be condemned to long-term unemployment with little chance of tertiary training close by.

Significant wetlands could be destroyed, the migration of internationally protected bird species be interfered with and an already stressed Hawkesbury River could potentially be worse off in terms of flooding and pollution. He notes that in the original Metropolitan Strategy the Scheyville area was specifically excluded from the North-West Sector proposals that now saw the imminent commencement of the Rouse Hill Development.

'Surely', he stated, 'these major development proposals should at least be deferred until these reviews are completed and until the air and water quality data, and the questions of employment and social infrastructure have been resolved.'

That is what happened. However, it took more than a submission from Hughes. The cause was helped by CRADLE activists.

At this early stage of studies into the development, the NPWS and CHANGE were on the front page of the paper commenting on the first of the reports on the development. Already there was a call to ban domestic cats, remove cattle from the area and questions about water quality controls.[46]

Interestingly, the same paper contained a story on land being cleared for the new John Morony Correctional Centre at Bligh Park. That 250-cell maximum security prison was built in the same general area as Scheyville. Three years earlier there had been plans to build a 400-cell prison at Scheyville.

CRADLE was formed when Scheyville land was committed to housing. CRADLE conducted an extensive letterbox drop, encouraging the community to rally against the development. The group predicted destruction of the natural environment and was cynical about results of air and water pollution studies, claiming 'the results would be biased because they are produced by consultants employed by the people who want the area developed – they will want to please,' Ms Daly, a spokesperson, said. They were joined in their opposition to the proposal by the NPWS who commented on the fact that a large block of box ironbark forest

---

[46] 'Scheyville habitat under scrutiny', *Hawkesbury Gazette,* 11 July 1990

would be cleared for the development and that domestic pets attached to the dwellings would have a huge impact on the native fauna in the area. 'The Dharug Local Aboriginal Land Council opposed the use of Longneck Creek as a water retention basin and demanded all Aboriginal sites in the area be protected.'[47]

Opponents commented that the development contradicted the Government's urban consolidation policies by developing the outer suburbs. Although the Hawkesbury Mayor said that a longer period of public consultation would be considered, it was stated that even if Hawkesbury voted against rezoning the State Government could press ahead with the development under the Environment and Planning Assessment Act. Critics also pointed out that both the consent authority, the Planning Department and the developer, the Department of Housing, came under the same Minister, Mr Webster, as did the Water Board, which all added up to a smoother decision-making process. A spokesman for the Minister said that 'This was done purposefully to facilitate a sensible approach to the long-term housing and planning needs for Sydney.'[48]

An article in the Hills News on 1 September 1992 suggested there would be a good roll-up to a Council meeting that night, and that the Council General Manager was surprised at the strength of opposition from Baulkham Hills Shire residents. Comparing the Scheyville development 'to house size 16,000 people as minimal compared to the 200,000 expected in the North-West sector. ... It is aimed at first-home buyers who aren't catered for in the Rouse Hill development where land prices are likely to be at least $100,000 whereas house and land prices at Scheyville would be an affordable $120,000.'[49]

An article by Baulkham Hills Council Mayor Peggy Womersley appeared in the Hills News stating that council shared the concerns of Maraylya and adjoining districts residents.[50]

---

[47] *Penrith Press* 25 August 1992
[48] Southam, Kate 'Group to block major housing development' *Northern Herald.* 27 August 1992
[49] 'Scheyville protest gathers force' *Hills News,* 1 September 1992 p 4.
[50] *Hills News* 8 September 1992

Articles in the Penrith Press and Hills Shire Times on 8 September commented on meetings the previous week attended by more than 500 Hills and Hawkesbury residents and a visit by Hawkesbury Council to Baulkham Hills Council to discuss the development. One Baulkham Hills Councillor even commented that he 'was very unimpressed with their lack of knowledge with what they were doing.' By now the Hawkesbury Mayor, Wendy Sledge commented to Penrith Press that the development 'would be delayed necessarily while arguments against it were investigated.'[51]

Baulkham Hills Council aldermen also commented against the proposal; Councillor Ron Gibbs raised concerns about the traffic implications and the fact that 'it's very isolated and the area is cut off by floods.'[52]

The deadline for public input into the controversial scheme was extended following strong pressure from local residents. More public comment on the proposed development was to be sought. Final vote was twelve to nil in favour of extending the deadline.[53]

The NPWS also reported in the Sydney Morning Herald that it had been campaigning since 1967 for the area to be a nature reserve. Its submission said: 'in all, 99 terrestrial and 42 wetland species of birds have been recorded within the Longneck Lagoon Field Studies Centre. An additional 68 species are reported for the general area of Scheyville. This is a high diversity for the Sydney Region.' The council's LEP [Local Environment Plan] said that bird habitat diversity will be ensured, but according to environmentalists 'we've already got a Hawkesbury River crisis situation and this – the impact of 20,000 people on top of that – will only add to the problem.'[54]

The implications of the development: lack of air pollution studies, social problems as allegedly existed at the Bligh Park development, lack of public transport, lack of jobs and the lack of suitable roads, all went against every

---

[51] *Penrith Press* and *Hills Shire Times* 8 September 1992
[52] *Hills Shire Times* 9 September 1992
[53] *Hawkesbury Gazette* 16 September 1992
[54] *Sydney Morning Herald* 12 October 1992

government policy on urban consolidation. These were cited by, and reiterated by CRADLE and CHANGE.[55]

Draft land assessment no 159 in October 1992 [56]

Under the NSW Crown Lands Act 1989 and Crown Lands Regulations 1990, the proper assessment of Crown Lands is carried out prior to the land being reserved or dedicated for a public purpose or disposed of by way of sale, lease or licence. The aim is to identify suitable land uses and provide a basis for the rational land use allocation of Crown land.

This was carried out on the 200 hectares within the catchment area of Longneck Lagoon. 'The objectives of the zoning are to protect and preserve remnant stands of Cumberland forest and to prohibit development that may damage or destroy significant portions of this forest.' The conservation values of the Longneck Lagoon catchment were first brought to the attention of the NPWS in 1973. The area was recognised as having uncommon vegetation assemblages as well as being an important faunal habitat within the context of the Sydney region. The Sydney Region North-West Sector Regional Environmental Study (1984) identified the largely undisturbed vegetation within the study area as one of the best two remaining examples of this complex in the Sydney region and was worthy of conserving. A value was placed on the vegetation in the vicinity of Longneck Lagoon by Benson and McDougall (1991) and Benson and Howell (1990) as important areas of grey box woodland; its value for catchment protection and it was seen as one of the most important examples of Cumberland vegetation. A subcommittee of the Heritage Council of NSW in recommending that the area be listed under the National Estate Register was of the opinion that the area contains vegetation that is significant to the state.

This study reported that urban areas have a higher rate of run-off due to large areas of impervious material. This urban run-off contains large quantities of

---

[55] *The Gazette (Hawkesbury Windsor)* 28 October 1992
[56] Land Assessment No. 159 Reference: MN89H216 dated October 1992 prepared by Sydney District Office of the then Department of Conservation and Land Management.

suspended solids, nutrients and oxygen depleting substances which can place a considerable pollution loading on the creek systems. It also noted that the Longneck Lagoon drainage catchment as being sensitive to any changes in land use in the Sydney Region North-West Sector Regional Environmental Study (1984 Dept of Environment and Planning). The study area fell within the catchment of Longneck Lagoon. The lagoon is regarded as a valuable resource in terms of nature conservation and education.

The study noted that the majority of the catchment was undeveloped and therefore expected to contribute little to problems of urban stormwater and sewerage run-off in its present state. However, it also reported that 'a site appropriated for future housing to the south of the study area could create potential pressures in the upper catchment. The lagoon's future viability would need to be studied in greater detail if parts of its catchment were to be further developed. Soils within drainage depressions have been identified as being prone to gullying if an increase in run-off developed (Logan and Luscombe 1984) with a resultant increased deposition of sediment in the lagoon.'

The above parts of the report meant that more thought had to be put into the Local Environment Plan. The findings are best summed up by the statement in the background to this report that paraphrased, states that the working party convened in 1990 by the Cabinet Committee on Urban Development to consider the possible allocation of land between housing and conservation recognised that the greater the area allocated for housing, the more pressure that would be exerted on any land set aside for conservation.

Consultants to the council, Gutteridge, Haskins and Davey said, 'we hope to educate residents so they don't dump grass clippings in drains or use excessive amounts of detergents. ... We intend to reduce the export of effluent – that is, sewage will be treated and reused to irrigate open spaces or pumped back to houses for use in flushing toilets or on gardens.' It was stated that arterial roads leading to

Scheyville, including Pitt Town Road and Boundary Road, would need upgrading.[57]

In the March 1992 'Summary of Findings – Water Cycle Management Studies' by Gutteridge, Haskins and Davey, it stated 'that the recommended proposals outlined in the studies could become, if not the standard for the future, at least a preferred and possible alternative for the resolution of problems facing further urban expansion in the Sydney Region.' The opening paragraph of the report states that 'a large part of the five-hundred hectare area drains to the environmentally sensitive Longneck Lagoon, and thence on to the Hawkesbury River which is itself already under some stress from point source and diffused pollution from agricultural and urban activities and development. Studies outlined in this and companion reports have confirmed that urban residential development at Scheyville can be achieved without adverse impact.'

To maintain the existing water cycle balance in the Scheyville catchment and minimise environmental impacts a framework of management of the water cycle of Scheyville was recommended. This recommended scheme involved treating sewage to a very high standard and re-using all of it in years of up to average rainfall, so that it wouldn't have any impact on catchment waterways. Effluent was to be reused totally, either by irrigating parks and open spaces or by first satisfying residential garden and toilet flush needs and then using the balance on open spaces. The latter would be costlier in terms of communal piping and reticulation systems and additional internal house and garden plumbing. Other claims made in the Management Framework were that: provision of raw sewage overflow storage meant that in almost all individual wet weather events there would be no pollutant discharge by overflow, and only in wetter-than-average years (less than fifty per cent) would small amounts of highly treated surplus effluent require disposal by onward discharge to catchment waterways; the Biological Sewage Treatment Plant would be of a superior standard, sited to give adequate buffer space and components to eliminate any release of odours. It was

---

[57] *Penrith Press* 18 March 1992 p. 10

also claimed that during the wetter-than-average years, the small surpluses of unused effluent would be released during periods of high run-off for mixing with stormwater discharges. 'On the basis of limited data currently available, these discharges would not worsen existing quality levels in Longneck Lagoon if released down Longneck Creek. Should further and better data indicate an adverse impact on the Lagoon, then the intermittent small discharges could be directed to the Hawkesbury River with no adverse impact.'

The consultants then covered themselves by stating that 'it is not possible to propose a system which will prevent the export of pollutants and nutrients during all significant stormwater run-off events. During high flow events in Longneck Creek the majority of the material exported from the development catchment would traverse Longneck Lagoon with minimal detention time and then pass on to the Hawkesbury River.' So, the consultants state in the opening paragraph that the Hawkesbury River is already under stress, and given that Scheyville is cut off by floods frequently (in years of greater than average rainfall), their report emphasises 'minimal' impact: 'the long-term annual effect on the Hawkesbury River, that complete mixing of any discharge from Longneck Creek and the Hawkesbury River would occur within a distance of two km and that at this distance the water quality would not be detectably changed'. The studies highlighted the need for further assessment of issues including ownership, operation and management of the effluent disposal system, detailed ongoing management of treatment wetlands and the need for public education and involvement with adoption of new preferred water management systems. In March 1992 there were obvious issues that still needed addressing.

This report did receive attention in 1997, when the CSIRO produced a report for the Council of Governments National Water Reform Task Force and Sustainable Land and Water Resources Management Committee as part of the move to clean up the Hawkesbury-Nepean catchment. The CSIRO said, 'housing developments at Scheyville will reuse effluents through irrigation of open space.

This becomes an alternative disposal option to otherwise discharging effluent into Longneck Lagoon and the Hawkesbury River.'[58]

The neighbouring municipality of Baulkham Hills Council raised concerns that the same environmental reviews being taken in respect of a development at Rouse Hill should be applied to the Scheyville development, following a letter from New South Wales Planning Minister Robert Webster.[59]

Another article concentrated on the background of the CRADLE protesters who included nurses, a marine engineer, the wife of a sewerage treatment plant engineer, self-employed businessmen, and trained welfare and employment counsellors, and painted them as being 'family activists'.[60]

Hawkesbury Mayor, Alderman Sledge, announced to a public meeting of 160 residents that work would stop on the Scheyville development and push for a development at Vineyard. She explained that the turnaround was because of reviews of the Metropolitan Strategy for Sydney and North-West Sector to be under taken in the following twelve months. She explained, 'rushing into the Scheyville development was premature in light of the strategy reviews. ... The only way the state government could provide housing at Scheyville would be by changing its Regional Environmental Plan. Mayor Sledge said the government would only do this if it felt it was significant for the whole of New South Wales.' Residents unanimously resolved at the meeting to establish a catchment management council for Scheyville and Longneck Lagoon, and call for a review of the Rouse Hill development.[61]

Residents celebrated as the Hawkesbury aldermen unanimously supported a report recommending council 'not rush into the Scheyville proposal'. Instead it would 'liaise with the Department of Planning regarding Scheyville's relationship

---

[58] CSIRO Land and Water Research Position Paper 1 1997, Appendices P.35
[59] *Hawkesbury Shire Times* 20 October 1992
[60] *Hawkesbury Gazette* 28 October 1992
[61] *Hawkesbury Gazette* 18 November 1992

to the Metropolitan Strategy, as well as undertaking more research into the environmental impacts of the Scheyville proposal.'[62]

Battle four: A giant tip!

In 1990 plans for the biggest rubbish tip in the southern hemisphere created a nightmare for the Greiner Liberal Government. Scheyville and Maroota, both sites in Liberal MP Kevin Rozzoli's Hawkesbury electorate, were first and second choices. This was after eight years of investigation by the Waste Management Authority. Once again strong public protest protected the site and in 1991 the third choice, Londonderry, in one of the safest Labor seats, was nominated to bear another 'undesirable' element. As there was a likelihood of electoral boundaries being re-drawn, and an upcoming election, Kevin Rozzoli (Hawkesbury) and Anne Cohen (Minchinbury) broke ranks to oppose the Londonderry tip in March 1991.

In March 1991 the government decided not to establish any new landfills with the responsibility for establishing new landfill sites passing to local government and the private sector. The Waste Management Authority was abolished when the Protection of the Environment Administration Act, 1991, reconstituted the Authority as the 'Waste Recycling and Processing Service'. The regulatory and licensing functions of the Authority were transferred to the newly established Environment Protection Authority and the operational side established as a Government Trading Enterprise to be conducted under the name Waste Service New South Wales. These arrangements became effective 1 March 1992.[63]

Scheyville was lucky compared to Penrith in the NIMBY stakes, as that city now had a liquid toxic waste dump and two gaols, with a third to be built at Berkshire Park. In the context of regionalism, residents of Western Sydney, including the Liberal members, were feeling that their backyard was getting more than its fair share of 'undesirable elements'.

---

[62] *Hills Shire Times*. 17 November 1992. P 3
[63] NSW State Records Agency 1147 file on The Metropolitan Waste Disposal Authority (1971-1990) and Waste Management Authority (1990-1992)

On 19 March 1992, Mr Downy (Liberal MLA, Sutherland) successfully moved a motion 'that this House notes, as a matter of public importance, the broad community debate on the future of waste minimisation, recycling and disposal and calls upon the Government to agree to establish a select committee into long-term waste strategies to be dealt with in the proposed Government policy paper on the waste stream.[64]

Thus, Scheyville and Londonderry were safe again – for the moment!

Vigilance needs to be ongoing! Some concluding thoughts

It appears that in a small sense, one of Rex Stubbs' ideas has come to fruition, that is, that Scheyville be converted into a museum complex.[65] Stubbs was a local doctor, Mayor of the Hawkesbury, and staunch supporter of preserving the Scheyville site. He claimed that the museum would benefit tourism, could be utilised by archaeology students, and that the historic buildings be utilised for the exhibits.

Under the Park Conservation Plan a number of buildings have been conserved and restored. These give an insight into what the buildings were like particularly in the migrant and OTU eras. Up till the early 1990s, the National Parks Department, which became the Department of the Environment and Conservation was only responsible for the natural environment. Then came the Conservation Plan. The draft plan outlines proposals for the management proposals of native plants and animals, Aboriginal and historic heritage, introduced species and recreational use.

Yet vigilance must be maintained. In June 2018 a public meeting was called by Oakville residents to express concerns over the implications of the Outer Sydney Orbital Transport Corridor Draft Strategic Environmental Assessment. This assessment affects suburbs surrounding Scheyville.

---

[64] New South Wales *Parliamentary Debates,* Legislative Assembly, 19 March 1992 pp. 1461 – 1473
[65] *Windsor and Richmond Gazette*, 13 July 1983

Residents feared the plan meant those properties not directly consumed by the Outer Sydney Orbital road would instead be swallowed up for industrial use.

One resident, Judy Ryan, reported that 'given the proximity of their proposed industrial zone to Scheyville National Park could be an environmental disaster. Not just for Oakville but the whole of the Hawkesbury.' Councillor Nathan Zamprogno posted on social media that residents had reported receiving speculative letters from developers 'asking if they can buy your land and "land bank" it'.[66]

There has been approval for 895 residential lots in Pitt Town and the North-West growth precinct has finally reached the Hawkesbury local government area. As Zamprogno stated in 2017, the growth marches towards rural holdings in Pitt Town, Oakville and Maraylya from both sides. Thus, there is a slow erosion of the rural amenity of the district.[67] A whole separate study is warranted into these threats to the National Park.

Scheyville has culturally historic values that reflect the development of the colony of New South Wales and later the nation. The site contains the most extensive remnant vegetation on the Cumberland Plain and provides endangered birdlife and vegetation with habitat. Approximately thirty per cent of the National Park and the majority of Pitt Town Nature Reserve are still covered with introduced and native grasses.

The Conservation Plan identified a number of structures and sites as being of considerable to high significance and that should be retained as archaeological sites relating to the use of the area prior to 1929, including the twin silos from the Dreadnought era; the Georgian revival–style masonry buildings and quadrangle; the palm trees and avenue of pine trees to and around the buildings, which may have been part of the architect's design for the buildings; the two large SAAR huts used during the migrant period; the 1929 electrical substation; and the small water

---

[66] Pollard, Krystyna *Hawkesbury Gazette* 7 June 2018
[67] Stubbs, Rex and Linda. A History of Scheyville. 1983. P35-36. Footnote added by Councillor Nathan Zamprogno January 2017.

storage tank built in 1911. Gates erected during the OTU period remain as evidence of the association of the site with the Vietnam War.

The New South Wales Department of the Environment has taken up the challenge of conserving all the values, including cultural heritage as well as natural heritage. They have provided informal recreational opportunities within the Park, are protecting Longneck Lagoon and Pitt Town Lagoon as habitat for migratory birds and aiming 'to create a lively, interesting and educational place that conserves and promotes the site's cultural and natural values'. They also wish to develop it as a 'key regional destination for cultural tourism and education in conjunction with other regional cultural organisations such as the Historic Houses Trust, the Powerhouse Museum and the Migration Heritage Centre.'[68]

Long live the National Park!

The first Silos

---

[68] *Scheyville National Park Conservation Management Plan,* Department of Environment and Climate Change, 2009.

Afterword

Of all Australian National Parks Scheyville must have the most diverse history. Located on the outskirts of Sydney the site was once part of Governor Macquarie's townships along the Hawkesbury. From the 1890s Scheyville became a training site for the unemployed, British migrant youth and then the Australian military. Roger Donnelly covers all these phases in detail examining the biography of the place as well as biographies of those who have influenced and occupied the site. The result is an understanding of the Australian experience in a semi-rural environment.

EMERITUS PROFESSOR GEOFFREY SHERINGTON
THE UNIVERSITY OF SYDNEY

References

Trove

'Concert at Pitt-Town.' *Windsor and Richmond Gazette (NSW: 1888–1961)* 28 November 1891: 5. http://nla.gov.au/nla.news-article72541562

'Pitt Town.' *Windsor and Richmond Gazette* (NSW: 1888–1961) 22 April 1893: 10. http://nla.gov.au/nla.news-article72546641

'The Village Settlements.' *Windsor and Richmond Gazette* (NSW: 1888–1961) 30 September 1893: 5. http://nla.gov.au/nla.news-article72543935

'Notes.' *Windsor and Richmond Gazette* (NSW: 1888–1961) 30 September 1893: 5. http://nla.gov.au/nla.news-article72543933

'The Village Settlements.' *Windsor and Richmond Gazette* (NSW: 1888–1961) 27 January 1894: 5. http://nla.gov.au/nla.news-article66442983

'Overdue Payments on Conditional Purchases.' *New South Wales Government Gazette* (Sydney, NSW: 1832–1900) 11 May 1894: 3094. http://nla.gov.au/nla.news-article222337570

'The Village Settlements.' *Windsor and Richmond Gazette* (NSW: 1888–1961) 9 June 1894: 10. http://nla.gov.au/nla.news-article66444005

'Picnic at Pitt Town Settlement.' *Windsor and Richmond Gazette* (NSW: 1888–1961) 30 June 1894: 6. http://nla.gov.au/nla.news-article66444129

'News in Brief.' *Windsor and Richmond Gazette* (NSW: 1888–1961) 10 November 1894: 3. http://nla.gov.au/nla.news-article66445202

'The Sydney Morning Herald.' *The Sydney Morning Herald* (NSW: 1842–1954) 14 February 1895: 4. http://nla.gov.au/nla.news-article14005268

'The Sydney Morning Herald.' *The Sydney Morning Herald* (NSW: 1842–1954) 16 February 1895: 8. http://nla.gov.au/nla.news-article14005680

'The Village Settlement Fiasco.' *The Daily Telegraph* (Sydney, NSW: 1883–1930) 22 February 1895: 4. http://nla.gov.au/nla.news-article236003226

'Pitt Town Settlement.' *Windsor and Richmond Gazette* (NSW: 1888–1961) 13 June 1896: 7. http://nla.gov.au/nla.news-article72548880

'A Government Labour Experiment.' *Australian Town and Country Journal* (Sydney, NSW: 1870–1907) 21 June 1902: 31. http://nla.gov.au/nla.news-article71525327

'Appeal to Country.' *The Sydney Morning Herald* (NSW: 1842–1954) 2 April 1909: 7. http://nla.gov.au/nla.news-article15047941

'Athletic Display.' *The Sydney Morning Herald* (NSW: 1842–1954) 14 April 1909: 9. http://nla.gov.au/nla.news-article15050672

'Hawkesbury 'Old Boys.'' *The Sydney Morning Herald* (NSW: 1842–1954) 19 April 1909: 7. http://nla.gov.au/nla.news-article15051793

'The Proceedings.' *The Sydney Morning Herald* (NSW: 1842–1954) 27 May 1909: 8. http://nla.gov.au/nla.news-article15061202

'Country Meetings.' *The Sydney Morning Herald* (NSW: 1842–1954) 26 April 1909: 7. http://nla.gov.au/nla.news-article15053261

'Sporting the Turf.' *The Sydney Morning Herald* (NSW: 1842–1954) 17 May 1909: 10. http://nla.gov.au/nla.news-article15058637

'Northern Suburbs.' *The Sydney Morning Herald* (NSW: 1842–1954) 25 May 1909: 7. http://nla.gov.au/nla.news-article15060641

'The Proceedings.' *The Sydney Morning Herald* (NSW: 1842–1954) 27 May 1909: 8. http://nla.gov.au/nla.news-article15061202

'Shire Councils.' *The Sydney Morning Herald* (NSW: 1842–1954) 28 May 1909: 10. http://nla.gov.au/nla.news-article15061688

'Farm Training for City Lads.' *Singleton Argus* (NSW: 1880–1954) 26 March 1910: 1. http://nla.gov.au/nla.news-article76912323

'Women Farmers.' *The Sydney Morning Herald* (NSW: 1842–1954) 25 August 1915: 5. http://nla.gov.au/nla.news-article15609411

'Agricultural Training for Women.' *The Daily Telegraph* (Sydney, NSW: 1883–1930) 1 September 1915: 6. http://nla.gov.au/nla.news-article239124035

'Week to Week' *Windsor and Richmond Gazette* (NSW: 1888–1961) 31 December 1915: 5. http://nla.gov.au/nla.news-article85859152

'The Dreadnought Farms' *Windsor and Richmond Gazette* (NSW: 1888–1961) 25 February 1916: 1. http://nla.gov.au/nla.news-article85881887

'Week to Week' *Windsor and Richmond Gazette* (NSW: 1888–1961) 10 March 1916: 3. http://nla.gov.au/nla.news-page8974130

'Female Farmers' *Windsor and Richmond Gazette* (NSW: 1888–1961) 12 January 1917: 10. http://nla.gov.au/nla.news-article85883054

'Farming for Women' *Windsor and Richmond Gazette* (NSW: 1888–1961) 2 March 1917: 1. http://nla.gov.au/nla.news-article85879143

'Scheyville Training Farm' *Windsor and Richmond Gazette* (NSW: 1888–1961) 29 June 1917: 8. http://nla.gov.au/nla.news-article85879205

'Week to Week' *Windsor and Richmond Gazette* (NSW: 1888–1961) 6 July 1917: 4. http://nla.gov.au/nla.news-article85879329

'Women Farmers.' *The Sydney Morning Herald* (NSW: 1842–1954) 9 July 1917: 5. http://nla.gov.au/nla.news-article15759272

'Week to Week' *Windsor and Richmond Gazette* (NSW: 1888–1961) 20 July 1917: 4. http://nla.gov.au/nla.news-article85882827

'Week to Week' *Windsor and Richmond Gazette* (NSW: 1888–1961) 6 July 1917: 4. http://nla.gov.au/nla.news-article85879329

'Week to Week' *Windsor and Richmond Gazette* (NSW: 1888–1961) 5 October 1917: 4. http://nla.gov.au/nla.news-article85882181

'Women Farmers' *Windsor and Richmond Gazette* (NSW: 1888–1961) 8 October 1920: 9. http://nla.gov.au/nla.news-article85877375

'Women Farmers' *Windsor and Richmond Gazette* (NSW: 1888–1961) 12 November 1920: 5. http://nla.gov.au/nla.news-article85874325

'Women Farmers' *Windsor and Richmond Gazette* (NSW: 1888–1961) 26 November 1920: 2. http://nla.gov.au/nla.news-article85876001

'Boy's Body Recovered.' *The Sydney Morning Herald* (NSW: 1842–1954) 2 December 1925: 16. http://nla.gov.au/nla.news-article16258312

'A Review' *Windsor and Richmond Gazette* (NSW: 1888–1961) 13 May 1927: 6. http://nla.gov.au/nla.news-article85951078

'Drowned in River.' *The Sydney Morning Herald* (NSW: 1842–1954) 27 March 1928: 12. http://nla.gov.au/nla.news-article16452317

'A Review' *Windsor and Richmond Gazette* (NSW: 1888–1961) 4 May 1928: 12. http://nla.gov.au/nla.news-article85928708

'Hawkesbury Jubilee Show.' *The Sydney Morning Herald* (NSW: 1842–1954) 9 May 1930: 9. http://nla.gov.au/nla.news-article16679985

'Farm Training.' *The Sydney Morning Herald* (NSW: 1842–1954) 16 October 1930: 12. http://nla.gov.au/nla.news-article16723008

'Windsor Council' *Windsor and Richmond Gazette* (NSW: 1888–1961) 26 December 1930: 7. http://nla.gov.au/nla.news-article85887809

'Blacktown Show' *Windsor and Richmond Gazette* (NSW: 1888 - 1961) 6 March 1931: 8. http://nla.gov.au/nla.news-article85884976

'Wood Week' *Windsor and Richmond Gazette* (NSW: 1888–1961) 5 June 1931: 10. http://nla.gov.au/nla.news-article85887083

'Football Notes' *Windsor and Richmond Gazette* (NSW: 1888–1961) 17 July 1931: 12. http://nla.gov.au/nla.news-article85886329

'Football Notes' *Windsor and Richmond Gazette* (NSW: 1888–1961) 14 August 1931: 13. http://nla.gov.au/nla.news-article85886040

'Week To Week' *Windsor and Richmond Gazette* (NSW: 1888–1961) 13 May 1932: 4. http://nla.gov.au/nla.news-article86057206

'Advertising' *Windsor and Richmond Gazette* (NSW: 1888–1961) 13 May 1932: 9. http://nla.gov.au/nla.news-article86057248

'Unemployed Boys.' *The Sydney Morning Herald* (NSW: 1842–1954) 10 June 1932: 13. http://nla.gov.au/nla.news-article16889844

'Scheyville Training Farm' *Windsor and Richmond Gazette* (NSW: 1888–1961) 8 July 1932: 12. http://nla.gov.au/nla.news-article86051469

'Employment.' *The Sydney Morning Herald* (NSW: 1842–1954) 15 July 1932: 12. http://nla.gov.au/nla.news-article16898804

'Stud Jerseys' *Windsor and Richmond Gazette* (NSW: 1888–1961) 22 July 1932: 2. http://nla.gov.au/nla.news-article86057715

'Personal' *Windsor and Richmond Gazette* (NSW: 1888–1961) 22 July 1932: 4. http://nla.gov.au/nla.news-article86057714

'Efforts Justified' *Windsor and Richmond Gazette* (NSW: 1888–1961) 5 August 1932: 1. http://nla.gov.au/nla.news-article86057439

'Week To Week' *Windsor and Richmond Gazette* (NSW: 1888–1961) 19 August 1932: 4. http://nla.gov.au/nla.news-article86053650

'Week To Week' *Windsor and Richmond Gazette* (NSW: 1888–1961) 2 September 1932: 4. http://nla.gov.au/nla.news-article86057165

'Windsor Council' *Windsor and Richmond Gazette* (NSW: 1888–1961) 7 October 1932: 6. http://nla.gov.au/nla.news-article86056163

'Obituary. Rev. P. C. Anderson.' *The Sydney Morning Herald* (NSW: 1842–1954) 27 December 1932: 6. http://nla.gov.au/nla.news-article16941068

'Scheyville Training Farm.' *Windsor and Richmond Gazette* (NSW: 1888–1961) 13 January 1933: 6. http://nla.gov.au/nla.news-article86051223

'Scheyville Training Farm.' *The Sydney Morning Herald* (NSW: 1842–1954) 27 March 1933: 7. http://nla.gov.au/nla.news-article16965663

'Doing Good Work' *Windsor and Richmond Gazette* (NSW: 1888–1961) 31 March 1933: 10. http://nla.gov.au/nla.news-article86057524

'Scheyville Farm' *Windsor and Richmond Gazette* (NSW: 1888–1961) 7 April 1933: 9. http://nla.gov.au/nla.news-article86055896

'Scheyville Farm' *Windsor and Richmond Gazette* (NSW: 1888–1961) 23 June 1933: 1. http://nla.gov.au/nla.news-article86052666

'Unemployed Youths.' *The Sydney Morning Herald* (NSW: 1842–1954) 8 December 1933: 15. http://nla.gov.au/nla.news-article17030823

'Week To Week' *Windsor and Richmond Gazette* (NSW: 1888–1961) 5 January 1934: 4. http://nla.gov.au/nla.news-article85799031

'Personal' *Windsor and Richmond Gazette* (NSW: 1888–1961) 19 January 1934: 12. http://nla.gov.au/nla.news-article85800587

'Scheyville Farm.' *The Sydney Morning Herald* (NSW: 1842–1954) 9 April 1934: 6. http://nla.gov.au/nla.news-article17056542

'Dr. Harbison' *Windsor and Richmond Gazette* (NSW: 1888–1961) 27 April 1934: 1. http://nla.gov.au/nla.news-article85794982

'Maraylya' *Windsor and Richmond Gazette* (NSW: 1888–1961) 27 July 1934: 3. http://nla.gov.au/nla.news-article85794874

'Unemployment' *The Mercury* (Hobart, Tas. : 1860–1954) 10 August 1934: 11. http://nla.gov.au/nla.news-article24955103

'Work at Scheyville' *Windsor and Richmond Gazette* (NSW: 1888–1961) 1 March 1935: 9. http://nla.gov.au/nla.news-article85797164

'Member for Hawkesbury's Fine Record of Achievement' *Windsor and Richmond Gazette* (NSW: 1888–1961) 3 May 1935: 2. http://nla.gov.au/nla.news-article85794270

'Week to Week' *Windsor and Richmond Gazette* (NSW: 1888–1961) 3 May 1935: 4. http://nla.gov.au/nla.news-article85794286

'The Success of Bundidup' *Sunday Times* (Perth, WA : 1902–1954) 20 October 1935: 15. http://nla.gov.au/nla.news-article58744165

'Maraylya' *Windsor and Richmond Gazette* (NSW: 1888–1961) 31 January 1936: 7. http://nla.gov.au/nla.news-article86047331

'A Scheyville Sunday' *Windsor and Richmond Gazette* (NSW: 1888–1961) 26 June 1936: 4. http://nla.gov.au/nla.news-article86045859

'Youth Employment System.' *The Sydney Morning Herald* (NSW: 1842–1954) 26 August 1937: 11. http://nla.gov.au/nla.news-article17389433 .

'Skilled Labour Shortage.' *The Sydney Morning Herald* (NSW: 1842–1954) 23 October 1937: 17. http://nla.gov.au/nla.news-article17413948

'Boy Migrants.' *The Sydney Morning Herald* (NSW: 1842–1954) 22 February 1938: 12. http://nla.gov.au/nla.news-article17442208

'Young Settlers.' *The Sydney Morning Herald* (NSW: 1842–1954) 25 August 1938: 17. http://nla.gov.au/nla.news-article17474125

'Young Migrants For N.S.W.' *The Sydney Morning Herald* (NSW: 1842–1954) 18 January 1939: 10. http://nla.gov.au/nla.news-article17552416

'Boys For Farming.' *The Sydney Morning Herald* (NSW: 1842–1954) 22 February 1939: 14. http://nla.gov.au/nla.news-article17548581

'Little Brothers.' *The Sydney Morning Herald* (NSW: 1842–1954) 2 March 1939: 10. http://nla.gov.au/nla.news-article17569277

'English Youths For Farms.' *The Sydney Morning Herald* (NSW: 1842–1954) 17 March 1939: 10. http://nla.gov.au/nla.news-article17575485

'Christian Refugees for Sydney.' *The Sydney Morning Herald* (NSW: 1842–1954) 15 May 1939: 12. http://nla.gov.au/nla.news-article17566993

'Overseas League Proposal.' *The Sydney Morning Herald* (NSW: 1842–1954) 30 May 1939: 10. http://nla.gov.au/nla.news-article17573995

'Modern Boy Voyagers.' *The Sydney Morning Herald* (NSW: 1842–1954) 3 June 1939: 13. http://nla.gov.au/nla.news-article27972464

'Compulsory Training Reintroduced.' *The Sydney Morning Herald* (NSW: 1842–1954) 21 October 1939: 15. http://nla.gov.au/nla.news-article17633620

'Army School at State Farm.' *The Sydney Morning Herald* (NSW: 1842–1954) 11 October 1940: 9. http://nla.gov.au/nla.news-article17710886 .

'Week to Week' *Windsor and Richmond Gazette* (NSW: 1888–1961) 18 October 1940: 4. Web. http://nla.gov.au/nla.news-article86064302

'Soldiers' Blocks' *Windsor and Richmond Gazette* (NSW: 1888–1961) 30 May 1941: 11. http://nla.gov.au/nla.news-article86065506

'How Our Paratroops Are Trained To Be Tough' *The Sydney Morning Herald* (NSW: 1842–1954) 24 July 1945: 2. http://nla.gov.au/nla.news-article17948210

'Cardinal Gilroy Opens Convent At Migrant Centre' *Windsor and Richmond Gazette* (NSW: 1888–1961) 23 January 1957: 7. http://nla.gov.au/nla.news-article256359776

'Pitt Town To Have Festival Week Effort' *Windsor and Richmond Gazette* (NSW: 1888–1961) 2 April 1958: 5. http://nla.gov.au/nla.news-article256357500

Journal articles

Costello, Lauren N. & Dunn, Kevin M. 'Resident action groups in Sydney: people power or rat-bags?' *Australian Geographer*, 25:1, 1994, 61-76

Forster, P.M. and Metcalf, W.J 'Communal Groups: Social Laboratories or places of exile?' *Communal Societies Journal*, Vol. 20, 2000, 1-11.

Nora, Pierre, 'Between Memory and History: Les Lieux do Mémoire, *Representations*, Spring, 1989, No. 26, 7–24

Sherington, Geoffrey, 'British youth and Empire settlement: the Dreadnought boys in New South Wales', *Journal of the Royal Australian Historical Society* 82, 1996, 12.

Books

Ayling, Robert I. *Rev. John Ayling Australian pioneer: the life of Rev. John Ayling clergyman, educator, beekeeper, 1825-1897* Robert I. Ayling Marco Island, Florida 1999

Braithwaite, B. M. and Hawkesbury Agricultural College. Old Boys' Union. *Challenge & change : the history of Hawkesbury Agricultural College 1966-1991* Hawkesbury Agricultural College Old Boys' Union, Richmond, 1991

Burford, Kathleen E. *Unfurrowed fields: a Josephite story, NSW, 1872-1972* St Joseph's Convent, North Sydney 1991

Dennis, D. J. *One day at a time: a Vietnam diary,* University of Queensland Press St Lucia, Qld 1992

Dickey, Brian. *No charity there: a short history of social welfare in Australia,* Allen & Unwin, Sydney. 1987

Donnelly, Roger. *The Scheyville experience: the Officer Training Unit Scheyville: 1965-1973* University of Queensland Press, St Lucia, 2001.

Harrison, Rodney. *Heritage: Critical approaches,* Routledge, 2013.

Karskens, Grace. *The Rocks: life in early Sydney* Melbourne University Press, Carlton, Vic, 1997

Proudfoot, Helen. *Exploring Sydney's west* Kangaroo Press, Kenthurst 1987

Smith, Laurajane *Uses of Heritage*, Routledge, 2006

Appendix A: Scheyville Centre School reports
Summary of the school inspector's annual reports from 1950 to 1964

Every year the Scheyville Migrant Centre School was the subject of an annual visit and report by a designated NSW Education Department School Inspector. All NSW schools were subject to these visits. Such reports give an insight into the "inner official workings" of the school. It wasn't just an "audit" of how the headmaster and teachers were coping, nor was it to find all the negatives of the school. Rather than simply reproduce the reports I have noted recurring themes and comments as well as items that appear unusual or interesting. These excerpts provide a glimpse into a time when political correctness had not entered the vocabulary of the NSW Education Dept. bureaucracy.

1950

The school opened at the beginning of the 1950 school year.

Accommodation at the school was missing teacher's tables and chairs in four rooms. There were thirty- nine dual desks in the school. The school had a piano and radio receiving set, but no readers had been supplied for second class, a good supply of reading material was needed and there was practically no kindergarten occupational material.

Ages of the pupils ranged from four years to fourteen. Classes corresponded to those in a normal school but the attainments of pupils were lower. The headmaster stayed in touch with the work of the school by taking a demonstration lesson daily with each of the three classes taught by migrant teachers, and visited each class at least daily. He reported that there were harmonious relations prevailing between the school and the Administrator of the Centre.

As with nearly every annual school report that followed, it was noted that "pupils are rapidly assimilating Australian ways, and that the school recently participated successfully in the District P.S.A.A.A. sports". Participating in these athletic and ball game carnivals not only allowed the students to compete against their Australian born peers but were another way of social inter-action. (In 1951 a girl won the senior championship and a boy was later fourth in the state championship high jump. In 1953 the school won the ball games competition. In 1955 the school won the marching event. In 1957 the school was successful in ball games, though not so good in athletics.)

Emphasis in the learning programme was naturally placed on the learning of English and an average class load of thirty students was endeavoured to be maintained..

Class 1 pupils read "Fay and Don". Handiwork, or craft work stimulated the pupil's interest.

1951

"Pupils in classes four, five and six are able to do reasonably normal English and mathematics work. Their standard was noted as being below corresponding normal classes owing to their using a new language. The Inspector wrote "that it was hoped that most of class six would be able to proceed to a normal first year class at Richmond High next year, as they will not require special tuition in English." A common observation was that "most pupils who leave the Scheyville school after about a year's attendance should be able to take their place without difficulty in a normal school".

A piano seemed to be a necessary item and the Centre Amenities Committee purchased a radiogram with extension speaker. This was used especially for music and occasional listening to other broadcasts such as Art and English Treasure House.

The school did work for the District Jubilee Celebrations and a successful function was held at the school. Approximately five hundred ornamental trees were planted throughout the Centre.

"Developing school discipline was difficult owing to the conditions under which the children live, and with the attitude adopted by many of the parents."

1952

The Inspector noted that "instruction is now being planned in accordance with the new syllabus. This year an effort has been made to broaden the curriculum to include all subjects taught in the normal schools, apparently with satisfactory results".

Reading was being taught mainly by the "phonic method" and Social Studies was introduced.

Good use was made of the school radio broadcasts and the children sang in "*The Good Neighbour Session* "from station 2BL.

A good range of work is covered in handwork and a large exhibit was forwarded to Canberra. Nearly all of it was retained for exhibition at other centres after being exhibited in Canberra.

1953.

It was recorded that "accommodation is now sufficient. The waiting list has twenty five names-almost another class, if a room and further teacher were available. I am not going to deprive the girls of a sewing room. Suitable furniture has now been supplied to all classes".

"Staffing has been a problem throughout the whole year.

Transfers of capable teachers and their replacement with most incapable assistants have made any definite planning well nigh impossible. During second term the school was short of two teachers making discipline difficult.

One other factor that has made organisation difficult has been the arrival of many children direct from the boats thus making Scheyville like a Reception Centre rather than a Holding Centre. Very few families are now coming from other Holding Centres. While it would seem that these people are classes above the Displace Persons, the fact remains that they have absolutely no English. Each class has been encouraged to do as much as possible with the new students and results have been encouraging and reasonable.

The wide variety of reading material available has been partly responsible for the generally improved reading standard throughout the school.

A definite attempt was made to improve the general speech standard. Poetry and verse speaking received good treatment."

"There are now seven New Australian teachers on the Staff and the headmaster endeavoured to visit their classes daily to demonstrate teaching methods and to discuss difficulties encountered and suggest ways of overcoming them.

Preparing teaching programmes one week ahead helped the New Australian teachers."

"It was with personal satisfaction that the Headmaster felt personal satisfaction that the school choir won at the Hawkesbury Eisteddfod. On the competition day there were thirty- six children in the choir and eight had been in the country for less than six weeks.

Of the eleven members of staff, seven are New Australians. The disappearance of national groups indicates a big step forward in the process of assimilation."

1954.

In 1954 it was noted that the pupils were principally of Polish and Baltic origin. These days an Inspector would probably not be allowed to comment that students of a particular nationality "are clean and good looking".

"Drama is used to advantage. An increase in impromptu acting and dialogue concerning simple day to day situations was deemed advisable."

A common observation was that "the staff comprises too many migrant teachers. They should be moved out to general schools quicker and the proportion kept to 40% migrant and 60% Australian teachers. The migrant teacher has the same speech and language difficulty as the pupil and has a limited knowledge of Australia and its customs. While he is inclined to be over-serious and directive for children brought up in an atmosphere of subjection".

It was also noted that "the settlement is isolated thereby hampering Australian community experience. Empire and Coronation Day celebrations and displays, concerts, national days, visit to the Queen's Review and participation in Richmond Eisteddfod and Combined Sports are all positive influences in moulding social attributes."

"The school is following a policy of training in English and in Oral Reading, Spelling and Poetry. Pleasing success is being achieved. Some other subjects such as Arithmetic and Social Studies were sacrificed a little for this end.

Scripture is taught exclusively by visiting teachers."

By 1954 it was noted that "the standard of the Sixth Class is the highest of any Sixth Class since the Centre opened. From the Sixth Class one girl gained admission to a Junior High School. This, and the high standard of work resulted from a definite attempt to follow the group teaching method to a logical conclusion".

1955.

In 1955 further re-grouping of the workload and classes was necessary owing to the arrival of large drafts of Greek migrants for whom a special class was formed.

The continual movement of migrants in and out of the Centre was not conducive to effective teaching.

"There are now only three New Australian teachers on the Staff. The appointment of a teacher with a knowledge of Dutch would be of great assistance owing to the large number of Dutch pupils passing through the school."

It was observed over the year that pupils from Holland seem to take much longer to settle down than those from other countries.

In 1955 "national grouping formed a serious problem during the latter half of second term". Teachers suspected that it was due to influences from outside the school. "In general, however, the children of the various nations play together well as soon as they have mastered enough English to use it as a common language. Until such times they tend to drift into national groups".

1956.

In 1956 it was again noted that there "is heavy pupil turnover. Since 31 January last, 309 have enrolled and 190 of these have left again".

"Core" classes of permanent pupils were established and special classes for language training of new arrivals.

"Advantage is being taken of the language ability of the members of the staff. School timetables have a bias towards verbal subjects. There are 55 pupils below the age for their class but this was being kept under close scrutiny."

"The social education of the pupils has received some attention by excursions, ANZAC and Empire Day celebrations with outside guest speakers, and a bonfire for cracker night. This aspect might be extended by increased team games with Houses, inter-school visits and public presentations as social integration is a need of these children."

"The formation of a parent organisation, despite anticipated difficulty, is a venture worth attempting. Without its aid the school is rather sparsely equipped and parental interest is not strong. "

1956.

In 1956 it was noted that a small group of stringed instrumentalists was being trained.

1957.

By 1957 the Centre had all but lost its Holding Centre status and become more of a Temporary Accommodation Centre. "The 'core' is slowly dwindling, and soon there may be insufficient pupils to maintain separate 'core' classes. Staffing was below that of previous years."

"Since last inspection two successful school concerts have been held, one in December 1956 following the opening of the new Recreation Hall, and another in August 1957 in connection with Education Week. Both were well attended and received favourable comment."

"There are many children in 'core' classes whose education is not helped by parental co-operation; many of the older Displaced Person residents have not taken the trouble to learn much English, and still speak their native tongue in the home. This tends to make the overcoming of structural errors in English very difficult."

In general, it was noted "that children from Scandinavian countries and from Germany are much easier to handle than Dutch children who tend to be noisy and restless.

The difficulties with national groups experienced in earlier years seems to be lessening though it has not entirely disappeared."

To give an idea of the diversity of teachers as well as students the 1957 report stated "the new Kindergarten formed in September is making fair progress and the teacher is a Dutch migrant who still has some slight difficulty with English.

The Transition or Upper Kindergarten was taken over in September by a Latvian casual teacher and First Grade is capably taught by a Polish migrant teacher who has a good understanding of infant methods."

1958.

In 1958 a small room adjoining the office was utilised for needlework, visual education and occasionally for remedial group teaching by the Headmaster.

"The 'core' classes are becoming more difficult each year as the old core of Displaced Persons is slowly diminishing. There is now in every class a group of pupils with a large degree of language disability. This is especially noticeable in Spelling and Composition.

Total enrolments during the year numbered 676, and pupils left totalled 516.

The school again participated in the Annual District Sports, and although not successful in winning any pennants, had two representatives in the Area Sports at Lidcombe."

During 1958 a stretch of ground near the Camp entrance was levelled and prepared as a football oval. "A team was entered in the District Primary Schools Rugby League Competition and accredited themselves very well in this, their first year in this sport."

The field was also used for the school's first School Sports Carnival. An annual School Concert was held on 3rd December and throughout the year two excursions were made to Taronga Park Zoo.

"There has been a slight improvement in the standard of the migrants entering the Centre this year, and the proportion of troublesome pupils has seemed smaller. The tendency to restlessness of Dutch children is still noticeable, and as new arrivals posted to Scheyville lately are predominantly Dutch, this tends to have an unsettling effect on the school."

"The progress of many children is still retarded by their parents not making the effort to learn English, and speaking Polish, Dutch etc in the home."

1959.

In 1959 it was noted that," there is a ready participation in singing and most renditions are melodious. The Headmaster is developing adequately the formal aspects of the Music Course for 6A-5A. The response being obtained in Art varies considerably. A suitable range of Poetry was covered and evidence of a developing interest in literature among the brighter pupils. Folk dancing in the infants is a strong feature, and dramatisation in Class 1A is very pleasing".

"Physical Education is being competently directed, Health Education is being fairly impressively treated., and suitable topics treated in Social Studies.

Instruction in Scripture is being left almost entirely to visiting church representatives who are giving instruction for an hour per week."

"The Centre Library is well stocked with suitable reading material for children and it is well patronised by the pupils of the school."

"In preparing the children for the Australian way of life the school is making a valuable contribution, and progress is being made with the development of acceptable standards of conduct."

1960.

In November 1960 it was noted that "the degree of assimilation is very pleasing indeed. After newcomers have achieved an elementary knowledge of English the various nationalities mix well in the playground. In some cases, home backgrounds have not helped where the parents have made little or no attempt to learn English and make friends of people of different nationalities".

"A few children in the school show a tendency to 'answer back' in a rather insolent manner."

"Pupil punctuality, though it has improved, still leaves much to be desired."

Spelling.

For migrant children, whose language is not normally English, I would regard the results as very satisfactory.

Mathematics.

Some weakness in recognition of coins and giving value of two or more coins.

Poetry.

Poetry, in addition to its literary value, can be a useful speech and vocabulary aid in this school. Frequent oral recitation is recommended.

Formal English in the upper classes was quite good.

Social Studies was noted as being well treated in the upper classes.

Physical Exercises.

Some special features have been the folk dancing and pattern marching.

Natural Science.

'Strip films' were used to advantage.by many teachers.

Scripture.

Each class has now one hour per week. Class teachers take a half hour for groups not visited twice by the Sisters. (i.e. The Roman Catholic nuns).

1961.

'The number of class units has reduced to eight with the falling off of numbers of newcomers."

"The rate of pupil movement showed a sharp drop this year. While 758 pupils were enrolled during 1959 and 681 during 1960, enrolments this year dropped to 416.

Outward movement was similarly affected."

"The Rugby League team was successful in gaining second place in the competition, whilst the girls came second in the softball competition."

"No school concert was held this year, but a group of girls and boys gave a folk dancing display, and a marching display in Education Week."

1964.

"The school serves a migrant hostel exclusively. All the pupils are foreign migrants: they arrive, stay a few days and then depart; others have remained too long."

It was noted that that "the tone of the classrooms and happiness of the students was evidence of efforts to ensure social adjustment and general assimilation; the policy is proving a practical instrument."

"There is a general downward trend in enrolments, and it appears likely that only three classes will be required soon."

"Three of the classes are normal, the fourth contains a group of older pupils for whom special language instruction is provided by an interpreter-teacher."

"Education Week saw a heartening body of visitors. The school is an active supporter of Stewart House and the principles of the Gould League and membership is encouraged.

"Control and discipline are not difficult: individual pupils are sometimes aggressive, but allowance is made for their backgrounds; tolerance, patience and firmness prevail in most instances. The pupils are relaxed and happy; communication flows readily and their social confidence is impressive. Corporal punishment is avoided."

"The Infants Group is taught well with withy full regard for the promotion of language skill, advancement of acquaintance with local customs and introduction to usage in number and money. In addition, social adjustment, pleasant group experiences and training in desirable values are provided generously."

"There is a lively interest among the various grades in Australian Studies, undertaken in units.

Self -expression through art, expressiveness in music and poetry and creative activities in crafts are significant strands at this school."

Interestingly, the migrant children at Scheyville were taught to support Stewart House at Curl Curl Sydney; a charity for people less fortunate than themselves. They were also encouraged to learn about Australian birds and wildlife protection by being members of the Gould League of Bird Lovers. Both organisations are still serving the NSW community in 2021.

Current Scope of Services of Stewart House in 2021.

Stewart House provides services to children from the public education system in NSW and the ACT who would benefit from a positive intervention to build their self- esteem and personal development. The service is a holistic model of care. Children stay at Stewart House for a period of two weeks. During that time they undertake a range of activities that include:

- Recreational and social activities to build self-esteem and resilience;
- Learning/school activities for social and emotional skills development;
- Preliminary and ad hoc counselling;
- Health screening (including medical, dental and optometric).

The facility accommodates 84 children at a time. Typically the majority of children are between the ages of eight (8) and 14 years.

The Gould League

Named to honour the work of John and Elizabeth Gould, 'The Gould League of Bird Lovers' (now Gould League) was formed in 1909.

Originally set up to prevent bird egg collecting and to educate for the protection of Australian birds, the Gould League has made a significant impact on generations of Australians and their environmental attitudes.

Appendix B: Giving the Migrants a Profile

From 1949 to early 1965 some 30,000 displaced persons and other Europeans had Scheyville as their first residence in Australia. For some, they stayed years, but for many it was merely a matter of weeks or even days. The Dreadnought Boys have a roll call with Geoffrey Sherington's research material at the Mitchell Library, the Parachutists are listed in the book *Eagles Alighting*, members of the Search Light units are in the book *Expose*, and those National Servicemen who graduated as army officers and were trained for Vietnam are listed in the book *The Scheyville Experience*. Yet, the largest group to inhabit Scheyville, the post–World War Two migrants have never had anyone compile a listing of them. Sadly, my research has not turned up any coherent lists for those people who were at Scheyville between 1949 and 1960. Yet groups of migrants have managed to connect and reconnect at various re-unions, although the size of the re-unions (perhaps 200 people) is small when compared to their overall numbers.

Below, in an attempt to remedy the deficiency of recognition of existence of the migrants I list those people that I have met, interviewed or know have paid a return visit to Scheyville (usually for an organised re-union) at some time over the past forty-odd years. This listing just gives a small number of people an acknowledgement of their existence at Scheyville! Maybe, one day a complete listing will be made. My apologies to the relatives and friends of those in the list who have passed on and to those whose names I have misspelled.

Here are the people who have returned to Scheyville that I am aware of: Gretha Witsen, Anna and Eric Koelbel, Andrew Janislewski, Maria Cebulski, Ciene Zematis, Mrs Eijkman, Maria Foreman Smolders, Zina Carr-Lawless, Jon and Alice Grabowski, Wally Goszko, Maria Koomen, M. Milizakowsky, Ernest Hoskin, Adrian Stalenber, Walter Schmidt, Amiela Star, Aneta Schmidt, Veronica Siemsen, M. Witt, Ken Berger, Eugen Alexandrow, Bernie May, Mary Parker, Anton Tang, Cathy Borgman, Martn Nijberg, B. and G. Mazanka, W. Herber, T. Vandenberge, Maria Hiep, Tinie Lammers-Hiep, Hans Stichter, Elvi Suviste (nee Thomson), Maria Foreman, Ellie Denning, Erik Hockstra, Herman Sprakel, Jackie

Scheyville Speaks

Martin, Grazyna Grzeskiewiez, Sophia Berg, Sinoy Gavin, Tonie Besters, Antonia Element, Jin Van Dramel, John Eijkman, Louise Debeck, Corrie and Tony Witlox, Betty Eady, Keith Cole, T and D Schiwiaski, Julius and Mary Hevesi, Mark Bradbury (son of Jean Izatt), Anne (nee Daczko) and Carl Birdsey, Stephania McDonald (Latka), Rita (nee Eizenbergs) and John Bulmanis, Catarina Sgangarella, Imre Kalandy, George Csanady, Cobie VanDenberge, Joe and Kim Wrona, Val and Barry Dollin, Don Roberts, Tiiu Kroon, Margaret and Michael Ginnings, Norm Dale, Anne Kurovsky, Viivi Kuru, Valda and Ivars Seibelis, Peter and Susanne Hledik and family, Jo Kowalczyk, Johan Luchters, John Eggers, Olga Green, Margita Dubabs, Yvonne Kinney-(Hilberding), Wally Colasa, Therese McKinnon, Valentina Plateris, Catherina Bonwick, George and Hazel Humphrey, Theodora Werle (Hoogenboom), Casey van der Mey and Anna Heller, Karma Rowe (nee Borg), Eva Lederman, Ivars and Valda Seibelis, Rutha Osins, Inara Zemitis, Alex Batch, Mrs Mazanka, Sylvia O'Connor, Ligita and Ilmars Legzdins, Jo Mulholland, Wadyslava Adamick, Maria Straub, Elizabeth Lazdans, Rick Gurtman, Helen Kroban, Bernadette Quinn, Jurco (George) Wenc, Erica Halezousky, Elizabeth and Adam Wosachlo, Marie Dierick, Elizabeth Baitch, Steve Lette, Katie Borgman, Elizabeth Lazdans, John Pohl,   Linda Straub, Thea Derksen, Jo KowalczykKlothilde Kowalczyk, Marie Pinkewich, Aarts Gloria, Maria Smolders , Gerry Smolders, Lillian Madsen, Mary and Julius Hevesi, Allan van Kraanen, Wally Placho, Mary Parker (Callus), Adrian van Asten, Marie SparkesMichael Del Haas, Barbara Betts, Marie Sparkes, Jo Gort, Sue, Couloumbis, Peer Toft, Cathy Reemst, Veronica Siemsen, Thea Lunney, Ada Hawkins, Walter Osiczak, Marie Seltenrych, John Seltenrych, Tony Bilokur, George Augoustinos, Francesca Moor (Samethini), Elie Treichler, Barbara Altorjai-Albury, Imre Kalandy, Ene Dioguardi (Elvie Suviste's sister), Rosemary Bergman, Eugenia Jeremiejczyky, Margaret Gurtman, Irene Gurtman, Robert Van Hese, Richard Gurtman, Eugene Alexandro, Dianne Beeken, Tony Derksem, Frank and Cornelius Aartz, Yvonne Kinney, Joanna Velt, Kurt and Jan Boesen, Gerit Biegel, Sjovkje Biegel, Johanna Mazanka, Katherine Zaje.

Scheyville Speaks

In 2010 I found a file in the National Archives with Arrival and Departure Sheets of migrants at Scheyville between 1961 and 1964. It is possible that some 3,000 families comprising perhaps 6,000 individuals are listed on these Sheets. In a separate spreadsheet I have listed some 300 families, all members of the families, their nationality and their arrival and departure dates. Time constraints mean I cannot list them all. If readers care to access File:

The following material that you wish to use in a book appendix is no longer in copyright.

C3939, N1954/25/75074 PART 3 - Aliens registration - transfer of aliens X [ex] Greta [migrant hostel] plus daily advice slips from Scheyville [file consists of the details of arrivals at - departures from - and meal refunds - at Scheyville Migrant Camp - not obviously to do with Greta - NSW Immigration policy file - 3 cm; box 1].

C3939, N1961/75078 - Immigration - Aliens Registration Transfer of Aliens ex Scheyville [5.0cm; box 137].

Copyright has expired in material that was made or first published by the Commonwealth Government before 1 January 1969.

I appreciate the service of Eve Terry at National Archives and acknowledge the National Archives of Australia as the source of this material. with the following citation [as in the example shown below].

In digital format people can see details of all the folk who went to Scheyville over that three-year period. Dates of Birth, religion and ship or airline that brought the family to Australia are also listed. For privacy reasons they are not listed here.

Scheyville Speaks

Extract from National Archives File C3939 N19542575074 Part 3 Daily arrival & Departure Sheets Scheyville Camp 1961

Family name	Family members	Nationality	Arrival date	Depart date
Aarts,	Johannes, Elisabeth, Johannes, Gerardus, Cornelis,	Dutch	Jul-58	Jun-61
Abspoel	Johanna, Maria, Franciscus, Hubertus Lena, Michiel, Jacobus	Dutch	May-61	Jun-61
Aguirre Garcia	Eduardo, Maria, Salvador, Maria, Eduardo	Spanish	Aug-61	Nov-61
Albers	Johanna, Jacobus, Johan	Dutch	May-61	Jun-61
Arizon Gonzalez	Felix, Lucia, Arenzaza	Spanish	Aug-61	9/11/1961
Babijn	Cornelia, Erna, Alex, Frank, Marian	Dutch	14/09/1961	9/12/1961
Baggeler	Peter, Anna Maria, Helmut, Angelika	German	23/09/1961	28/10/1961
Bakker	Menne	Dutch	May-61	Jun-61
Balzamo	Anvonio, Concetta, Maria, Guiseppe	Italian	19/07/1961	27/10/1961
Behiels	Andre, Anthonia	Belgian	Jan-61	Sep-61
Bendick	Leon, Dorothy, Hanson	American	8/07/1961	4/10/1961
Beney	Sylvia	Swiss	May-61	1/11/1961
Benjamins	Jan	Dutch	Dec-60	Jul-61
Benning	Erwin	German	Dec-60	Oct-61
Benning	Erwin	German	Dec-60	Jul-61
Berksen	Johannes, Maria, Theodorua, Antonie, Johannes, Annemarie	Dutch	Apr-61	Jul-61
Binkiewicz	Antoni, Janina, Bernarda, Marta, Helena, Krystyna, Bronislav, Jerzy Stefan	Nat'ed Australian		Jul-61
Boering	Margarete. Jurgen, Rainer, Michael, Iris, Alfred	German	Mar-61	Aug-61
Bos V.D.	Johanna, Wilhelmina, Hendrik, Sjoerd, Johanna, Willem	Dutch	Apr-61	Jun-61
Bosgra	Siebren, Maria, Frederika, Harm	Dutch	Jul-61	Jul-61
Braam	marianus	Dutch	May-61	Aug-61
Bran	Roland	Swiss	Apr-61	Sep-61
Breukel	Petrus, Anna, Anna Louise, Elisabeth, Petrus	Dutch	4-Sep	30/09/1961
Brose	Helga, Heinz, Helmut, Harry	German	Jun-61	9/11/1961
Bucholtz	Jacobus	Dutch	3/04/1961	27/11/1961
Buijn	Cornelis, Elizabeth, Cornelis, Johannes, Elisabeth	Dutch	Jul-61	Jul-61
Buitelaar	Ursula, Patricia, Frans	Dutch	14/09/1961	5/10/1961
Butts	Floyd	American	Jun-61	Jun-61
Caccavano	Giuseppina, Renato, Giuseppe	Italian	Apr-61	Jun-61
Cano Alonso	Antonio, Inocencia, Jose, Ma Christina, Ortega Calvo	Spanish	Jan-61	Aug-61
Cappello	Bastista, Maria, Rosaria, Vita, Pietro, Salvatore	Italian	Aug-61	Sep-61
Cesnik	Franc, Ida, Romana	Yugoslavian	May-61	9/11/1961
Christopher	Mary	American	26/09/1961	28/09/1961
Cicic	Uras	Yugoslavian	Jan-59	28/10/1961
Cok	Jan, Sophia, Jan, Willem, Ronald, Maria	Dutch	2/11/1961	17/11/1961
Cosse	Jan, Catharina, Donata	Dutch	Sep-61	Sep-61
Costerhout	Wijnand	Dutch	Jul-61	Aug-61
De Best	Hendrik, Adriana, Johannes, Hendrik	Dutch	Jan-60	Sep-61
De Geus	Cornelis, Henddrikje, Jacoba, Peter, Linda	Dutch	18/07/1961	20/10/1961
De geus	Cornelis	Dutch	18/07/1961	10/09/1961
De Las heras De Castro	Agustin, Honorina, Ma Angeles, Francisco, Fermin, Miguel, Ma Pilar, Alfonso, Ma Mercedes, Julian	Spanish	Aug-61	20/10/1961

De Pater	Johannes, Elizabeth, Catharina, Johanna, Payulina, Eduardus, Joannes, Emme, Antonius	Dutch	26/09/1961	11/10/1961
De Pater	Ferdinand	Dutch	Mar-61	1/09/1961
De Rooy	Hermanus	Dutch	7/08/1961	29//10/1961
De Vroome	Martha, Marinus, Dirk, Johannus, Hans, Willem	Dutch	Apr-61	Sep-61
de Vroome	Willem	Dutch	Apr-61	Jun-61
De Wit	Adrianus, Elisabeth, Gerrit, Henk, Klasina, Adriana	Dutch	14/09/1961	7/10/1961
de Wit	Adrianus	Dutch	14/09/1961	1/10/1961
De Wit	jan, Anna, Andreas	Dutch	Jul-61	Aug-61
Deden	Petrus	Dutch	30/10/1961	17/11/1961
Di Bella	Salvatore, Francesca, Gaetano, Francesco, Claudio	Italian	Aug-61	29/12/1961
Dittman	Werner, Rita, Peter, Elvira	German	Jun-61	12/10/1961
Donk V.D	Matheus, Cornelia, Maria, Johannes	Dutch	14/09/1961	12/10/1961
Drtina	Gisela, Jeiko, Herbert	German	Apr-61	Jun-61
Dusseldorp	Kurt, Mathilda	Dutch	Aug-61	Aug-61
Eggens	Johan	Dutch	11/09/1961	22/10/1961
Eneriz Perez	Nieves, Eugenie, Ma, carmen	Spanish	Jan-61	9/11/1961
Ernst	Erwin, Elsa, Haaselau, Uwe, Ute, Michael, Heike, Gisela, Sonja	German	22/01/1959	24.10.1961
Ernst	Frieda	German	14/05/1961	24/10/1961
Ernst	Erwin, Elsa, Haaselau, Uwe, Ute, Michael, Heike, Gisela, Sonja	German	22/01/1958	16/10/1961
Erwich	Willem, Edith, Willem, George, Marianne	Dutch	14/09/1961	12/10/1961
Evenhuis	jan	Dutch	Mar-60	Aug-61
Faber	Lydie	Dutch	May-61	Jun-61
Feenstra	Kornelis, Hielkje, Andrieske, Anariesje, Andre	Dutch	Sep-61	30/09/1961
Feenstra	Kernelis	Dutch	Sep-61	Sep-61
Flack	Deborah, Mona	American	Jun-61	Jun-61
Fleck	Kurt, Ingeberg, Wolfgang, Iris	German	23/09/1961	28/10/1961
Fonnenbergh	Theo, Elfride	Dutch	16/05/1961	4/11/1961
Frenken	Theodorus	Dutch	14/09/1961	26/09/1961
Gabel	Adolf, Irmgard	German		6/10/1961
Galar Gomez	Francisco, Saturnina, Joaquin, Lopez Curie	Spanish	Jan-61	Aug-61
Garrido Perez	Leonelo, M Luisa, Jesus, Araceli	Spanish	Aug-61	9/11/1961
Geldhof	Jan	Dutch	Apr-61	Sep-61
Giubin	Angelo	Italian	Mar-61	May-61
Golnar	Matijas, Antonija, Danica	Yugoslavian	Mar-61	9/11/1961
Gomes	Reinier, Maria	Dutch	Sep-61	Oct-61
Gonzales Aguero	Venancia, Mercedes, Luis	Spanish	Aug-61	9/11/1961
Gordon	Harold, Ann, Richard, Patricia, Ronnie, Kathy	American	Jun-61	Jul-61
Gover	James, Yvenee, John, William	American	11/12/1961	11/12/1961
Graft	Cornelis, Engelbertas	Dutch	14/09/1961	21/10/1961
Griffith	Tim, Jim, Bina, Ada, Timothy, William	American	21/11/1961	2/01/1961
Groot	Maria, Albertus	Dutch	Sep-61	Oct-61
Groot	Albertus	Dutch	15/09/1961	3/10/1961
Haag	Heinrich	German	16/11/1956	17/09/1961
Haahti	Rauno, Eewa, Markku	Finnish	28/11/1960	3/11/1961
Haanstra	Gerardus, Johanna, Gerard, Edith, Aletta	Dutch	14/09/1961	14/10/1961
Haanstra	Gerardus	Dutch	14/09/1961	3/10/1961
Haanti	Raune	Finnish	28/11/1960	28/10/1961
Hanson	Hendrik, Francina	Dutch	Jul-61	Jul-61
Harbach	Wilhelm, Anita, Willy, Irma	German	23/09/1961	1/12/1961
Hartgers	Tjaltje, Gerritje, Evert	Dutch	May-61	Jun-61
Hartgers	Evert	Dutch	May-61	May-61
Hauri	Petar, Beatrice, Erich, Rolf, Liliane	Swiss	Jun-61	19/10/1961

Scheyville Speaks

Heath	Don, Lydia, Daniel	American	Jun-61	Jun-61
Hernandez Ramos	Manuel, Manuela, M Angeles, Manuel	Spanish	1/08/1961	9/11/1961
Hernantes del Rincon	Angel, Candeles, Ma Pilar	Spanish	Jan-61	Aug-61
Heuse	Giselle, Chrislaine, Francine, Roger	Belgian	Apr-61	Jun-61
Hiitola	Marjatta	Finnish	Jun-61	4/12/1961
Hilgers	Johannes, Paulina, Wilhelmina, Johanna, Nicephera, Elizabeth, Katharina, Mary	Dutch	Aug-59	Jul-61
Hofbauer	Diether, Gunda, Reiner	German	Mar-61	Jun-61
Hogelin	Brigitte, Roger, Nils	Swedish	Apr-61	Sep-61
Homoet	Johan	Dutch	16/05/1961	16/09/1961
Hornung	Egen, Josee, Robert, Michael	German	Jun-61	Aug-61
Houben	Jan	Dutch	Jul-61	Aug-61
Houterman	Hendrikus	Dutch	Jun-61	Jul-61
Hulsegge	Hendricus, Bernadina, Gradus, Edith, Ronald	Dutch	Aug-59	Jul-61
Isken	Adriana, Stephanus, Pieter, Johannes, Evert, Francina, Stephanus	Dutch	Feb-61	Sep-61
Isken	Stephanie	Dutch	Feb-61	Aug-61
Jambrovic	August, Ljudmilla, Marijan	Yugooslav	Aug-61	9/11/1961
Jankowski	Feliks, Maria, Halina, Zbigniew	Polish	23/09/1961	7/12/1961
Johannessen	Asbjorn	Norwegian	23/09/1961	16/10/1961
Johansen	Reitar, Bodil, Vigdis, Karl	Norwegian	Mar-61	14/11/1961
Jokinen	Pirkko-Liisa	Finnish	5/10/1961	13/10/1961
Jongejan	Martinus	Dutch	Aug-61	Aug-61
Jongkin	Theodorus, Agnes, Anna, Desiree, Alexander, Leattia, Lucia	Dutch	Apr-59	Aug-61
Jonker	Janette, Robert	Dutch	May-61	Jun-61
Juvakka	Jorma	Finnish	3/11/1960	24/10/1961
Juvakka	Einar, Viene Kyllikki, Tarja Marjut, Anne Maria	Finnish	Nov-60	Aug-61
Juvakka	Jeouke Kalevi	Finnish	Nov-60	Aug-61
Kaffa	Karel, Maryia, Kitty	Dutch	Aug-61	Sep-61
Kalkreuter	Hermann	German	May-61	Jun-61
kelka	Antun, Steja, Drag, Alexander	Yugoslavian	Apr-61	9/11/1961
Kemnitz	Hans	German	8/07/1960	28/10/1961
Kemnitz	Hans	German	Jul-60	Jul-61
Kirchberger	Eduard	Austrian	22/08/1960	27/12/1961
Klijnsoon	Charles	Dutch	30/10/1961	4/11/1961
Koenraait	Karel, Maryia, Kitty	Dutch	Jul-61	Aug-61
Kroesken	Gerhardus, Johanna, Geertruida, Albertus, Gerhardus, Wilhelmina, Maria	Dutch	30/12/1960	26/09/1961
Kromhout v.d. Meer	Alt Wiebren	Dutch	Jul-60	Sep-61
Kromhout van der Meer	Jana, Lodewijk, catharina, Alt Wiebren	Dutch	4/07/1960	6/10/1961
Kubrak	Rudolf	German	Dec-60	Jul-61
Kujat	Albert. Inge, Karin, Hans	German	Jun-61	9/11/1961
Kunkel	Manfred	German	15/10/1960	28/11/1961
Lammers	Gerardus, Frederika, Gerarda, Hendrik, Olga, Andreas	Dutch	Apr-61	Jun-61
Lampe	Axel	German	Aug-60	Sep-61
Ledermann	Gerd, Isla, Jeffrey	British	5/10/1961	20/10/1961
Lelliott	Ronald, Kathaleen, Caron, Murtel, Michael, Patrick, Kathaleen	British	30/10/1961	17/11/1961
Lemajic	Petar, Milunka, Jovanka	Yugoslavian	20/03/1961	18/11/1961
Lemmens	Jacoba, Petrus, Willem, Johannes	Dutch	May-61	Jun-61
Lev	Clinton	American	Jun-61	Jun-61

Surname	Given names	Nationality	Arrived	Departed
Lewis	Ann, Jennifer, Linda, Wendy, Jillian, Vivian, Sheila	British		13/12/1961
Liefting	Hendrikus	Dutch	Feb-61	Jul-61
Loonstra	Trijntje	Dutch	Jun-61	Jul-61
Loonstra	Trijntje	Dutch	Jun-61	Jul-61
Lubbers	Frederikus	Dutch	May-61	Jun-61
Luckerhoff	Pieternella, Elly, Robert, Frederik	Dutch	Jul-61	Aug-61
Luckerhoff	Frederik	Dutch	Jul-61	Aug-61
Luebke	Ingeberg, Wilfried, Harald, Heinrich	German	Jun-61	Aug-61
Lupton Smith	Anthony	British	30/10/1961	1/11/1961
Marsman	Burend	Dutch	14/09/1961	9/12/1961
Marsman	Hendrik	Dutch	14/09/1961	30/10/1961
Marsman	Hilegenda	Dutch	14/09/1961	25/09/1961
Martens	Matneus, Jacoba, Wilhelmus, Henri, Christina	Dutch	14/09/1961	6/10/1961
Martens	Matheus,	Dutch	Sep-61	Oct-61
Maurer	Karl, Vaino	Austrian	Aug-60	Sep-61
McKay	David, Helene, Kathlene, Gloria, Debbie	American	26/09/1961	19/10/1961
Meijerink	Hendrik	Dutch	May-61	Jun-61
Meljer	Philomena, Inga, Johannes, Cathy	Dutch	May-61	Aug-61
Mellenbergh	Johan	Dutch	16/10/1961	24/10/1961
Melzer	Herbert	Austrian	Apr-61	Sep-61
Menesch	Franz	German	27/01/1960	22/12/1961
Menesch	Franz	German	27/01/1960	18/11/1961
Meuwese	Henricus, Josephine	Dutch	Jun-61	Jul-61
Meyerink	Hendrik, Johanna, Reintje Anton, Hendrik, Johannes	Dutch	May-61	Jul-61
Michel	Mare, Nelly, Philippe Johannes, Adriana, Johannes, Jozef, Everardus, Charles, Bernardus, Felix, Maria, Leonardus,	Belgian	Apr-61	16/10/1961
Morris	David, Emma, Terry, Gwendolyn	American	May-61	Aug-61
Morris	David	American	May-61	Jul-61
Mulder	Albert, Jantje, Werner, Albert	Dutch	3/04/1961	6/11/1961
Neey	Richard, Frances, Lavid	American	Sep-61	Oct-61
Niedermeier	Erika, Jutta, Juer	German	Jul-61	9/11/1961
Nisius	Boris, Manuela, Sylvia	German	Aug-61	14/10/1961
Nissila	Laimi, Seija, Kirsti, Pauli	Finnish	Apr-61	Jun-61
Noordeloos	Willem, Jantje, Fempje	Dutch	1/05/1961	22/11/1961
Oosterhout	Nijnand, Maria, Wijnand, Elixzabeth, Frida, Barend	Dutch	31/07/1961	7/11/1961
Opreij	Johannes	Dutch	Apr-61	Aug-61
Ouwerkerk	Mijndert, Johanna	Dutch	Jul-61	Jul-61
Ovaa	Willem, Elly	Dutch	14/09/1961	23/09/1961
Paes	Willem	Dutch	14/12/1961	20-Dec
Paijmans	Aaltje, Netty, Henny	Dutch	Jun-61	Jul-61
Paijmans	Cornelus	Dutch	Jun-61	Jun-61
Palomaki	Alpo, Maria, Elisabeth, mack, Donald, Hannele, Mia	Finnish	Sep-61	18/10/1961
Patona	Rosalia, Rudolph, Rosalia, Istvan, Sander,	Hungarian	Jun-61	Aug-61
Paulus	Johannes, Erma, Nikolaus, Christoph, Johannes	German	Jul-61	9/11/1961
Pavlovic	Andre, Anthonia	Yugoslavian	27/07/1959	6/12/1961
Pershouse	Gerald, Eulalie, Anthony, Jonathan	British	Jun-61	Jul-61
Peters	Willy	Dutch	May-61	Jun-61
Peters	Jan	Dutch	May-61	Jun-61
Piekar	Elisabeth	Dutch	Jul-61	Jul-61
Piekar	Antoon	Dutch	Jul-61	Jul-61
Pietersma	Gerritje, Sicstke, Dirk, Tjitje	Dutch	Jul-61	Jul-61
Pinkus	Percival, Margaret, Donald, Derrick	South African	24/09/1961	28/09/1961
Poeber	Cabele, Cornelis, Benno, Martinus, Marcel	Dutch	Apr-61	Jun-61

Poen	Cornelis	Dutch	14/09/1961	28/11/1961
Poll V.D	Jan	Dutch	14/09/1961	10/10/1961
Pouw	Gerardus, Maria, Johannes, Anna	Dutch	Dec-60	Jul-61
Prins	Frens, Frans, Johanna, Alfred, Marcel, Tiber	Dutch	Jan-61	Sep-61
Ramon	Joannes, Aaltje, Klaas, Joannes, Jan, Leendert	Dutch	14/09/1961	28/09/1961
Rauker	Werner, Ruth, Hartmuth, Baerbel	German	Jun-61	90/61
Rebellon bernal	Sebastian, Eduardo, Jesus	Spanish	Jan-61	Aug-61
Remme	Hendrika, Johannes	Dutch	30/10/1961	7/12/1961
Ribic	Milan, Marija, Rudolf	Yugoslavian	May-61	9/11/1961
Ricke	Franciscus, Cornelia, Carla, Franciscus	Dutch	23/10/1961	17/11/1961
Rieck	Ewald, Ingeberg, Rainer	German	Jun-61	Oct-61
Roos	Jacob, Margaretha, jan, Birkje, Jacob	Dutch	Mar-61	Sep-61
Ros	jan	Dutch	Aug-61	Aug-61
Salden	Johannes	Dutch	14/09/1961	30/09/1961
Scheepers	Maria, Petrus, Wilhelmus, Hubertina, Johanna, Hubertus, Antonius	Dutch	May-61	Jun-61
Scheepers	Hubertus	Dutch	May-61	Jun-61
Schering	Ewald,	German	Dec-60	Jul-61
Schmitz	Christiaan, Lena	Dutch	8/05/1961	9/12/1961
Schmitz	Christiaan, Lena	Dutch	May-61	Aug-61
Schomburg	Robert, Elizabeth, Carlton, Mark, Lisa	American	5/10/1961	10/10/1961
Schoocharit	Herbert	German	Aug-60	Aug-61
Schouten	Albert	Dutch	2/11/1961	3/11/1961
Seidel	Anton	German	28/12/1960	6/11/1961
Sengers	Christisan, Jo, Martha	Dutch	Jul-61	Aug-61
Seroka	Stanley, Elizabeth, Elizabeth	American	Jun-61	Jul-61
Smallegange	Jan, Lena, Helena, Therese, Mylene	Dutch	Feb-61	Jul-61
Smith	Robert, Elsie, Sarah, Penelope, Jeremy, Simon	British	4/10/1961	3/11/1961
Smolders	Josephus, Johanna, Gerardus, Maria, Jacoba, Johannees	Dutch	3/11/1957	28/12/1961
Snel	Herminus	Dutch	Jul-61	Jul-61
Solleveld	Sophia	Dutch	Jul-61	Jul-61
Stachowiak	Bronislawa, Irena, Theresa, Susanna	Australian	30/01/1951	30/12/1961
Staffeleu	Bernardus, Maria, Bernardus, Maria, Julius, Victor	Dutch	May-61	Sep-61
Staffleu	Bernardus	Dutch	May-61	Sep-61
Stanton	Annie, Dorit, Vanciscia, Patrick	British	24/09/1961	4/10/1961
Stanton	Patrick	British	24/09/1961	2/10/1961
Steinke	Arno, Irmgard, Juergen, Monika	German	May-61	Oct-61
Stojanovic	Miodrag, Otojanka, Verica, Tomislav	Yugoslavian	Aug-61	9/11/1961
Strybom	Raymond, Maria, Aubrey, jeanne, Bawn, Yvonne	British	Jul-61	Jul-61
Stubbe	Wilfred	German	Mar-60	Oct-61
Stubbe	Hubert	German	Mar-61	Oct-61
Stuber	Heinrich	Swiss	Apr-61	1/09/1961
Sving	Julia, George, Robert	Yugoslavian	25/10/1957	2/11/1961
Szeles	Mattias, Elisabetta	Hungarian	Jul-61	15/11/1961
Tesse	Euge	Belgian	22/06/1960	30/10/1961
Till	Franjo, Olga, Zlata, Evonimir, Suzana	Yugoslavian	Aug-61	9/11/1961
Toomsalu	Bruno, renee, Inge, Gita, Evald, Alida	Naturalised Australian	Dec-49	Jun-61
Toth	Nander, Johanna	Dutch	31/07/1961	13/10/1961
Truter	Daniel, Leonie, Felicity, Michael, Glynis, Martine	South African	24/09/1961	9/10/1961
V. D. hooven	Johannes, Helena, Wilhelmina, Jacob, Helena, Bernhard	Dutch	3/07/1961	6/10/1961

Scheyville Speaks

Surname	Given names	Nationality	From	To
V. laarhoven	Adriaan, Gerda	Dutch		Sep-61
v. Unen	Jan	Dutch	14/09/1961	25/09/1961
V. Vlimmeren	Gerrit	Dutch	14/09/1961	3/10/1961
V.D. Anker	Jantje, Martinus, Gerrit, Maris, Cornelia, Antonius	Dutch	Jul-61	Aug-61
V.D. Neut	Cornelis, Wilhelmina, Henry, Johanna, Thomas, Ida, Paulina	Dutch	May-61	Jul-61
V.G. Slys	Freddy	Dutch	Jul-61	Sep-61
Van Brummelen	Johannes, Victoria, Soraya	Dutch	19/06/1961	12/12/1961
Van Bussel	Henri, Theodora, Maria, Wilhelmus, Hubertaus, Paulus, Henrica, Theodorus	Dutch	14/09/1961	27/10/1961
Van Den berg	Gerhardus, Johanna, Geertruida, Albertus, Gerhardus, Wilhelmina, Maria	Dutch	Aug-61	Sep-61
Van Den Bosch	Evert	Dutch	Sep-61	Sep-61
Van den Heerik	Johannes	Dutch	May-61	Jun-61
Van der Anker	Hendricus, Jesina, Marinus, Theodorus	Dutch	Jul-61	Aug-61
Van Der Anker	Antonius	Dutch	Dec-60	Jul-61
Van Der Brande	Willem	Dutch	23/10/1961	30/10/1961
Van der Donk	Lambertus, Femia, Adrianus, Anne, Jacobus	Dutch	May-56	Aug-61
Van der heerik	Elizabeth, Johannes, Elizabeth	Dutch	May-61	Jun-61
Van der heiden	Gijshert, Cornelis, Maria, gerda, Dieuwke	Dutch	Jul-61	Sep-61
Van der Heiden	Gijsbert	Dutch	Jul-61	Jul-61
Van der Neut	Alfonsius	Dutch	May-61	Jun-61
Van Der Poll	Gretha	Dutch	14/09/1961	20/11/1961
Van der Sluijs	Freddy	Dutch	Jul-61	Aug-61
Van der Stap	Adrianus, Anna	Dutch	Jul-61	Jul-61
Van Der Stok	Marius, Cornelia	Dutch	2/11/1961	18/11/1961
Van der Vlag	Bart, Sietske	Dutch	May-61	Jun-61
Van Der Zwet	Alphonsus, Annie, Franciscus, Maria	Dutch	19/03/1961	10/11/1961
Van Eynde	Maria, Antoom, Jaques, Jean-Marie	Belgian	Jun-61	25/11/1961
Van Geijt	Jan, Emma, Ludwig	Dutch	May-61	21/10/1961
Van gent	Hendrike, Johannes	Dutch	May-61	Jul-61
Van gent	Johannes, Hendrika	Dutch	May-61	Jul-61
Van Girschot	Franciscus, petrenella	Dutch	Jul-61	Aug-61
Van Haeren	Willem, Anna, Gerard, Mathias, Noel, Adele	Dutch	14/09/1961	16/09/1961
Van halen	Robert, Elsie, Sarah, Penelope, Jeremy, Simon	Dutch	16/10/1961	21/10/1961
Van heeswicjk	Wilhelmus	Dutch	26/03/1961	28/10/1961
Van Helden	Kornelis, Cornelia, Petronella, Adalbertus, Gerrit, Anna	Dutch	4/04/1961	9/12/1961
Van Opijnen	Johannes	Dutch	16/01/1960	3/01/1961
Van Rompaey	Jaa, Denise, Dorothy, Lue	Belgian	Jul-61	Aug-61
Van Schaik	Arnoldus, Klazina, Gerardus, Gijabertus, Wilhelmina, Arnoldus, Klazina	Dutch	Jul-61	Jul-61
Van Steenhoven	Anthonius	Dutch	Jul-61	Jul-61
Van Tienen	Arthur, Magdalena	Dutch	Aug-61	Aug-61
Van Tongeren	Hendrick	Dutch	Jan-61	Aug-61
Van Unen	Jan, Gerritje, Gerardus, Berend	Dutch	14/09/1961	2/10/1961
Vanaudenaerde	Edouard, Maria, Marcel, Charel, Alexander, Marcella	Belgian	Jun-61	9/11/1961
Veenhuis	Adrianus, Hendrika, Maria	Dutch	14/09/1961	20/10/1961
Veenhuis	Adrianus,	Dutch	14/09/1961	6/10/1961
Veld	Elisabeth, Johannes, Antonius, Maria, Peter, Koert	Dutch	Apr-61	Jul-61
Veld	Johannes	Dutch	Apr-61	Jun-61
Versteeg	Clara	Dutch	Jul-61	Jul-61
Vetters	Bruno, Margarete, Karin, Angelika, Helmut	German	Dec-60	14/11/1961
Viljakainen	Naine, Lyyli, Sari	Finnish	8/09/1961	10/11/1961
Viljakainen	Vaino	Finnish	8/09/1961	8/10/1961
Viljakainen	Karl, Vaino	Finnish	Sep-61	Sep-61

Visser	Helena	Dutch	May-61	Jun-61
Vogel	Ernst, Liselotte, Elke, Ulrike, Michael	German	Sep-61	Sep-61
Vos	geert, Harmke, Trijntje, Jan, Annechiena, Albert	Dutch	Jul-61	Aug-61
Vreedenburgh	Robert	Dutch	Jan-61	Aug-61
Vucko	Ivan, Terezija, Katarina, Ivan	Yugoslavian	Sep-61	9/11/1961
Vujcic	Svetomir	Yugoslavian	1/07/1960	28/10/1961
Waaijer	Albertus, Johanna, Wilhelmina, Johannes, Robertus, Alberta	Dutch	Sep-60	Jul-61
Wagner	Martinus	German	Mar-61	Jul-61
Walthuetter	Otto, Anna, Otto, Norbet, Gerhard, Manfred	Norwegian	May-61	14/11/1961
Warne	Pieter, Rosmarie, Kristina, Patrick	Belgian	Aug-61	Sep-61
Weber	Jules, Flore, Marie Louise	Belgian	17/04/1961	13/12/1961
Weise	Joachim	German	Nov-60	Oct-61
Wenet	Siegfried	German	Mar-61	Sep-61
Wijnand	Jan		14/05/1961	26/09/1961
Wildeboer	Wijbe	Dutch	2/11/1961	9/11/1961
Wildenburg	Johannes, Martina, Maria, Antonius, Agnes	Dutch	2/11/1961	16/11/1961
Wilke	Bernardus, Geertuida, Johannes, Theodora, Gerhard	Dutch	21/10/1960	28/10/1961
Withuis	Cornelis, Maria, Johan, Ronald	Dutch	17/11/1961	15/12/1961
Withuis	Cornelia	Dutch	17/11/1961	11/12/1961
Witt	Albert	german	20/06/1958	13/10/1961
Wolf	Guenter	German	14/06/1953	28/10/1961
Wooley	Ellis, Dorothy	American	26/09/1961	6/10/1961
Wuennerlein	Rosemarie, Gabriele, Helmut	German	Mar-61	Jun-61
Zentrich	Georg, Wilma, Georg	German	Apr-61	9/11/1961
Zonervan	Johannes	Dutch	May-61	Jul-61
Zwitser	Cornelius, Catharina, Cornelis,	Dutch	14/09/1961	21/09/1961
Zwitser	Willem, Clasina, Augustinus, Clasina	Dutch	14/09/1961	21/09/1961

www.ingramcontent.com/pod-product-compliance
Lightning Source LLC
Chambersburg PA
CBHW061131010526
44107CB00068B/2903